IDENTITY, ATTACHMENT AND RESILIENCE

Identity, Attachment and Resilience provides a timely foray into the new field of psychology and genealogy, exploring the relationship between family history and identity. The field encompasses family narratives and researches family history to increase our understanding of cultural and personal identity, as well as our sense of self. It draws on emotional geography and history to provide rich yet personalised contexts for family experience.

In this book, Antonia Bifulco researches three generations of her own Czechowski family, beginning in Poland in the late nineteenth century and moving on to post-WWII England. She focuses on key family members and places to describe individual experience against the socio-political backdrop of both World Wars. Utilising letters, journals and handwritten biographies of family members, the book undertakes an analysis of impacts on identity (sense of self), attachment (family ties) and resilience (coping under adversity), drawing out timely wider themes of immigration and European identity.

Representing a novel approach for psychologists, linking family narrative to social context and intergenerational impacts, *Identity, Attachment and Resilience* describes Eastern European upheaval over the twentieth century to explain why Polish communities have settled in England. With particular relevance for Polish families seeking to understand their cultural heritage and identity, this unique account will be of great interest to any reader interested in family narratives, immigration and identity. It will appeal to students and researchers of psychology, history and social sciences.

Antonia Bifulco is professor and co-director at the Centre for Abuse and Trauma Studies at Middlesex University, London. She is a psychologist with expertise in lifespan development, and utilises an attachment model to examine relationships. She has had extensive research funding and publishes on issues concerning childhood and adult adversity, stress/trauma and clinical depression.

IDENTITY, ATTACHMENT AND RESILIENCE

Exploring Three Generations of a Polish Family

Antonia Bifulco

LONDON AND NEW YORK

First published 2018
by Routledge
2 Park Square, Milton Park, Abingdon, Oxon OX14 4RN

and by Routledge
711 Third Avenue, New York, NY 10017

Routledge is an imprint of the Taylor and Francis Group, an informa business

© 2018 Antonia Bifulco

The right of Antonia Bifulco to be identified as author of this work has been asserted by her in accordance with sections 77 and 78 of the Copyright, Designs and Patents Act 1988.

All rights reserved. No part of this book may be reprinted or reproduced or utilised in any form or by any electronic, mechanical, or other means, now known or hereafter invented, including photocopying and recording, or in any information storage or retrieval system, without permission in writing from the publishers.

Trademark notice: Product or corporate names may be trademarks or registered trademarks, and are used only for identification and explanation without intent to infringe.

British Library Cataloguing in Publication Data
A catalogue record for this book is available from the British Library

Library of Congress Cataloging in Publication Data
Names: Bifulco, Antonia, 1955– author.
Title: Identity, attachment and resilience : exploring three generations of a Polish family / Antonia Bifulco.
Description: Abingdon, Oxon ; New York, NY : Routledge, 2017. | Includes bibliographical references.
Identifiers: LCCN 2017014291 (print) | LCCN 2017030943 (ebook) | ISBN 9781315203935 (Master eBook) | ISBN 9781138701700 (hardback) | ISBN 9781138701724 (pbk.)
Subjects: LCSH: Polish people—Ethnic identity—Case studies. | Polish people—Psychology—Case studies. | Polish people–Cultural assimilation—Great Britain—Case studies. | Families—Psychological aspects—Case studies. | Group identity—Case studies.
Classification: LCC DK4121 (ebook) | LCC DK4121 .B54 2017 (print) | DDC 929.20941—dc23
LC record available at https://lccn.loc.gov/2017014291

ISBN: 978-1-138-70170-0 (hbk)
ISBN: 978-1-138-70172-4 (pbk)
ISBN: 978-1-315-20393-5 (ebk)

Typeset in Bembo and Stone Sans
by Florence Production Ltd, Stoodleigh, Devon, UK

In memory of my mother, father and grandparents.

With thanks to my family, far and wide, for the gifts handed down.

*In Warsaw in Poland
Half the world away,
The one I love best of all
Thought of me to-day;
I know, for I went
Winged as a bird,
In the wide flowing wind
His own voice I heard;
His arms were round me
In a ferny place,
I looked in the pool
And there was his face—
But now it is night
And the cold stars say:
'Warsaw in Poland
Is half the world away'.*

Sara Teasdale, 1844–1933

CONTENTS

List of figures	*xi*
Preface	*xiii*
Acknowledgements	*xviii*
Spelling and pronunciation of Polish names	*xx*

1 Trust: introducing family narratives ... 1

SECTION I
Poland: the first generation — 23

2 Autonomy: living under partition (1886–1913) ... 25

3 Initiative: fighting on the Eastern Front (1914–20) ... 51

4 Industriousness: life in independent Warsaw (1921–39) ... 72

SECTION II
Poland and England: the second generation — 95

5 Confusion: Nazi occupation of Warsaw (1939–43) ... 97

6 Identity: resistance in France (1939–43) ... 118

7 Isolation: England fights, Warsaw rises (1943–45) ... 136

SECTION III
England: the third generation — 159

8 Intimacy: marriage and migration (1945–50) — 164

9 Generativity: family reunion and loss (1951–71) — 186

10 Integrity: reminiscence and reflection (1972–2016) — 214

Index — *242*

FIGURES

1.1	Erikson's stages of identity development and book structure	15
1.2	The family in 1900, and analysis of themes	16
1.3	Map of modern Poland	20
2.1	The first phases of Erikson's development as applied to the family	23
2.2	Map of Polish partitions	27
2.3	Map of Belarus, previously Polesie, East Poland	29
2.4	The Czechowski family tree	32
2.5	Summary of the themes in Chapter 2	46
2.6	Maria-Victoria with baby Tadeusz, 1886	48
2.7	Władisław Czechowski	48
2.8	Felicija Cygler, with daughter Maria	48
2.9	Maria and Tadeusz marry, 1911	48
2.10	Tadeusz, Maria and Jurek, 1918	49
2.11	Stas and mother Julia	49
2.12	Grazyna and Maria, defence of Warsaw, 1920	49
2.13	Maria and Jurek, 1923	49
2.14	Maria and Jurek in Warsaw, 1931	50
2.15	Jurek at University, Warsaw 1932	50
2.16	Myszka and Jurek marry, Warsaw 1938	50
3.1	Summary of the themes in Chapter 3	68
4.1	Plan of Warsaw	77
4.2	The O'Neill family tree	86
4.3	Summary of the themes in Chapter 4	92
5.1	Erikson's phases of development, midpoint	95
5.2	Summary of the themes in Chapter 5	116
6.1	Summary of the themes in Chapter 6	134
7.1	Summary of the themes in Chapter 7	154

8.1	Erikson's final stages of development	159
8.2	Stas Leinweber, 1939	161
8.3	Myszka, 1942	161
8.4	Jurek mobilised to French army, May 1940	161
8.5	Jurek (left) in the French army, 1940	162
8.6	Jurek's student card, Grenoble, 1941	162
8.7	Jurek in SOE as A. Bronisz, 1944	163
8.8	Jurek and Jonny, SOE training, 1944	163
8.9	Summary of the themes in Chapter 8	184
9.1	Third generation of the Czechowski family tree	193
9.2	Summary of the themes in Chapter 9	206
9.3	Christine O'Neill, 1945	210
9.4	Jurek and Christine marry, Derby 1948	210
9.5	O'Neill family, with baby Yolanda, Swansea 1949	210
9.6	Jurek (left) with Gen Bor-Komorowski, Polish Club Derby	211
9.7	Jurek with Princess Lee Radziwil, Derby 1966	211
9.8	Christine, Jurek and children, Derby 1962	211
9.9	Grazyna, Marysia and Maria, Falenica Warsaw, 1958	212
9.10	Małgosia with family, Warsaw 1961	212
9.11	Barbara, Karolina and Ania Cygler, Gdansk, 1977	212
9.12	Jurek and family visit to Falenica Warsaw, 1965	213
9.13	Marie, Joanna, Yolanda, Antonia, London 2015	213
9.14	Małgosia and Piotr, Warsaw 2016	213
10.1	My DNA cultural analysis	229
10.2	Summary of the themes in Chapter 10	230

PREFACE

Aims

This book is about certain aspects of cultural and family identity and our sense of 'who we are' as explored through family narrative. 'Identity' is a broad concept; it includes how we see ourselves and how other people see us, in terms of our cultural, social and personal characteristics. It is what makes us individual. Our sense of identity is varied and can involve complex layers. For example, cultural identity can include more than one cultural inheritance and may vary depending on where we live and with whom we interact. We can encompass a number of inter-related identities, for example in our family, friends, work and leisure roles. Our sense of identity is dynamic, it changes over the life course as roles grow or reduce and become more or less integrated (Rosenberg, 1988). Understanding our identities becomes an important psychological task, ideally to enhance our sense of self, or if a source of negativity, to understand the conflict between roles or their source of stigma or shame.

Integrating our different identities often occurs through our self-narratives, the story we tell about ourselves (McAdams, 1988). Cultural identity, we inherit from our family and related social group. Whilst often nationally based, it can also refer to subcultural differences: for example that class-based, location-based or rural versus urban. We all have such cultural identities and when people move, this can create a dislocation from the cultural source. Through family narrative, and the experience of prior generations, we can make links to our cultural roots. The family narrative developed may explain reasons for leaving a home location, the costs, losses and benefits associated with the journey, the demands of settling in a new home and the nostalgia for the original location. The narratives may refer to a single location but change of class through education and entrepreneurial activity across generations. These narratives can be a source of inspiration, personal growth and 'grounding'. For some it can be a source of disappointment, rejection, loss or stigma.

It seems that most of us prefer to know about previous generations of our family in order to create a sense of completeness and 'grounding' of self. Our family roots may lie nearer or further from where we now live, but it is rare in the UK for families to remain in the same small area over generations. It is also rare to retain the same levels of poverty or disadvantage; or even wealth and social elitism. Public interest in such movement in family and in family history occurs in the television programme *Who do you think you are?* This shows individuals' searching their family antecedents with the help of professional archivists and has proved of interest to the public in general. Original documents and photographs are uncovered to give an account of the lives of historical family members. A family tree is created. Often there are visits to significant places and an outline of political events of importance to the family. These experiences seem to touch a common chord, even for those watching. Frequently the individual involved (usually a well-known figure) will cry when they hear of trauma, loss or poverty-stricken circumstances. It seems that this is often an unexpected emotional response, often given that the family member concerned may be long dead. There appears to be an awakening of empathy around experience of loss, trauma and severe deprivation, for people who are related to us and who share DNA. It seems to create an expanded and enriched sense of identity and position in the world. A new emotional dimension appears from putting one's self in their shoes. This is a form of 'emotional history', which looks at past events through the eyes of someone like us to provide an emotional link to past events.

It is novel to apply psychological method to such investigation, as planned in this book. For psychologists, understanding the development of identity through life stages is important. This impacts on how it is expressed at different points during the life course in terms of our perception of our roles, relationships, behaviour and sense of self. Erik Erikson, one of the first psychologists to define identity, was particularly interested in its social aspects, its change over time and with development, and its positive and negative aspects. I have taken his labelling of life stages and identity development to structure the family story presented here. These stages are applied to particular family members, but also in parallel to the unfolding of political events, forming a national and European narrative to the developing context which has shaped lives.

The materials utilised in this project include archival approaches, family documentation, photographs and letters, and it uses these to provide the narrative of events and the core around which psychological interpretations around issues of identity are discussed. It represents a newly developing branch of psychology as related to genealogy (P. Nicolson, 2017). The interpretations have a triple focus: for the individuals' described, for later family members and for other individuals with similar or related experience. It is hoped it will trigger additional psychological debate about topics and methods. This type of qualitative analysis using a single case study is unusual, but accepted in the broad church of psychological method (N.A. Frost, 2011). Given also that the analysis is of my own family, there are also personal interpretations and impacts involved which can present challenges to systematic analysis and interpretation, and requires a degree of self-reflection or 'reflexivity'. It does, however, provide a new structure for understanding individuals in their wider socio-historical context over time, from an in-depth personal perspective. It also seeks to observe the way human beings react under extreme circumstances, as well as their adaptability for survival and resilience.

The three themes, identified prior to the project are all related concepts in psychological functioning. Identity is about 'who we are and where we belong', attachment is about 'who we love and to whom we belong' and resilience is 'how we cope with adversity and survive' where belonging can be a great aid. These concepts apply to the individual, the family and the wider community. Sub-themes also emerged in the course of developing the narrative, for example around heroism, both military and of the everyday variety, and resistance to hostile forces where subterfuge is involved and identity hidden, of trauma, and being able to speak about it. These are interspersed with political dimensions – for example, hidden identity in the Polish state until it achieved independence; the state imposition of forgetting in communist East Europe; understanding the two world wars from the Eastern European perspective; and understanding Polish immigration to the UK in a recent 'Brexit' context.

The method utilises a retrospective, lifespan and intergenerational approach to the experience of my own family, developed through a family narrative woven round the family tree. The concepts of 'emotional geography' and 'emotional history' are also utilised to denote attachment to certain places and certain historical events. These help focus and narrow the time and places involved. In covering a century, a continent and three generations, it is necessary to be selective. Only key places where family members lived are included, down to the city, and sometimes district, level. Only key historical events in which the family members were involved are included. This has meant omitting many significant historical events and many places key to history and to other groups targeted at times of strife. There is no implied minimisation of these experiences, simply that by chance they did not apply to my forebears. Similarly, for focus and simplicity, as well as in relation to the documentary evidence, not all of the broad family tree is included; I have selected certain lines, for depth rather than breadth, in analysis. No doubt I have missed other important family stories, and may have overlooked important family members on the basis I know little about them. This is unfortunate and I hope I have not given offence to people whom I am related to. In this I am constrained both by selection of those closest, and by the documentation I have available.

The book serves as a 'cross-over' between disciplines including Psychology, Sociology, Social History, Cultural Studies, Genealogy and Family Memoire. Its focus is on charting the political events and associated adversity in Eastern Europe and then Britain, across three generations of my family in times of political turmoil. It utilises historical references, Internet searches and eye-witness accounts to chart the events of the time (from 1886 to the present day), and family letters, diaries, journals, photographs and archival documentation to complete further detail from my family perspective. I have quoted published accounts from eye-witnesses to these historical events, to provide more vivid context and opportunities for empathic understanding.

Contents

The book progresses chronologically from the birth of my grandparents Maria and Tadeusz Czechowski in 1886/7 in Russian Poland. The three sections represent the three generations of the family and the move of my branch of the family from Poland to England. The characters described include:

- Władisław and Maria-Victoria Czechowski (my great-grandparents), and their three children:
- Tadeusz (my grandfather), his brother Olgierd and youngest sister Grazyna.
- Maria Cygler Czechowska, my grandmother
- Jurek Czechowski, my father, an only child, and his cousins, Stas and Marysia
- Myszka (Maria Janiszewska), Jurek's first wife, married before WWII
- Christine O'Neill, Jurek's second wife and my mother, married after WWII
- My three sisters (Yolanda, Marie, Joanna) and myself (Antonia), daughters' of Jurek and Christine
- Małgosia and Jan (grandchildren to Grazyna); Piotr (from the Czechowski line), my second cousins
- Ania and Karolina (great-nieces of Maria Cygler), my second cousins.

I also briefly outline my mother's family background: her parents, my other grandparents, Hugh and Barbara O'Neill and their five children from Sheffield. This is to complete the family picture, but also because of a strange quirk of fate whereby my Anglo-Irish grandparents visited Poland both before and after the Second World War, and provide additional description of the country in those times and whose support of Poles probably led to my parents meeting.

The book progresses chronologically, the sections relate to the generations and location (Poland, then England). The chapter structure relates to the Erikson stages of identity, each with a particular focus on an individual family member with analysis of the three themes (identity, attachment and resilience) as indicated by experience.

Biographic sources

I have had the benefit of substantial family documentation, including photographs dating from 1900, as well as numbers of papers, official documents, letters and mementos, and two brief biographic accounts, which have survived time and political and geographic upheaval. These came to life once I understood more of the social and historical context and had translations made from the Polish to English. Much I had never read before.

Public records of historical events and geographical locations can now be easily accessed through the Internet. There is surprising detail, and mining of such sources provides numerous sub-stories. For example, rich information about the ship the MS *Stefan Batory* on which my grandmother sailed to England, or about the Red Cross hospital where my grandfather died and where Myszka worked during the Second World War. The Red Cross provided interventions at various critical points in this narrative.

Most of those I write about here are now dead – my grandfather having died many years before I was born, my grandmother when I was just seven years old, my father when I was aged sixteen. My mother, when I started the account, no longer had conscious access to specific memories despite a positive view of her past with 'no regrets' and still romantic about meeting her 'handsome Polish airman' husband. She died in the course of writing this account. However, my sisters and I have memories of conversations with our parents and grandmother about the family. Other stories are taken from conversations with elderly Polish relatives, recalled here by my Polish-speaking brother-in-law Grigoris.

I am not a historian. I have accessed good historical texts as much as possible, and have been particularly reliant on Norman Davies's extensive work on Polish history. In order to provide context for the events that unfold, I have looked more widely at biographical and eye-witness accounts, both published and available on the Internet. For example, a biography of Marie Curie's Polish childhood (Quin, 1995) is used to describe family and school life in the Russian partition of Poland prior to the First World War. Published accounts of both adults and children who lived in Warsaw during the Second World War are also utilised, particularly those focused on Warsaw and areas where my relatives lived. I have liberally used quotes from these to describe scenes that occurred to capture context more vividly. I hope it serves to convey both a personal but also a cultural narrative, and I am grateful to the authors of these accounts.

ACKNOWLEDGEMENTS

I have a number of people to thank for helping me in this enterprise. First, Paula Nicolson, close friend and psychology colleague, who herself was publishing on genealogy and identity and encouraged me to think of publication rather than simply writing some narrative for my family. My sisters Yolanda, Marie and Joanna, have been highly supportive of the project and provided various sources of help. Yolanda and her husband Grigoris were able to give valuable information about the family origins, locations and stories from remembered conversations; Marie accompanied me to Warsaw on two fact-finding missions and read drafts; and Joanna read drafts of the account, giving helpful feedback and additional factual information.

My Polish cousins were also of great assistance: Piotr Radwan-Rohrschef supplied substantial information about the Czechowski family origins, having himself researched the archives, constructed a detailed family tree, spoken at length to family members and visited the site of the original family country house now in Belarus. He provided many photographs I had not seen before and family information that was new to me. Małgosia Miliskiewicz and her mother Marysia Szypowska supplied additional photographs and context, including some reminiscences. Cousin Ania Kanthak (née Cygler) provided links to the Płock archives to determine the Cygler family tree, and supplied photographs. My Polish friends in London, Irena and Kazik Bojanowski, came with me to Warsaw and discussed their family narratives from the Second World War. They introduced me to Jola Malin's account of a family fleeing through Siberia. I am grateful to Bozena Chomiuk, who translated and deciphered a number of letters and documents from the original Polish and accompanied our friend Irena and I on our Polish lunches. Various university colleagues, including Julia Davidson and her husband Glen, have been encouraging and supportive. Thanks are due to Nollaig Frost, for discussion of method and immigration; to Pnina Sheinbourne and Fiona Starr for talking about their own histories in Poland; to Geraldine Thomas for inspiring the heroism theme in relation to her own family's Dutch experience in war; and to Helen Stein for discussions of Jewish experience in Poland. Nicola Boyce introduced me to the work of Janusz Korczak and social pedagogy, and Yael Ilan-Clarke gave me the link to the '23andme' DNA service. Sam Oram was a good listener and was impressed with the tales! I am grateful to all.

However, the text is bound to have accumulated some errors, historical, biographical or in faulty interpretation, and these are entirely my own.

SPELLING AND PRONUNCIATION OF POLISH NAMES

Polish names can be difficult for the British reader. I have mainly retained Polish spellings but with some simplifications; see guide below.

Accents: I have dropped accents for simplicity of production where it makes minimal difference (to my non-linguistic sensibilities) to the pronunciation (e.g. Zoliborz/Żoliborz; Stas/Staś; Mokotow/Mokotów; Krasinski/Kraśinski; Bor/Bór).

First names: In Polish these are changed in to an affectionate diminutive. I have made use of such diminutives to differentiate people with the same name (for example, the various Marias) and to make names easier to follow in English. Jurek (Yurek) is a diminutive of Jerzy (George) and is how his mother referred to him. Staś (Stash) is a diminutive of Stanisław; Bogus (Bogush) of Bogusław. I have used Jurek's first wife, Maria's, nickname 'Myszka' (meaning ironically 'mouse' – she had an outgoing personality but small stature). My grandmother was apparently known as 'Marychna', but I have used the simplified 'Maria' as she signed herself. I have called my sister baptised Marie-Christine, 'Marie', even though in the family she is called 'Maria' like our grandmother. Surnames with a 'ski' ending change to 'ska' for women.

Pseudonyms: During WWII, in clandestine operations, pseudonyms were commonly used. This was to preserve anonymity and protect relatives but also helped simplify long Polish names for Allied use. My father changed his name twice – to Jerzy Krause when in France and then to Andrzej (Andrew) Bronisz (Bronish) when in Special Operations Executive (SOE). He often used the name Andrew after the war, at work and with friends. Members of the Polish Home Army and SOE all used pseudonyms. For example 'Bor' (meaning forest) was a pseudonym for Komorowski, although it has since been added to his given name (Bor-Komorowski). 'Wira' (Vera – a non-related eye witness) is a girl's name and pseudonym for Danuta Szhlachetko, her account published by her son.

Pronunciation: Some indicative pronunciations are given in the table below. It can be seen that in Polish 'w' is pronounced as 'v' and that the crossed l (ł) sounds like 'w' in English; similarly (Polish to English sound): sz = sh; cz = ch; ę = en and ą=an.

Polish names	English	Polish names	English
Czechowski	Chekovski	Małgosia	Mawgoshia
Cygler	Tsygler	Sikorski	Shikorski
Jurek	Yurek	Komorowski	Komorovski
Myszka	Myshka	Ciechochemni	Cheeko-chemni
Marysia	Marysha	Wira	Vera
Rodziewicz	Rodgevich	Krasinski	Krashinski
Stas	Stash	Krysia	Krisha
Tadeusz	Tadeush		
Władisław	Vwadiswav		
Wacław	Vatswav		

Polish place names	English		
Wisła	Viswa (Vistula)	Pruszkow	Prushkof
Płock	Pwotsk	Mokotow	Mokotuf
Krasinski	Krashinski		
Łódz	Woodge		
Częstochowa	Chenstohova		

1
TRUST

Introducing family narratives

> Hope is both the earliest and the most indispensable virtue inherent in the state of being alive. If life is to be sustained hope must remain, even where confidence is wounded, trust impaired.
>
> Erik Erikson

A famous Polish ship

In April 1958, a Polish transatlantic passenger ship, the MS *Stefan Batory*, docked in Southampton, England. The liner had crossed the Baltic Sea from its base in Gdynia, North Poland, leaving behind a grey communist Poland locked behind the 'Iron Curtain' of East Europe. It was one of the first ships transporting Polish nationals to visit their displaced families in England. It brought my grandmother Maria Czechowska to her only son and his family after a separation of nearly twenty years. This ship had a history of its own – one that mirrored not only an important piece of Polish modern history, but also the eccentricity, heroism, hospitality, determination and flair for being at the centre of events, typical of Poland and the Poles.

I only learned about this ship when checking the facts of my grandmother's journey to England from Poland in researching our family story. I had in my possession one first class ticket, a list of personal items to follow on as freight and a letter recalling difficulties of leaving the country. One of the delights about such research is that seemingly peripheral elements can prove to be a rich source of cultural interest. The MS *Stefan Batory* is one such instant. Named after a 16th-century king of Poland, the ocean liner was built for luxury, comfort and culture, and in the 1930s transported passengers across the Atlantic. The ship was 160 metres long, several levels high, with seven decks, guest cabins, dining halls, dance halls, a reading room, three bars, a swimming pool and a gym. The interiors were elegant and modern for its time, decorated with silver art deco by famous artists of the day, giving it a name as a floating art showroom[1] (Aksamit, 2015). A tourist attraction when it arrived at the Polish Baltic seaside town of Gdynia in 1936 from Italy, it was among the best-known Polish ships of the time. Her sailing route was from Gdynia to Southampton, and then across the Atlantic to New York. The ship sailed for 34 years, undertaking hundreds of transatlantic crossings.

The aspects that carried it into legend include an eccentric captain (Borkowski), a large-hearted mariner crew and a list of daring escapades. It pirated illegal liquor from Canada to the USA during prohibition. When war broke out in 1939, the *Batory* was in Canadian waters and was one of the few free Polish ships in the conflict, being refitted as an Allied warship and then spending 652 days continuously at sea. All the luxurious interiors were stripped out, and it was refurnished with guns and sailors' accommodation. It was given the name 'the lucky ship' because of the number of times it evaded the German U-boat submarines and bombers throughout the war. Its escapades involved transporting treasures to Canada from Britain and Poland for safekeeping away from the Nazis, and taking injured French and British soldiers from the ill-fated battle of Narwik in Norway to safety in England. It also evacuated 500 British children to safety in Australia in the summer of 1940. The children enjoyed a happy eleven-week voyage and called it the 'singing ship' (Aksamit, 2015). They later remembered the *Stefan Batory* with affection and formed a reunion on the ship in 1968 for its final voyage. In the early post-war years, the ship carried more than 100 people to asylum in foreign cities from East Europe behind the Iron Curtain. During the communist years the ship was a more sombre affair used only for the political elite of the regime, and for those artists and writers who found political favour. The atmosphere on the ship grew grim. The ocean liner finally went to China to be scrapped in 1971. Its importance is only now being recognised, and a replica is being built and housed in a museum in Gdynia.

Its most valuable cargo for my family in April 1958 was my grandmother, Maria. She left her homeland from the port in Gdynia and settled with us in England for the remaining four years of her life. She had last seen her son, my father Jurek, on the eve of war in September 1939. She was to meet my mother Christine for the first time, and my two older sisters (aged 9 and 6) and myself (aged 3). Like the ship, my grandmother had been in the centre of the historical cyclone in the first half of the twentieth century. She had lived through three wars in each of which her city of Warsaw had been threatened, until eventually razed to the ground. The ship reunited a family. The lady and the ship were both carriers of their culture and history. Both were survivors.

While I have no memory of meeting my grandmother for the first time, the family story tells that my parents; two older sisters and I piled into our second-hand black Buick car and drove from our home town of Derby in the English Midlands to Southampton docks. My grandmother arrived in style, first class on the ocean liner, quite an occasion in austere 1950s England and more so for passengers used to far greater austerity in communist Poland. This marked the first year that people could cross the Iron Curtain. My grandmother had sold all her possessions in Warsaw, travelled by train to stay with her Cygler relatives in Gdansk and sailed alone for a new country. She brought with her beautifully made Polish presents for us children, and to my mother she gave her jewellery collected from more affluent times: aquamarine from Russia, a *Longine* Swiss watch, a diamond bracelet, coral and amber. She was giving away her few treasured possessions to her only daughter-in-law. Maria returned with us to our modest 1930s three-bedroomed, semi-detached house in Chaddesden, Derby.

All four grand-daughters (my youngest sister, Joanna was born the year after she arrived) learned Polish and benefitted greatly from the additional care and culture she provided in the home. My mother Christine found it less easy. The understandable female competition in the household was perhaps a burden for her, but her own strong Irish Catholic sense of familial duty kept her steady. Indeed, it was Christine who insisted my grandmother come to England to live with us. I knew little of my grandmother's earlier life and, like many of her generation, she seldom spoke about her past. I was to learn much more. Having started with the aim of writing about my father, one of the unexpected treasures along the way included the story of my grandparents and their extraordinary times.

The biographic enterprise

The story behind my father's family and how we came to be living in England involves a fairly common tale of people transplanted across Europe, propelled by the key political events in the middle of the twentieth century. The story is a variant on a well-known European theme about wartime displacement and movements of populations due to fight or flight, but the details vary for each family or individual. Many of the details remain largely unfamiliar to a British audience, particularly those of a younger generation. Behind the sketchily known historical facts about Poland lies the more complex detail of individuals and families caught in the historical drama. Focusing history on particular times, places and contexts reveals additional detail of the mechanisms around travel, resistance and survival to provide insight into how individuals coped, the choices they made and the determinants of resilience. For my generation (I was born in 1955), we feel a relatively close connection with the Second World War. I was born ten years after the war ended, my eldest sister only four years after. During childhood, it seemed an age later, a different world and time. Now looking back it seems only a relatively short time after, and many of the post-war impacts were certainly present.

Somewhat harder to grasp, personally, is the experience of our grandparents' generation who lived in the late Victorian era emerging from a traditional to a modern mechanised world at the turn of the twentieth century. Much has been written and televised about the trauma and hardship suffered in the First World War starting soon after the century began. In Britain, we mainly think of the trench warfare in Flanders, with gunfire that could be heard across the English Channel from Hampstead heath, and needless slaughter of large numbers of men. Less attention is given to the Eastern Front (the war in fact having been triggered in Serbia), the warfare involving cavalry, as well as early armoured cars and machine guns, at the confluence of the German, Austro-Hungarian and Russian empires. The fighting on the Eastern Front was mainly on Polish territory. For complex reasons, Poles found themselves' fighting in these three different armies, at times directly against each other. The (now) capital Warsaw has been one of the most threatened cities in the last century. The only European capital invaded by the German army during the First World War, under attack by the Red Army in the Polish–Soviet war, and then under siege by the Nazis at the start of the Second World War. The city of Warsaw takes centre stage in much of the family narrative.

My aim is to turn a personal family account into a narrative woven through with the historical and social context of the time, to add to our understanding of cultural narrative as related to psychological themes. This can provide a more empathic way of understanding the past to aid our continual redefining of our sense of identity as a nation or culture. It also touches, of course, on the European enterprise – a brave consolidation of states united after the war to make a further world war unthinkable. It has now evolved into a more complex entity that recently had triggered very diverse passions.

A psychological approach

As a lifespan psychologist, I have been involved in the collection of many hundreds of life history interviews in the course of research to develop understanding of life stress, trauma and psychological disorder. These narratives have provided essential information about the impact of the social environment on individuals across lifetimes and generations. It has shown the long-term ill-effects of childhood trauma, which impairs adult well-being, relationships and parenting of the next generation (Bifulco, Bernazzani, Moran and Ball, 2000; Bifulco, Moran, Jacobs and Bunn, 2009). These stories from 'ordinary' people, living mainly in London, were provided willingly. The speakers were conscious of the importance of their experience, and of the intrinsic value of narrating such life stories to aid understanding of the experiential basis of clinical disorder or well-being. A lifespan model emerged showing how individuals deal with loss, trauma, rejection, neglect or abuse, sometimes with damaging personal impacts, sometimes with resilience, but always going through personal and psychological change (Bifulco, 2009). One recent analysis examined just two individual cases to illustrate key themes, involving the Second World War experiences of two women, one in Germany and the other, Jewish, in England (Bifulco, 2015). This was a spur to the current narrative. Whilst no life story is the same, patterns emerge that give us important messages about aids to survival, including the importance of close support and loving relationships – that is, our attachment context. Good coping strategies are important, as are competence, planning and emotional control to deal with adversity. Optimism is key. This book is an attempt to explore such resilience.

The book outlines a period from the time of my grandparents' birth in 1886 through to my father coming to England in 1943, his marriage to my mother in 1948 and my grandmother's voyage to England in 1958. It will conclude with an outline of my family's life in England after the war up to the 1970s, and the current family contacts between Poland and England in 2016. Throughout, I will relate the family events to the political-social context of the times with a focus on Poland and East Europe and then West Europe and Britain.

Sociology and context

This approach, of understanding people within their social context, also borrows from a very long British sociological tradition (Mayhew, 1851). In this tradition, Young and Willmott studied poverty in East London through extensive detailed interviews and by this changed social policy (Young and Willmott, 1957/2007). This approach was also voiced in the research tradition where I first learned my skills, with Brown and Harris's contextualised study of stress in London working-class women (Brown and Harris, 1978). In a similar vein, the mass observation documents of the Second World War, originally initiated to monitor morale, have been a rich source of data about day-to-day experiences for ordinary people in wartime (Koa Wing, 2007). The difference with the present narrative is that I will talk about a professional and upper-class family who lived through trauma, and the vilification and victimisation produced alternately by Bolshevism (regarding class) and Nazisim (regarding race), and how this impacted on them individually and as a family and led to their uprooting and replanting. The proposition is that individuals born into privilege can also suffer trauma and victimisation, which is psychologically no less meaningful.

Genealogical study and family narrative

Paula Nicolson has recently published a genealogical study of both her family and her husband's family, in order to use personal material to highlight important psychological themes (P. Nicolson, 2017). This represents a new branch of psychology. It brings together diverse writers like Erikson, emerging from the psychoanalytic tradition of the 1950s, to the sociology of Giddens forty years later, investigating the development of a sense of self (Erikson, 1950; Giddens, 1995). Zerubavel, more recently, has looked at how culture drives our understanding about relatives and genealogy. He points to society rather than human nature shaping our mental lives, with social groups involved in shared patterns of thinking (Zerubavel, 2011). This is a broad span of theory in which to consider the impact of the social environment on the individual and family over time. Much of it develops through the family narrative created in family conversation across generations, but is also open to verification through public record. This interdisciplinary approach seeks to extend the usual psychological approaches to understanding individuals and groups.

Family narratives have also been used to develop individual well-being in therapeutic contexts. Understanding of our own past, but also that of our parents or previous generations, can generate self-knowledge (Fivush, Bohanek and Duke, 2008). Having the ability to share our memories with others enables us to incorporate a sense of past experience, which expands our own sense of self to take into account those common to the family as a whole. Personal narratives are often told by parents to their children, in the family setting. These can be about shared experiences, but can also include parents' accounts of their past, creating a sense of self through historical time. The family story thus goes beyond personal recall. By the time children are old enough to go to school they begin asking for stories about their own parents' childhood (Fivush et al., 2008). Studies of adolescents confirm that those with such family narratives show higher levels of well-being (Fivush and Zaman, 2011). They aid in the development of the self and a sense of identity. They also aid with socialisation though seeing things from others' points of view. Whilst this relies on language for narration, increasingly we also have access to photographs and even video capture of earlier generations. These stories and images of prior generations became part of our own personal self-definition.

Claims have been made for family narrative and genealogy as an aid to psychotherapy (Mcgoldrick, 2011). The telling of life narratives can be used effectively, particularly in relation to trauma and clinical disorder (Neuner, Schauer, Klaschik, Karunakara and Elbert, 2004). This is because there are often blocks to thinking about our traumatic experience, and this can interfere with the coherence of narrative accounts. In the course of therapy, the client provides an initial chronological account of their experience, in as much detail as they can, and this is recorded for future comparison. The story is then revisited with the therapist and revised over time. The aim is to transform a fragmented account into one which is coherent, through such reworking. The client is then asked about their emotional response, thoughts and even physical response to the story, and then to relive the experiences in a supported environment. Eventually there is a synchronising of emotion with the final, coherent account of the experience. This aids insight and the 'working through' or processing of the trauma, which can lead to recovery.

More generally in counselling, use of narrative therapy explores people's stories and the impact on their self and functioning ability. Because these stories are often initially 'thin' in terms of detail and description, the purpose of the therapy is to develop 'thicker' and deeper narratives and to explore alternative stories or interpretations (Freedman and Combs, 1996). These are subjective accounts that improve through further recall, organisation and understanding of information. They are not reliant on independent corroboration. The purpose is that of self-understanding, as well as therapeutic validation. The accounts are not open to independent scrutiny.

There are many published biographic enterprises and memoires, many of which involve famous individuals and which do not look towards psychological interpretations. For example, the Jewish banking family of Edmund de Waal, in the 'Hare with the Amber eyes', provides a chronological account of the rise and fall in family fortunes related to the Second World War. It discusses art collections as a sub-theme (de Waal, 2010). Juliet Nicolson describes her female family members over generations with a chapter focused on each individual, including her famous forebear Vita Sackville-West, in exploring women's influence on society and the family (J. Nicolson, 2016). There are also highly innovative approaches to telling such family stories, such as the 'Maus' pictorial book about the author Art Spiegleman's parents' Jewish Holocaust experience. This is drawn as a strip cartoon of mice and other animals, to represent the victims and protagonists, and has amazing immediacy and impact. It is used to describe the Holocaust experience, but also importantly through the author's conversations with his father, their relationship in older age (Spiegleman, 1996/2003).

Collecting information

Using secondary sources, this qualitative investigation seeks depth of context to derive meaning from events for both the reader and the individuals involved, which can be used to generate further understanding and possible ideas for future study (Travers, 2001). The aim is that the themes emerging have wider application than for just my family alone, and may hold meaning for the general interested reader.

The approach is exploratory and in-depth to encompass idiosyncratic experience as well as that more common to a population and to more universal factors. The data collection and analysis occur simultaneously in order to develop general concepts to organise the data and then to integrate these into a more formal set of concepts as the study progresses (N. Frost, 2016). It is hoped that a single family history can be systematically investigated and to have some wider application (Bifulco, 2015). Nollaig Frost, an expert in pluralism, advocates a creative approach to method in social science. She justifies the wide use of different approaches in order to gain a richer understanding of human experience. The challenge is then to 'knit' these approaches together to fill in gaps which exist in any research findings (N. Frost, 2016). A single case study may fill such gaps.

Engaging in qualitative work, particularly when the topic and participants are close to the researcher, requires an exercise in 'reflexivity'. In other words, the investigator needs to be aware of how they may be influencing the course of the data analysis, and in turn be personally influenced (Finlay, 2002): 'There may be some conscious realisations about one's self arising from the process as well as some insight into your relationship with the research (p. 146) (N. Frost, 2016). Researchers who engage with experiential data are involved in the process of continually reflecting upon interpretations of both their experience and the phenomena studied. An awareness is needed of how this occurs, with the aim to effect a more direct contact with experience as lived (Shaw, 2010).

The geography of where families originate, and the historical events that affect their behaviour, are also of central concern. Given that these are applied to the

8 Trust: introducing family narratives

personal narrative, the emotional or personal aspects of geography and history are now outlined.

Emotional geography

Emotional geography is a recognised academic subdiscipline within human geography. It deals with the relationship between personal emotion and geographic places and locations (Gregory, 2011). It focuses on how human emotions relate to their physical environment. It can take many forms and determines how the relationship to particular places can embody identity (Davidson, Smith and Bondi, 2007). It also investigates feelings in various environments and landscapes. Davidson and colleagues (2007) identify three core themes: the location of emotion in bodies and places, the emotional relation of people and environments, and the representations of geography in emotional terms.

Emotional geography thus locates places in personal proximity, and according to their meaning and emotional significance for the individual or group. This can also be considered attachment to place. Such proximity can be on a different scale and metric from the more familiar map-based ones. For example, places where we are born, live, work, take holidays, have friends, emigrate to or from, may all seem close in proximity. They feature in an emotional 'map' with different scaling and positioning of significance to their actual size and distance. Frequently travelled routes to relatives may make those places appear closer and more connected. There are cities we know intimately and others less distant we have never visited and about which we know little. Our personal geography of a region, showing only those places we feel connected to, would look very different from a traditional map.

A nation can also have an emotional geography. Poland has a long and illustrious history but, for a hundred years, it disappeared as a political and geographic entity. It was not visible on any map of Europe. Yet the population within the original (and current) borders retained their language, culture and customs, considered themselves Polish and agitated for independence. The rest of Europe knew of Poland, was in no doubt of its location, and the 'Polish Question' of autonomy was debated in parliaments across Europe. Yet it had no formal map reference or political recognition and its occupying neighbours made substantial attempts to delete its identity.

Emotionally Poland was clearly in existence for the 30 million or so people living in its designated area between Germany, Russia and Austria throughout the 1800s, despite being geographically non-existent as a map reference. This cultural and emotional idea remained real during many years of unsuccessful armed uprisings, sabotage attempts and passive resistance by its population, but between 1772 and 1920 Poland was only an emotional ideal of home for the people living in its territory and those exiled. Finally, in 1920 it achieved political independence and briefly achieved the autonomy it had craved. Whilst fraught with social problems on an immense scale, it nevertheless preserved a democracy, and a liberal and socially benevolent society with a flourishing of learning, culture and art for twenty years. Then it fell again under Russian Soviet control, and despite having a formal national identity (unlike the Baltic States) it was locked behind the Iron Curtain with constraints on democracy and freedom of movement and communication. The emotional geography of Poland has had continuous existence. In this book, when I write about Poland I will refer to the peoples and territory approximately within its current boundaries. For most Poles this is the enduring emotional concept of Poland.

Emotion and history

A related concept, though not an acknowledged subdiscipline, is that of emotional history. This is where individuals and cultures fasten on particular historical events that affect their sense of identity, or their moral sense of right and its transgression. There are a number of such emotional historical events from our Islands – for example, the Battle of the Boyne for the Irish, maybe Glencoe for the Scots and the Battle of Hastings for the English, and the Battle of Britain for the UK as a whole. But the Holocaust, from modern times, is perhaps the most obvious example known internationally. Individuals and cultures choose to remember the genocide and to retain a strong (albeit negative) emotional attachment shown for example on Holocaust Memorial Day. This commemorates 'the six million Jews murdered in the Holocaust, and the millions of people killed in Nazi Persecution and in subsequent genocides'.[2] The date chosen, 27 January, marked the liberation of Auschwitz, the largest Nazi death camp.

Most of those killed in the Holocaust came from Poland, and indeed the Nazis located Auschwitz and other death camps in Poland. The Poles keep the memory of this alive. They have established museums in Auschwitz, and other death camps, as a memorial and lesson to the future. The Holocaust and its eleven million victims included six million Polish nationals, and the near obliteration of the Polish nation. This is inclusive of both its Jewish and Christian members, its Semitic and Slavic population. Nazi genocide was applied to both Jews and Slavs, on the basis of supposed racial inferiority. It was more viciously and extensively applied to Jews, but the Nazi plan to eradicate the Poles once no longer needed for slave labour was clearly articulated by Hitler. As well as racial genocide there was also wholesale obliteration of particular groups under threat—'politicides', including academics in Poland. Given my profession, this is another personal link to history. But German apology to Poles for Nazi genocide and the destruction of Warsaw was slow in coming, due to barriers formed by the Iron Curtain. East Germany admitted no Second World War responsibility until after reunification in 1990, when it apologised for the Holocaust and to Poland. A formal apology from united Germany was given in 1994 by the visiting President Herzog for the destruction of Warsaw and the killing of millions of Poles, on the 50th anniversary of the Warsaw Uprising.[3] No reparations were paid to Poland after the Second World War. It seems unfair. This is emotional history.

Ethical consideration

All psychological investigations start with a consideration of ethics. This balances the degree to which the endeavour is of benefit to knowledge against costs to participants. Most studies ensure confidentiality and provide at least a degree of anonymity. All usually provide informed consent about participation. So how does this apply to a detailed case study of one's own family, in which the main actors are no longer alive but all are identified? To whom does the story belong? Who can give consent?

The documents and photographs used have all come into my hands, either gifted or as a consequence of my power of attorney of my mother's estate in her declining years. So the documents are in my possession. However, I still needed to check how the family felt about this possible invasion of privacy. I contacted my own generation to get their agreement, and the only living member of my father's generation, an aunt in Poland. There is always the danger of uncovering something detrimental about the family, and individuals, but in fact this did not occur. There are also issues of privacy. I quote from letters that were written and sent privately, and were kept safely for over 60 years in their original envelopes, which suggests they were considered precious and of significance. I only hope their writers would have had no qualms about making these public. I do not probe into the lives of my sisters and cousins in relating this account. My own generation is examined in more general terms, not by individual characteristics. I see us as the recipients of the story and its events, not as its main actors. I hope my family will remain magnanimous about the project when they see the final product! I expect it will spark family discussion, the future unearthing of more information or interpretation, refutation of some of the 'facts' presented and a dynamic discourse which may lead to alternative conclusions. I am happy with that.

Materials

In this investigation of my family I have mainly used secondary methods comprising the following.

Journals, diaries and unpublished biographies

I have had access to several journals, diaries or biographies. A significant one was a brief handwritten biography of my grandfather Tadeusz written by his father Władysław, soon after his son's death in the early 1920s, and added to in the following few years. He dedicated it to his grandson Jurek. In addition, my mother Christine wrote a brief summary of my father's life based on her conversations with him and her cataloguing of various documents about his life. A recently acquired fragment from my Aunt Marysia in Warsaw, recounting how her father found my grandmother after the war, is also included. My maternal grandfather (Hugh O'Neill) wrote a full account of both his early life and his visits to Poland in his unpublished autobiography. [This was printed and distributed to family members by my mother's cousin, Christopher O'Neill.]. His early history also appears in a published text (O'Neill, 1967).

Letters

I have a number of letters written in Polish: a handful from Myszka, my father's first wife in Warsaw in 1942, and from my grandmother Maria, also during the Second World War and delivered through Red Cross couriers to my father, Jurek, in France. There are another five or so letters from Maria post-war to Jurek in England; seven or eight letters to Maria from her close sister-in-law Grazyna and niece Marysia, after 1958 when Maria came to England. A few other letters survive from relatives such as Maria's sister-in-law Jadwiga, married to her brother Jan. There are also a number of letters in English from Jurek to Christine during their courtship in 1945–8 when he was in London and she in Derby. Also some remain from 1949 when Christine went back to her parents in Swansea to give birth to their first daughter whilst Jurek was working in London. These are largely quoted in full; I have not edited the letters (apart from keeping consistency with names/diminutives). My mother's family would send a monthly round robin group letter, and I quote from this her account of our family trip to Poland in 1965.

Archived material

Archived material was mainly discovered by my cousin Piotr in Warsaw, who undertook his own family investigation and travelled to the places where the family originated, including those now outside Poland. Another Polish cousin, Ania, sent me the link to the Płock archive, now digital, which gave details relevant to my grandmother (her great-aunt) Maria's family tree in terms of births, deaths and marriages. In a few instances I accessed materials at the Kew national archive – for example, passenger lists of ships crossing to England from Gibraltar during the war. Disappointingly, there are no relevant records of SOE, these records having been lost in a fire in Baker Street after the war. Some think this was so that information could not get into Soviet Russian hands. However, books have recently been published on SOE training (Crowdy, 2016) and on the Polish division (Valentine, 2006), and I quote this as relevant. However, I did receive a copy of a possible SOE document (Jurek's identity card listed as in the Polish army) and more detailed copies of Jurek's Royal Airforce activities from the RAF at Northolt.

Formal documents

Christine had carefully collated all the family documents from Jurek and his mother Maria. This included my grandparents' marriage certificate, grandfather's death certificate, Jurek's school identification records, university identity card, and the death certificate of Jurek's first wife from Auschwitz. Documents relating to

Jurek's wartime activities have also been preserved. My grandmother, father and mother all seemed intent on keeping these as historical documents.

Photographs

Whilst photographs are of limited use in a written narrative, they give a very evocative idea of time and place. Various ones have come into my hands from the Polish family extending from the early twentieth century. A number were collated by my grandmother Maria, but I have also been given many new ones from the family in Warsaw. Some are of individuals and houses I had never seen before. This gives some clue to character, social circumstances, leisure activities and family likenesses. There are many photographs of good-looking people in wonderful uniforms or stylish hats and coats, sometimes seated in large cars. Others are informal, at picnics or by lakes, or in one, my father and his cousins dressed for tennis. It reminds us this was the first generation to have family photographs taken at home. We don't know who took the photographs, although Jurek's cousin Stas is remembered as a keen photographer. How the photographs survived the various wars, occupation and destruction of Warsaw is a mystery. It does show, however, their importance to the family members who preserved them, under very difficult conditions.

DNA 'cultural analysis'

Finally, I acquired a source of information different from the others. I sent to '23andme' a saliva sample for a genetic cultural analysis to see whether the cultural elements of the story I have researched are evident in my own genes. Whilst this may yet be at a speculative stage of development, gene-based cultural analysis would indicate the physical transmission from generation to generation to symbolise genetic inheritance through families. It provides a source uninfluenced by subjective family interpretation.

Published eye-witness accounts

Other information utilised includes many personal quotes from autobiographic documents of individuals who witnessed and were involved in events and have put these into the public domain. Some are published biographies by others (e.g. Marie Curie describing Warsaw in the 1880s), others personal wartime accounts (e.g. Jan Karski who witnessed both the Jewish ghetto and the lead-up to the Katyn massacre, or Wira who was a teenage soldier in the home army in Warsaw). Others are archived interviews with wartime survivors collated on the Internet.[4]

Developing thematic analysis

The challenge is to analyse this secondary information in such a way to speak to common themes of interest to other people. The pre-selected main themes are all academically current in psychology, and other social sciences, all relevant to families, family history and genealogy. They are also areas which I have researched in my career. These three themes will be applied to the individuals described in the chapters, to others of their time and to the later generation, including to me and my siblings. They will also to some extent apply to the Polish nation and at times to the Polish community in England. Other subtopics emerge. One is heroism and protecting others. Another is the forgetting of trauma and re-remembering; another is immigration and relocation, taking family stories to other countries. The three main organising themes are described further below. Much has already been said about identity, so I will begin with the other two.

Attachment: loving one's family

Attachment theory was devised by John Bowlby, a psychiatrist and psychoanalyst working in the UK in the 1940s. In this he was aided by Dr Mary Ainsworth, a developmental psychologist from Canada who came to work with him at the Tavistock clinic in London (Holmes, 1993). Attachment theory emphasises the key importance of care in childhood and the close bonding relationship with the mother/main carer for later healthy development. When positive, the baby experiences feelings of security, the mother is able to regulate the baby's negative emotions by soothing behaviour (for example, when the baby is crying over hunger or cold) and in time the developing infant gains the confidence to explore the environment and learn (Bowlby, 1958, 1988). The first carer is usually, but not necessarily, the birth mother, with fathers, substitute fathers and siblings all having a part to play in the child's learning to relate. A secure child will then develop, accompanied by trust in others and the ability to share confidences and thus grow with support (Bifulco and Thomas, 2012). This is a lifetime benefit, which also develops resilience against adversity.

Loss of key attachment figures is a threat to attachment and development, and is experienced as painful by the child. Both separation and bereavement are challenges to the child's coping and adjustment and can engender lasting insecurity. However, the presence of good care and sympathetic concern can mitigate risk associated with loss (Bifulco, Harris and Brown, 1992). When the initial bonding is hampered, or when later childhood experience includes neglect or hostile actions including abuse, the baby shows insecurity in their way of relating. This insecurity can show itself as anxious (clinging), avoidant (distancing) or disorganised (a mixed, confused) response (Ainsworth, Blehar, Waters and Wall, 1978; Main and Hesse, 1990). These relating styles can persist into adult life and result in poorer quality of close relationships (for example, involving conflict or indifference in marriage) or poor emotional control by the adult (for example, uncontrolled anger or anxiety under stress) (Bifulco and Thomas, 2012). Mistrust is typically high among those insecure, which forms barriers to confiding in others and closes off sources of support and help. Individuals with insecure attachment styles are more prone to psychological disorder as well as relationship difficulties around isolation, partner violence, parenting; and to the negative impacts of separation and loss.

Certain key concepts from attachment theory are used to help develop interpretations of family members experience and actions in this project (see Figure 1.2). These include a secure base (comfort from the mother and family); safe haven (a place of perceived safety, contrasted with my own notion of 'hazardous haven'), caring (both caregiving and care receiving from parents and support figures) and trust. Another aspect is loss and its impact, involving separation and bereavement, and reunion. Finally, the attachment concepts of autonomy (development of self-reliance), emotional regulation (having a cool head in relationships, and to address adversity) and exploration (in the wider sense of enjoying the environment, travel and learning).

Resilience: how to cope and survive

Resilience is connected both to attachment and identity. Its key element is positive adaptation in the face of adversity. At its most basic it is about survival, but in everyday life it is about functioning well under stress or adversity (Rutter, 2007). Studies of resilience first identify the adversity or stressors involved and then look at the positive coping responses in relation to well-being, positive relationships and high self-esteem (Masten and Curtis, 2000). Usually this concept is applied to the individual, but the same principle can apply to families and even nations, these are resilient when showing positive adaptation in times of stress.

Most investigators agree that positive elements in childhood can confer resilience – a secure family background, with stable features and positive relationships. Sometimes it is partial or limited – for example, one close parent with another hostile; or through support from other relatives or family friends in the absence of closeness to parents (Bifulco, 2009). School can also be a source of protection against adversity in developing self-esteem and competence. Religion too can play this part as a basis for support from the religious community, but also through faith and hope. Personal characteristics, such as high IQ and humour, have been noted (Fonagy, Steele, Steele, Higgitt et al., 1994). The aspects of resilience followed are support (positive relationships, social appeal), economic advantage (education, community resources) and positive functioning (self-worth, self-efficacy and self-determination). Underlying these are the themes of hope, faith and optimism.

Identity: who we are and where we belong

Erik Erikson was a psychologist in the mid-twentieth century and the first to take a lifespan view of human development and to explore issues of identity. Identity involves a sense of 'who we are' but also 'where we belong'. This includes personal identity in the sense of self, including the idiosyncrasies and features that identify each of us from one another. It also includes our social identity comprising social roles, including cultural identity, which speaks to our sense of belonging. Questions include 'To which group are we a part?' and 'With which groups do we feel like-minded and at home?' Both aspects can be more or less positive or negative. We may develop feelings about our own identity, which we may cherish and of which we feel proud. Conversely we may attach shame and a sense of inferiority about who we are. This can be subjectively determined (for instance, by low self-esteem) but it can also mirror, or be triggered by, discrimination from others. It can happen at the personal or group level. People can also idealise their sense of self or the group to which they want to belong. This can lead to distress at not belonging. Conversely, to security and a value for belonging.

Erikson describes the development of identity in the individual through eight life-stages. Each stage describes both a positive and negative psychological characteristic (for example, trust vs mistrust) as well as a 'virtue' (for example, hope). Each describes a step towards autonomy and maturation in the life of an individual from the earliest years. It does not proscribe where problems in development might occur, but gives a normative view – all stages have positive or negative elements. These eight stages are identified in Figure 1.1, and each is used as a chapter heading in this book. The stages cover the events in both my family's story and those of the Polish nation. This serves to convey a trajectory from my grandparents' birth through to my own upbringing in the UK. In fact, two of the eight stages

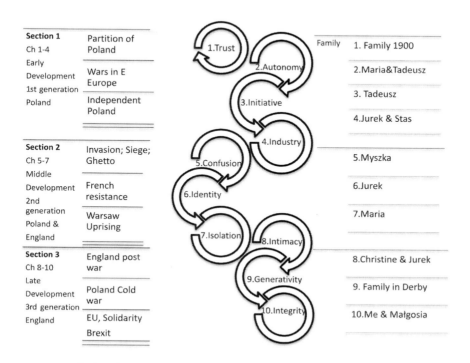

FIGURE 1.1 Erikson's stages of identity development and book structure

are represented twice to show their positive (identity, intimacy) and negative (confusion, isolation) features to give ten chapters in all and reflect experiences at times of conflict.

The stage covered in this chapter is the first: 'Trust'. Erikson considered the development of trust to be the first task of the emerging child, with this persisting throughout development. Trust is also a central principle of attachment: where trust develops between the child and mother or primary carer, then there is much greater likelihood that the child will be able to make close supportive relationships in later life with trusted others. If there is a failure of trust due to neglect or maltreatment of the child, this can hamper the child for years to come. Trust allows the child to have confidence that when the mother is briefly away, she will return. The balance of trust with mistrust depends largely on the quality of the maternal relationship and with family in early life. The 'virtue' associated with trust is said to be *Hope*. In this book, the issue of family trust, trust in the past and the people who preceded me, is the starting point of the endeavour. The aim is to see how the extra knowledge derived will enhance a sense of cultural and familial identity and hope for the future. Trust in the past is believed to aid moving into the future. This extends to hope for the European enterprise.

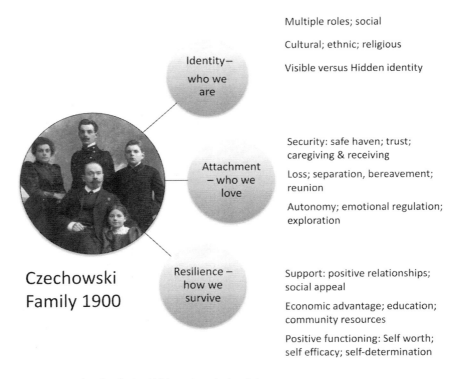

FIGURE 1.2 The family in 1900, and analysis of themes

Polish cultural narratives

Cultural identity can be transmitted through cultural or family narratives. This involves the transmission of stories about a culture, or a key event in a culture, which becomes a defining feature that leads to a particular type of story and solidarity in the group. It often involves a retelling of recent history from the group's point of view and may entail narratives around journeys, survival, resilience or maybe victimisation. There is research on the Polish cultural narratives among immigrants to England (White, 2011a, b). This differentiates the group identity of the three successive communities of Poles who came to England: in 1945, 1989 and 2004. Each has a different tale. One relevant here is the 'long journey' (Galasinska, 2010) told by the earliest generation about the Second World War, how they travelled to England through difficult routes, of trauma and persecution in Nazi and Soviet labour camps, stories of wartime struggles in the Battle of Britain, Monte Casino or the Warsaw Uprising. Of how they became a marooned community of pre-communist Poles abroad, on their resilience, adaptation and survival in their new country. Fictional accounts have been produced, often involving extensive research of Poland in the Second World War era (Furst, 1995/2005). My youngest sister has written two novels set in the Polish community in England post-war describing the experience of later generations (J. Czechowska, 2006, 2012).

The families from this generation of Poles settled all over the UK, in highly organised communities – for example in the Midlands (where I was raised) and in West London (where I now live). Complex relations between Britain, communist Poland and the Soviet Union meant that the community members in the UK could not return to live in Poland post-war, with most not even able to visit until the mid-1960s. They also held onto a different version of modern Polish history of the twentieth century than that taught in Poland under communism. For example, whilst the world professed ignorance, the local community had witness evidence of Soviet genocide and brutal repression (e.g. the Katyn massacre), as well as suffering the denigration of Polish resistance (e.g. in the Warsaw Uprising) among leaders still resident in the UK.

Many newly published accounts of Poles in the Second World Ware are emerging. These give eye-witness accounts about wartime experiences, including those from teenagers in the armed Warsaw Uprising. This includes accounts by 'Wira' a pseudonym for Danuta Szhlachetko, her account written by her son (Szhlachetko, 2015), and 'Warsaw Boy', whose author fought in the Uprising as a teenager and subsequently lived in the USA working as a journalist (Borowiec, 2015). Both describe Warsaw, central to the family narrative described in this book. Many other accounts emerging are self-published, such as Jola Malin's account of her family being deported to Siberia at the beginning of the war, to be released in Anders 'army' to trek from the East Soviet Union through the Middle East and then being evacuated to Uganda (Malin, 2013). I quote her in relation to the Polish community in London. Many other recent accounts are provided by Jewish survivors of the period (Olczak-Ronnier, 2004; Wittenberg, 2016), who give an informative and different slant on Polish politics.

These accounts describe the trauma of people who struggled through the Nazi invasion of their country, who suffered German concentration camps, Russian labour camps, slave labour and separation from families often dispersed around the world, as far afield as Kenya or Australia, before settling in Britain. Each story is different and extraordinary. The hardships suffered are often greater than that of my family, who had privileged origins and therefore access to resources, and in some instances (for example, with my father Jurek) the luck needed for survival. However, not all experiences emerging from these war accounts are negative. Resilience comes from being able to hold on to positive experience of attachment and identity and sense of self, to support people through stressful times. Many of the experiences related are positive – for example, warm and affectionate childhood experiences, close marriages and family relationships, which increases resilience. There are also a thousand kindnesses, bestowed in war-torn contexts. It is by no means a 'misery memoire'.

The Polish community in 1950s and 1960s Britain created a safe Polish haven in the heart of England. Whilst having the usual English influences, children in this community went to Saturday Polish school, played in Polish youth football teams, attended the Polish guides and scouts, and went to Polish Mass and to Polish social clubs for social events and dances. My father Jurek was a founding member and chairman of the 'Dom Polski' social club, a community resource for the Poles in Derby which both my parents supported enthusiastically. The club provided for the community and was a focal point for the Poles who lived in the city. We moved in a Polish setting – our decorator was Polish, as was the local photographer for weddings and family occasions; our priest was Polish, we bought from Polish food shops and my father got the weekly Polish paper. My parents' friends were Polish, and the Catholic primary school I attended had children only from either Polish or Irish backgrounds. This community was readily accepted by the practical, and friendly, Derby population. These refugee/exiled families did well, but with numerous challenges – mothers and grandparents who did not learn English, parents whose basic education had been interrupted by war and struggled with the new language, families who dropped social class, families damaged by the unacknowledged and untreated trauma. As Polish Midlanders, the community learned to fit in with English neighbours, with ties to an imagined and idealised pre-war Poland, far from the reality of its communist incarnation. A somewhat marooned community, in danger of fossilisation.

Modern Poland

In some ways the issues tackled here are wider and of contemporary concern. Our current society has many debates about immigration. Often economic migration is confused with political exile, refugee status or asylum seeking. Each poses different questions and challenges, moral, economic and social. Whilst Poles have in the past been largely welcomed, and clearly contribute to British society through their diligent work ethic, loyalty and pro-social values, after the more recent arrivals post- 2004 and the anti-immigration newspaper headlines of the last year or two, this is no longer holding true. All of this has come to a head as Britain is poised to exit the European Community after 45 years as a member. In direct contrast, Poland's active role in the European community since accession in 2004 as a growing economy with a large and young population is increasing as it holds the Presidency. Time will tell how the EU will affect both countries and how the relationship between our two countries is sustained.

To introduce Poland to those who have only sketchy knowledge: it is a democratic republic, now often labelled as being in Central Europe (once Eastern Europe), which emerged from Soviet communism in 1989 and acceded into the European Community in 2004. At the time of writing it holds the Presidency of the European Union (under Donald Tusk) and has a female prime minister (Beata Szydło). The country is the ninth largest in the EU in relation to land mass, with the sixth largest population. Its name *Pola* means a field or rural plane. It is now bordered by Russia to the north east, Germany to the west, with the Czech Republic and Slovakia to the south. It also borders Baltic countries to the north east, and Belarus and Ukraine directly to the east (Figure 1.3). It is a stunningly beautiful country: it has more lakes in the north than any other country, 23 national parks, is the fourth most forested country in Europe and has 58,000 miles of sandy Baltic Sea coastline. It has the Carpathian Mountains in the south, of which the Tatra Mountains on its southern border are the highest, with views rivalling the Alps. It has extensive wildlife – not only beaver and game animals such as deer and wild boar, but also the largest stork population in Europe (these can be seen in their large nests balanced in trees and even on farmhouse roofs). These coexist with brown bears, grey wolves, lynx and moose and even bison living in the wild. It is blessed in its natural green resources.

On the map shown of modern Poland (Figure 1.3), the cities key to this family story have been circled. Most of the story is about Warsaw, the capital, located centrally on the river Wisła (or Vistula). Other key cities are Płock, where my grandparents were brought up and where my father was born, and Ciechanow, where my grandfather was born and where his parents and siblings lived for some years. Gdansk, at the end of the Wisła where it meets the Baltic Sea, is where my Cygler cousins lived, and nearby is Gdynia where my grandmother Maria departed by ship to England. Other significant places in the East of Poland, include Suwałki, where my great-grandmother Maria-Victoria lived, still in Polish territory, and not far from modern Lithuania and its capital Vilnius (at one time in Poland). Further east in this region are other places of significance but no longer in Poland. These include Rudzk (near Pinsk), from where the Czechowski family originated and where they had their country home; and Mohylew, further east, where Maria-Victoria, my great-grandmother's family, had their country house. Other notable places are Grodno and Augustow in the north east and Łódz, south of Warsaw where my grandfather was involved in military action. Częstochowa in the south, a famous religious site, was a place where my grandparents lived for a while after exile in Romania.

20 Trust: introducing family narratives

FIGURE 1.3 Map of modern Poland

Poland has always been a Western-looking country. Its religion is Roman Catholic, its political tradition democratic and parliamentary, its alphabet Roman and its historical allies France, Sweden and the UK. For much of its history it had a liberal and welcoming policy towards Jews (hence the large numbers settled there from the twelfth century through to the Second World War). It has a proud political history – a successful democracy with a commonwealth at one time encompassing Lithuania and Ukraine and a land mass extending from the Baltic to the Black Sea. But Poland has had a cursed modern history through its aggressive political neighbours in the 1800s and 1900s: its submersion under partition with years of resistance and struggle trying to keep its language and cultural identity; its near annihilation under the Nazis; its threat from the Red Army; and repression under Soviet communism. Poland seems to exist in a historical vortex where the population is thrown about by the convergence of huge opposing forces. Norman Davis calls it 'God's playground' – the place where the ancient gods chose to play with humanity for their sport. It is also described as being between the 'hammer and the anvil', a reference to its vulnerable position between its German and Russian neighbours. Yet Polish survival attests to it being tempered in the heat and the pounding of the blacksmith's hammer produces strength and resilience. This has shown itself not only in its continuous reinvention and resurrection, but also in the story of its families in both Poland and the diaspora. I believe mine is one such family.

The following chapters follow chronologically in three sections to represent three generations, starting from my grandparents' lives, placing their experience in both a historical and geographic context to examine themes in these narratives, and ultimately themes in the genealogical enterprise as a whole.

Notes

1   http://culture.pl/en/article/lucky-ship-rebellion-desertion-and-love-on-the-ms-batory
2   http://hmd.org.uk/page/about-hmd-and-hmdt#sthash.hWFEpdwd.dpuf
3   http://articles.latimes.com/1994-08-02/news/mn-22740_1_warsaw-uprising-poland
4   http://hmd.org.uk/content/19041943-start-warsaw-ghetto-uprising?gclid=CNn55u PN59ACFWgq0wodwQcDjw

SECTION I
Poland
The first generation

This section will outline the first phase of development, which includes autonomy, initiative and industry (Figure 2.1). This part of the narrative is set in Poland and extends from 1886/7, with the birth of Maria and Tadeusz, to 1939 before the outbreak of the Second World War. It covers the upbringing of my grandparents,

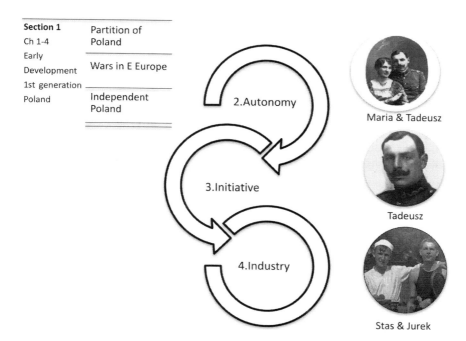

FIGURE 2.1 The first phases of Erikson's development as applied to the family

and then of my father Jurek and his cousin Stas. It describes Polish conditions in the Russian sector of Partition, when my grandparents were growing up. It then follows Tadeusz's experience fighting in the First World War and the Polish–Soviet war. Finally, it ends with an independent Polish state and the rebirth of culture in Warsaw at a time of economic challenge. The themes of autonomy, initiative and industry reflect the development of Poland as a nation, as well as my grandparents' independence and then my father's growing autonomy. It relates the psychological developmental themes with challenges and adaptation required of the volatile socio-political context.

2

AUTONOMY

Living under partition (1886–1913)

> Will, therefore, is the unbroken determination to exercise free choice as well as self-restraint.
>
> Erik Erikson

Introduction

This chapter explores the theme of 'autonomy', the second stage in Erikson's developmental scheme. It describes my grandparents' birth, background, childhood and early adulthood in Poland in the late 1800s and early 1900s. It also covers the debates over Polish autonomy, both in terms of my grandparents' developing identity as Poles and the drive for Polish national independence at the end of the nineteenth century. Learning autonomy is one of the key tasks of development, when a child can learn to become a separate entity from its parents, to acquire competencies and grow self-reliance. If this task should fail or be incomplete, then there are impediments to competence, coping and relationships.

Autonomy, when underdeveloped, results in a high level of dependency, lack of a sense of responsibility and often an exaggerated estimate of other people's worth at the expense of one's own. Individual action is impeded, others' opinions and approval sought at every turn, personal competence and confidence stunted. If, on the other hand, autonomy is overdeveloped, this can lead to over-self-reliance, lack of trust in others' competence and overdevelopment of solitary behaviour to the exclusion of others. This can form a barrier to social support. The ideal is the middle path: a growth in self-reliance and confidence balanced by good judgement about one's own limitations. This requires an understanding of when to approach others for help and advice. This latter depends on developed trust, the task of the earlier developmental stage. The ability to trust and seek help appropriately is a key challenge of attachment. Similar points apply on a national level: allies are needed and cooperation required among states, but ultimately nations need to forge their own future and take action to secure it.

Erikson relates the sense of autonomy to an awareness of justice. It is through growing independence and responsibility for those around that moral authority needs to grow and justice be applied. For Erikson the virtue associated with this stage is 'Willpower'. It is through willpower that autonomy can achieve its end. The negative psychological characteristics are Doubt and Shame, both of which impede autonomy. In this chapter the theme of autonomy is discussed in relation to my grandparents' developing independence as they grew up – particularly my grandfather, who became a highly independent and self-motivated man. This was in difficult political circumstances, where Poles were refused access to power and were legally and constitutionally denied autonomy by the Russian state. My grandfather, Tadeusz, proved to have had a strong will to succeed for his country and developed a high level of autonomy. In her own way, within the family, my grandmother also achieved this.

In terms of identity it will be seen that national identity had to be hidden given the political situation at the time; in terms of attachment the families described are close; the elements for resilience are built up for adversity in future years.

Poland partitioned

My grandparents were born within a year of each other, my grandmother Maria in 1886, and my grandfather Tadeusz in 1887. Both spent most of their childhood in Płock, some hundred kilometres north west of Warsaw, on the banks of the River Wisła as it flows north to the Baltic Sea. It is a beautiful Renaissance city, sitting high above the wide river, and an ancient capital of the region, dating from the eleventh century. Its castle, cathedral, abbey and ancient monuments remain, bordered by a Polish national park and area of outstanding beauty. In the Victorian era the city had elegant boulevards and a medieval market square. It was a centre of culture and learning hosting the oldest high school in Poland, dating from the twelfth century and a Scientific Society dating from 1820. In many ways a fine place for my great-grandparents to settle and my grandparents to live and flourish.

At this time, Płock and all 'Polish' lands and cities to the east, including Warsaw, were under Russian control, as one of the three partitions of Poland from 1795 (Davies, 2005; Figure 2.2). Since the last failed uprising in 1863, when tens of thousands of Poles were taken in chain gangs to Siberia and 100,000 forced into exile in France, the Russification of East Poland followed. This attempted to expunge every trace of Polish consciousness – in education, in government, in intellectual and religious life. For example, all signs in Warsaw were forcibly changed from the Roman to Cyrillic (Russian) alphabet. Many of the population wore black in mourning (Quin, 1995). However, the population remained tenacious in resistance and the narrative tales around the uprising and enforced deportation served to reinforce a sense of national identity both at home and abroad. The Poles had not forgotten their country's proud history, its prior prestige in Europe, its large

Autonomy: living under partition   **27**

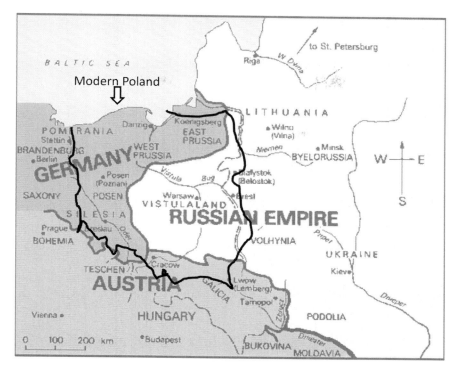

FIGURE 2.2 Map of Polish partitions

land mass and established democracy. The population knew itself to be Polish. It had a strong national identity resistant to occupation, which increased its sense of identity through a cultural narrative around reistance to oppression.

Technological advance

The last years of the nineteenth century in Europe were ones of excitement and energy, with leaps forward in invention and mechanisation. This increased individual autonomy over the environment. Such innovation led to social change and marked the beginning of the modern world we might recognise. Thus the 1880s saw revolutions in communications specifically through transport, printing, photography and generation of electrical power. In Germany, Benz's first three-wheel automobile and internal combustion engine, a predecessor of the four-wheeled automobile, was developed. In England, John Kemp Starley from Coventry designed the Rover Bicycle with a modern chain drive to make the cycle an efficient mode of travel. (These must have been exported widely, as I recently learned that 'bicycle' in Polish is still called a 'Rover'). Boyd Dunlop in Scotland patented the first practical inflatable tyre. Whilst rail travel was already established, a new national rail network was underway in the UK, and the Orient-Express running between Paris and Constantinople emerged in 1883. Such recent inventions of cycles, cars and trains would become great enthusiasms of my grandfather Taduesz, who was both a keen sportsman and engineer.

Other communication in the form of printing was developing at equal speed. The first Linotype machine revolutionised the art of printing for large-scale numbers, realised in the *Wall Street Journal*, but also in the printing of classic books. By 1880 these were in wide supply including, from that era: the original *Oxford English Dictionary*, the *American Adventures of Huckleberry Finn*, Dostoevsky's *Brothers Karamazov*, Tolstoy's *Anna Karenina* and *War and Peace*. In the UK, Robert Louis Stevenson published both *Treasure Island* and *The Strange Case of Dr Jekyll and Mr Hyde*, whilst Conan Doyle published his first Sherlock Holmes tale. All these books are still popular nearly 140 years later.

Photography also grew in both technique and popularity, with family photographs becoming newly available. George Eastman made cameras accessible to the masses through the Kodak No 1. From this point we can track families, and family likenesses, through the photographs available. This became an important way of recording family life by the end of the nineteenth and beginning of the twentieth century. Whilst many photographs were formally posed in studios, others showed family house interiors and exteriors and holiday settings. These are great documentary sources. Radio too was in development, with Heinrich Hertz in Hamburg having built a basic transmitter and receiver device in 1888. Other advances came through the development and commercial production of electric lighting in the late 1800s. The Edison Illuminating Company in New York created a central power plant for electricity distribution, and this became more commonplace in Europe. Therefore, the elements of our modern world were in production by the late 1800s – a great leap ahead in mechanisation, technology and communication.

However, politically the times were unstable and dangerous. Royal families were still very much in evidence in Europe, many famously related through the British Queen Victoria, including those responsible for Poland, such as Kaiser Wilhelm I (Germany), Emporer Francis Joseph I of Austria-Hungary and Tzar Alexander II (Russia). There were also royal families in Spain (Alfonso XII) and Italy (Umberto I). The 1880s were marked by several notable assassinations, including Tsar Alexander II of Russia, President James Garfield of the USA and Lord Frederick Cavendish, British Chief Secretary for Ireland. An attempt to assassinate Queen Victoria in 1882 was unsuccessful. These events provoked political instability.

Other sources of social instability were due to rapid industrialisation and movement of people to cities, which led to poverty, pollution and illness. These were rife among London's population of six million people. The fifth cholera pandemic in the 1880s resulted in 5,500 deaths in the East End of London alone. It killed a million people in Russia. Thus the experience of new mechanisation, innovation and communication collided with deteriorating social conditions. Europe, whilst becoming smaller and more accessible due to increased transport and communication possibilities, was also a more dangerous continent.

Autonomy: living under partition 29

Family background

Tadeusz Czechowski, my grandfather, was the oldest of three children born to Władysław and Maria-Victoria. Both his parents' families originated in Eastern Poland in the Polesie district, also known as the Krecy region. This borderland, between Lithuania, Ukraine and Russia, is now in the country of Belarus (Figure 2.3). It is a lowland area, stretching east along the course of the River Prypet to the Dnieper. An ancient region, it is where the Slavonic tribes are said to have originated. It is an area of forest with age-old oak and fir, clear rivers, blue lakes and the impenetrable Prypet marshes and wetlands, which run along the Ukrainian border. Key cities in the region are Minsk, located centrally (now the capital of Belarus), not to be mistaken with Pinsk in the south west of the region near the marshes. The Czechowski estate and farm was near Pinsk at Rudzk, five kilometres from a village called Janow Poleski. Tadeusz's mother's family, the Rodziewiczes, had their country house in Mohylew, in the same district but further north and east, on the very border with Russia. Whilst both great-grandparents were born in their country estates, they subsequently moved further west to Płock and Suwałki respectively, when adult. Throughout Tadeusz's childhood, his family would visit both country houses for holidays and festivals. Close to this location are sites of historical interest important to the family narrative. These include Grodno (Hrodna) on the western side of the region, the site of an important battle in 1920, and Katyn, a forested area northeast of Minsk in Russia, forever now associated with a massacre.

My grandfather Tadeusz was born into landed gentry. This *szlachta* class was traditionally powerful (having independent authority and participating in the

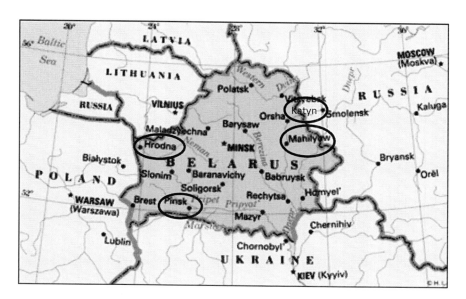

FIGURE 2.3 Map of Belarus, previously Polesie, East Poland

Parliament or *Sejm*). However, it had been dispossessed by the Polish Partition and defeat of the uprisings, and was greatly reduced in numbers. Many of the populist uprisings up until the late 1800s had been coordinated by the gentry, who used their manor houses for this purpose. Untitled, this class represented a larger minor nobility than in other European countries. It included the rich as well as those who had become quite poor under the Partition. However, most owned country houses. These varied in scale and opulence – the most extravagant were termed 'palaces' and were probably like English country estates or large hunting lodges. The more modest were small wooden houses. Families would congregate at these houses in summer, Christmas and Easter to foster strong family relationships and to appreciate the land in Tolstoyan style, before returning to apartments in towns and cities.

The Czechowski family, documented from the twelfth century, had an entitlement to use the Oksza coat of arms (featuring an axe, shield and crown). The surname was originally double-barrelled (Oksza-Czechowski). My grandfather simplified the name to Czechowski, but wore the crest on a gold signet ring passed down through the family. Their country house in the late 1800s is described in the publication *Wedding in Rudzk*, written by Tadeusz's aunt Helena (H. Czechowska, 1895). The house at Rudzk was located close to a village which then boasted one main road and a narrow-gauge railway line, the daily train taking one and a half hours to reach the nearest major town. On one side of the village was a river, surrounded by vegetable gardens and nearby a chapel with a well-known icon of the Virgin Mary. The family house was approached by an avenue of old trees. It was a single-storey property built of brick and wood with a whitewashed stucco exterior, its gabled roof covered in shingle. The distinctive front porch, supported by two wooden columns, was echoed by a similar porch, which led onto the back garden. The house had ten rooms, including rooms for servants. The layout was typical, comprising a centrally located corridor and rooms to the right and left leading on to the garden and orchards. There was an office, bedrooms, including guest rooms, a maid's room, pantry and a kitchen, which led to the stairs going up to the attic rooms. The living room and dining room had traditional wooden and upholstered furniture made earlier in the nineteenth century. The dining room, hung with dark paper and bright stripes, had at its centre a large table, upholstered chairs, richly carved sideboards and a decorative clock. The family clock, in ornate gold under its glass dome, is still with the family in Warsaw. The most important room of the house was the living room; its floors were stained mahogany, its walls were painted white. It housed a Bechstein grand piano, sofa, armchairs, rocking chair and paintings. A number of family members were musical, including my great-grandmother Maria-Victoria and her daughter Grazyna.

Blossoming cherry trees and a small garden of fruit bushes grew in front of the downstairs windows. The driveway leading to the house then turned towards a tennis court. Not far from the main house were outbuildings which included an icehouse, stables, barns, smokehouse and a large number of beehives. The land was both arable and pasture, but also had extensive forest, and originally covered an area of nearly 2,000 acres in the 1880s. It included the Awulsk farm; a large and productive enterprise. It had a smokehouse where different kinds of meats were prepared, which together with the yellow cheese produced were sent to the Pakulski brothers for sale in Warsaw. The estate also incorporated a cloth factory and a nail factory.

Taduesz's grandfather Alexander was born in 1825 in the house at Rudzk, which he came to own. A surveyor by profession, he married Countess Paulina Półhowska, seven years his junior, and both lived until early the following century; both are buried in the local cemetery in Janow Poleski near to the estate. They had three sons, Stanisław, Justin and Władysław; the latter was father to Tadeusz. Their only daughter Helena, the youngest in the family, became both a teacher and writer, and later lived and died in Geneva, Switzerland. The manor house at Rudzk was inherited by Justin (uncle to Tadeusz), a veterinary surgeon, who lived there at the end of the nineteenth century. He had six children, Julia, Jarosław, Zofia, Wacław, Paulina and Henryk. In terms of the family narrative, Julia is important as mother to Stas, and she spent much of her adult life living with her sister Zofia (known for her extremely long hair) in Warsaw. Paulina is also significant in the narrative as grandmother to my cousin Piotr.

Władysław, my great-grandfather, was born in Rudzk in 1852. Photographs show him to be fair in looks, tall and strong, with a sensitive face, elaborate moustache, smartly dressed (not in uniform) and photographed later in life informally dressed as a country squire, often wearing a straw hat. After finishing local school in Pinsk, he went to study architecture at St. Petersburg University. He graduated in 1885 leaving for Ciechanow, where he started his own architectural practice, and later took the role of Chief Architect in nearby Płock. He married Maria-Victoria Rodziewicz, whose family roots were in the same eastern border area of Poland, so the families may have known each other as neighbours. The Czechowski family tree is shown in Figure 2.4.

Maria-Victoria, born in 1859, was the daughter of an engineer, Bolesław Rodziewicz and an aristocratic mother, Princess Woroniecka. The family was said to be of Polish, Russian and even Tartar origin. The male side of the family was professional – military generals or engineers. Maria-Victoria was related to her famous namesake, the Polish writer Maria Rodziewicz, born four years later. As a writer, the other Maria is listed as one of the most influential of Polish women; born in Grodno in 1863, her writings reflecting the eastern border populations of Poland and the personal and political struggles endured.[1] The themes developed in her writings are love of democratic ideas, hard work as a means to national strength and how the thread of the present is interwoven with the tradition of the past – effectively a national cultural narrative.

We do not know how well the two cousins knew each other. My great-grandmother Maria-Victoria was a talented musician – she studied at the Conservatoire in Russia and became a music teacher. The house where she was born at Mohylew was said to be large, but surviving pictures only show the wide

Poland: the first generation

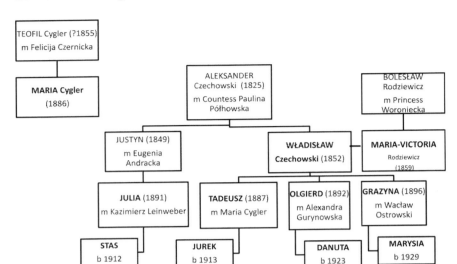

FIGURE 2.4 The Czechowski family tree

veranda at family gatherings. It is likely she would have visited her cousin Maria at her house in Hruszów, built forty years earlier by Antoni Rodziewicz. It was grander than the house at Rudzk – a neoclassical, two-storey stucco mansion with a distinctive four-column portico inscribed 'God bless the residents'. The outbuildings included a two-storey granary, orangery and icehouse, all built in the same neoclassical style. The manor park was surrounded by old trees: limes, oaks, maples and ash, above flowering gardens. The writer Maria is buried in Pawązki cemetery in Warsaw, her tomb not far from that of the Czechowski family and that of her namesake cousin, my great-grandmother.

Władysław and Maria-Victoria married in 1886 and lived in Ciechanów, where Władysław practised architecture. The following year their first child Tadeusz (my grandfather) arrived. When their second son, Olgierd was born ten years later, the family moved to nearby Płock on the Wisła, where Władysław was appointed chief architect for the city. We have a photographic portrait of Maria-Victoria holding baby Tadeusz, her first-born. She is dark haired and handsome, with a broad Slavonic face, large dark eyes and full figure, but not tall. Tadeusz was also dark-haired and brown-eyed like his mother, and all three children have her colouring. A family picture shows mother and two sons standing, while Władysław sits in the centre of the picture with little Grazyna, their third child and only daughter, sitting by his knee. They look a close and contented family. By the end of the nineteenth century they owned a villa in the town of Płock where, in addition to his professional work, Władysław gave lectures in technical drawing. He also gave several items to the Museum of Science Society. Grazyna, the youngest and only daughter, was born there in 1897. They were neighbours of the Cygler family, who were later to be related by marriage.

My grandmother was Maria Cygler; her father, Teofil, was a notary involved in civil law and official documentation. His responsibilities included traffic across the large bridge across the river Wisła. He and his family lived well in a house near the centre of the city. Teofil was later to commission an engraving of his daughter Maria's profile in silhouette carved into the plaster on an inner wall of the house, an indication no doubt of his pride in his daughter and her startling beauty. Teofil married Felicija Cernicka and they had many children, but also lost many. Of those surviving four were boys and only two were daughters: Julia the eldest, who later became a nun in a closed order, and Maria, the third surviving child who was to marry Tadeusz. Her younger brother, Jan, is significant to the narrative as grandfather to my cousins Ania and Karolina; and also her youngest brother, Wacek, whom I met when I was a child, in Warsaw. My great-grandmother, Felicija, came from an old Płock family, resident there since the twelfth century. Felicija was born in 1857, married Teofil when aged 22 and was nearly 30 when Maria was born, her second surviving daughter. The archives from Płock indicate eleven children born to Teofil and Felicija, with five dying in infancy. The loss of so many children must have had a major impact on the family. There is no documentation about the reasons for these losses, some within weeks of birth – one at a year and one at the age of four – but it is likely due to disease.

In Poland in the 1880s, illnesses such as tuberculosis, dysentery and diarrhoea are listed as common killers, these being more prevalent in urban areas (Budnik and Liczbin, 2006). Tuberculosis in particular was the major infectious killer of this period in Europe, and typhus epidemics were also common. There were several epidemics in Poland, including one in 1874, when babies would have been particularly vulnerable. This seems to have hit the Cygler family particularly hard.

The Cygler family were believed to have originated in Spain in the fifteenth century, having travelled north east through Europe and settling in Germany for a period. The name in its German spelling, Ziegler (meaning 'tile-maker'), is a common Jewish name, so I assume this was the family's cultural origin although this was never described in the family narrative. It is, however, consistent with the fact that when the Sephardic Jews were expelled by the Catholic Kings during the Spanish inquisition in the fifteenth century, many emigrated to Germany and then Poland. However, they may also have been part of the Aszkenazhy Jewish community who settled in Germany from other routes. We do not know. It is also possible the name is German. All documents about the Cygler family have been lost – the family story says they were lost in a fire. (My father's version was that they were used as fuel for the fire at a time of severe deprivation; my cousin Ania talks of a house fire.) If they did have a Jewish background then they were assimilated as Poles, and had been Catholic for some generations.

Jewish and Polish history are closely intertwined. In the late 1800s there was a large community of Jews in Płock, where the Cyglers and then Czechowski lived, with as many as 40 per cent of the city having Jewish origins. The large number of Jews there and in other parts of Poland (at times the largest congregation in

Europe) resulted from the historically enlightened policy of Polish monarchs from as early as the twelfth century welcoming Jewish immigrants from Spain, Italy and Turkey, and a large contingent from England and other Western countries. The Jews were offered a degree of refuge and tolerance and for many years experienced peaceful coexistence. The territory (of modern Poland) was to remain the home of many Jews. Under Russian control, this area was instituted as the 'Pale of Settlement' in 1772 by Catherine II, and restricted Jews to living in the western parts of the Russian Empire, including much of Poland. By the late nineteenth century, over four million Jews would be living in the 'Pale'. By the end of the nineteenth century, 14 per cent of Polish citizens were Jewish although proportions were substantially higher in cities, as high as 40 per cent in Warsaw and 63 per cent in Białystok, near the eastern borderlands (Davies, 2005). The relationship of the Jewish, assimilated Jewish and Slavic populations in Poland has gone through various phases denoting both closeness (when there was tolerance, and when Jews and Poles fought together against oppression) and antipathy (when there was anti-Semitism, and Jewish activism in Bolshevism). My reading of any modern antipathy (often emphasised more than the flagrant anti-Semitism of Poland's neighbours) is that is derives from a shared history of closeness and thus disappointment of expectation. It should be noted that some Jews did not feel Polish, or identify with their national desire for independence, but under Partition adopted German, Austrian or Russian identity. Anti-Semitism also occurred under these colonising forces.

My grandmother, Maria, remained a very religious Catholic all her life. There are a number of photographs of her: she was tall, with a willowy build, long chestnut-coloured hair and wide green eyes, in a narrow face with an aquiline nose. She was very beautiful, and very stylish. In one photograph, Felicija and Maria, mother and daughter, lean together to face the camera as a dual head portrait, indicating their closeness. In the photograph Felicija is about fifty, her silver hair combed back severely into a bun, her facial features broader and more Slavic than her daughter's, with deep-set dark eyes, a straight nose and narrow lips. She radiates strength but also sadness; the picture is a little severe, the face of a woman who has suffered the loss of several children. We have no pictures of Teofil, but Maria is likely to have looked more like her father, and many of her siblings and later generations share her looks.

Cultural identity

Language had become a political issue in the Polish territories now ceded to other foreign powers. Poles viewed their language as the touchstone of nationality, and the enforced use of Russian in the gymnasium high schools caused the intelligentsia to delay secondary school education as long as possible. As a famous Pole of that era, and a woman for whom there is much published biography, the Nobel prize-winning scientist Marie Curie (née Skłodowska) reported dark memories of the school she attended in Warsaw, where the teachers were 'hostile to the Polish nation and treated their pupils as enemies. What was taught was of questionable value and the moral atmosphere was unbearable' (Quin, 1995, p. 48).

Whilst women were generally excluded from university, in 1882 a clandestine academy for women was started with 200 women meeting in secret in the private apartments of supporters in Warsaw. The women were taught by prominent scientists, philosophers and historians, with sessions also including Polish literature and culture. Marie Curie was involved in this academy, and this may have been instructive in her later brilliance as a scientist. Polish women were observed by commentators to be outspoken, political and confident. Feminism had taken root in Poland in 1800, with more traction than in Russia. Women took a more prominent role in the Polish territories, because of the expulsion and execution of so many of the men. Women often took over their husband's roles and, whilst not allowed to operate in the public sphere, retained an independence of mind and action. Those with an education were more likely to have been privately educated and thus less subject to the Russification dominant in public schools. Education and training of the Polish population was recognised by the population as the hope for a Polish future.

Marie Curie's father, also called Władisław, was a scientist, but 'unhappily he had no laboratory and could not perform experiments' (Quin, 1995, p. 24). He never attained a university degree since the Russians had closed Warsaw University after the November Uprising in 1830. However, he studied in a biology department, which continued to operate without official status. Many academics had to decide whether to take up academic posts and work for the alien Russian government, or give up their professions to Russian tutors always willing to take the role. Marie's father became an academic, but was later demoted because of his pro-Polish sentiments and transferred after a school inspection. It was common then for an illicit double timetabling to be followed, with the Polish curriculum hidden below the obligatory Russian one. Marie's mother, Bronisława, went to the only private girls' school in Warsaw and received a good education, becoming a headmistress herself in her early twenties. Marie is quoted as saying:

> Private schools directed by Poles were closely watched by the police and overburdened with the necessity of teaching the Russian language even to children so young they could barely speak their native Polish.
>
> Quin, 1995, p. 26

Marie Curie recalls an atmosphere at her school with children 'constantly held in suspicion and spied upon . . . a single conversation in Polish, or an imprudent word, might seriously harm, not only themselves but also their families' (*op cit*, p. 48). Polish history was an ineligible subject for study. Lessons delivered in Russian history or culture commanded higher salaries, and the use of a biased Russian textbook on Polish history became the butt of local jokes. My grandmother in Płock was no doubt similarly affected by these problems in education. However, for girls from affluent households, there was a greater possibility of private and more Polonised education, which may have benefited my grandmother. For my grandfather, his secondary education was conducted in St Petersburg, the heart of the Russian Empire and therefore devoid of Polish elements.

My grandparents' upbringing

Maria and Tadeusz probably met as neighbours. My grandmother remembered how, in the winter, she would take her ice skates to school so she could skate with her friends on the frozen river Wisła after lessons ended. We know Tadeusz was also a keen skater as well as a sportsman in general. He became a strong swimmer and tennis player, as well as a cyclist. This is proudly described by his father, Władysław, in the short biography he wrote of his son. He does, however, emphasise many accidents:

> In Płock in the fourth or fifth class he went skating on the frozen Wisła as far as the sugar factory at Borowiczki eight kilometres away. However, while he was skating, the ice cracked and he fell into the freezing water and it was only through his presence of mind and his skill as a swimmer that he survived. When he arrived home he said nothing about this incident.

Tadeusz was both very active and, it would seem, very self-contained and autonomous. Władysław also recalls other accidents befalling his active eldest son: 'He was the best cyclist in Płock and nobody there could beat him in a race'. (I wonder, was this a Rover bike, from Coventry?). However, he adds: 'Once during a race he fell off at high speed but was not hurt'. Other accidents were unrelated to sport. For example, in the family summers spent in Rudzk as a child, there is an account of Tadeusz running into a barn where the farm workers were loading hay when suddenly a large pitchfork fell from the top of a wagon and hit his foot. He seems to have survived with no lasting ill effect. Another time he fell off a hay cart and the cartwheel hit his leg and left a 'lump as big as your fist, which he had for the rest of his life'. As an era with modern mechanisation and lack of any health and safety awareness, it must have been nearly as dangerous on the domestic front as on the political one.

Władysław gives some details of his eldest son Tadeusz's early life. He recalls a family game of tossing his young son into the air, twisting and turning him, to the boy's delight. He writes for his grandson Jurek:

> When your father was a little boy, I played with him as I did with you, lifting him up on one arm, and swinging him up and around, a game he called 'turn around'. I taught him to do somersaults and other gymnastic tricks. I also taught him, as with you, to always do what was right and if for example another boy deliberately hit him that he should never cry even when he was hurt. To do this he must grit his teeth and forebear because tears are

a sign of weakness and will serve as triumph to a spiteful bully. I also taught him, as with you, not to be afraid of the dark, or shadowy forests, or insects or reptiles such as frogs or lizards, but to handle them freely. I even allowed him to play where there was some danger, in order to get used to managing his fear. For example, when we were travelling on a steam ship I allowed him to lean over the side while holding tightly to his legs.

So Władisław adopted a Victorian ideal of manliness in bringing up his son to have high autonomy and little fear. We have no record of how his wife, Maria-Victoria, felt about such risks, not something most mothers would enjoy, even if the aim was to instil courage. What is interesting is that this form of acrobatic play was also something my father did with his daughters. I remember the thrill of it myself, never fearing for a moment of being dropped. A small family tradition, seen through three generations of father–child play.

It seems that Tadeusz also survived serious childhood illnesses, including two bouts of measles, scarlet fever and typhoid fever, where he was at times 'close to death'. This must have caused great strain for his parents, particularly when we note how many of the Cygler children died in infancy. But Tadeusz seems to have been destined to grow up to be strong and healthy.

I believe both my grandparents had a loving and happy childhood. Certainly both families seem to have been close and doted on their children. Both were also affluent, educated and privileged for the time. They would have enjoyed traditional Polish festivities at Easter and Christmas. At a later time of extreme privation, Maria says how lonely and poor Easter had been that year in a letter, adding wistfully: 'I remember well the Easters when I was a girl, we won't see those again'. Therapists often use the devise of a 'go-to' memory, which can be comforting at times of stress or loss. Easter celebrations may have been one such for Maria.

Easter was a special celebration in Poland, bigger even than Christmas. It extended from Palm Sunday to Easter or 'Wet' Monday. On Easter Saturday, baskets of traditional Easter food were taken to church to be blessed then eaten as a part of the Easter Sunday meal or 'Breakfast'. Tables were decorated with decorated eggs handcrafted in traditional designs recalling pagan symbols of fertility and spring. The breakfast included eating hard-boiled eggs, together with cold meats and other dishes, including a cake in the form of a symbolic Christian lamb. Easter Monday was a family holiday and called Wet Monday, after the practice of men and boys throwing water all over the women and girls. Despite privations under Russian domination, families would have enjoyed such times, the children in particular.

Christmas would have been similarly festive. Winters in Central Poland are very cold so there would have been snow and ice with temperatures far below freezing. Polish homes typically had large, tiled stove heaters in every room, coal or wood fired, and were a type of central heating running throughout the houses or apartments. My grandparents' homes are likely to have been warm and comfortable in winter, and Christmas celebrations would have been festive and joyful. The celebration was held then, as now, on Christmas eve, a *Wigilia*, triggered by sight of the first star, the meal comprising twelve courses of soup, fish, vegetables, fruit and cake lasting to midnight to herald in the birth of Christ. The Christmas tree (a Polish as well as a German tradition) would be decorated by the adults for the *Wigilia* and revealed ready decorated to the children late on Christmas Eve as if sent by an angel. In the Czechowski household it was Władysław who was credited for his excellent tree decorating, the tree lit with bright candles. The *Wigilia* is then followed by midnight Mass. Poles have retained such traditions, carried with them when they emigrate, and these markers of the passing of seasons of the year are a source of grounding and security.

Schools and trains

Maria went to primary school in Płock, probably later attending a private gymnasium or high school for girls. We know less of her schooling, but later she does relate having a school friend, Jadwiga, whom she introduced to her brother, Jan, and they later married. Tadeusz went to primary school in Ciechanow before the family moved to Płock, but at secondary level he was sent to a gymnasium boarding school in St Petersburg many miles away, where his father had also studied. The gymnasium trained pupils for admission to university with a seven-year educational plan, the subjects including theology, Russian literature, Latin and contemporary European languages, mathematics, geography, history, physics, drawing and technical drawing. It seems a broad education. Sending Tadeusz to school, and later university in St Petersburg, followed his father's footsteps. It also suggests ambition in the family. It required a high level of autonomy for Tadeusz, being so far from home at a young age. It also entailed Russification – immersion with similar upper-class Russian youth and Russian culture.

Sending upper-class young men away to boarding schools to be instructed as future leaders was common in both East and West Europe. The travel was substantial: Warsaw to St Petersburg is over 1,000 kilometres and would involve rail travel through the Eastern lands, close to the family country house, and across Russia. Train locomotives would have left from Warsaw's St Petersburg Station, in the Praga area of Warsaw on the right bank of the Wisła. Most of the stations of the day were imposing (often called palaces rather than stations), and this one was an elegant, two-storey, white-painted Italianate building with its tall, arched windows and colonnades.[2] It was linked by a horse-drawn tramway line to the Warsaw–Vienna railway, later becoming the basis of Warsaw's electrified tram network. Tadeusz and his family presumably got to know it well.

It is an oddity of the region that there was more than one gauge of railway lines. Of these the 'normal' (i.e. standard, or Western)-gauge railways headed from Vienna station south, with the broad-gauge (Russian) from St Petersburg station going east. The steam locomotives were imported first from England, having been built in Manchester, but later also from Paris and Belgium. Pictures of the first locomotives in the 1860s look primitive to our eyes – long, with low cylinders and large chimneys. By the 1900s they look more like the large, black, smoking locomotives shown in *Dr Zhivago* and would similarly be equipped for ploughing through snow.

The steam locomotive from Warsaw to St Petersburg travelled through Białystok, to Grodno, Belarus, Vilnius and finally St Petersburg. The journey probably took two days, a lengthy journey for a teenager to undertake several times a year. Tadeusz may at times have travelled from his mother's family home near Białystok to lessen the journey. The impressive railway station at Białystok still stands; built in the early 1860s, it has a white decorated façade, long arched windows and spacious interiors, richly decorated with marble. This station had covered platforms and even by 1908 there were automatic ticket machines. Tadeusz's early familiarity with train travel was to have a profound effect on the growing youth.

Tadeusz's grammar school was located in Tsarskoe Selo, 24 kilometres south of St Petersburg. It was the location of the Russian Royal Palaces, the baroque Catherine Palace and the neoclassical Alexander Palace, and their adjacent parks, surrounded by exotic architectural features: the Garden a la Française, an English landscape garden, the Creaking Pagoda, and the Chinoiserie including a Chinese Village. The city was dazzling in its architecture and with the abundance of palaces, cathedrals, grand buildings and gardens. It also held an army barracks and military arsenal. More important for Tadeusz was that its railway station was one of the first in Russia.

Tadeusz developed a great love for railway locomotives. This was not unusual in Victorian times, when train travel was becoming widespread and enthusiasm for this new technology seized the popular imagination. But Tadeusz wanted to do more than just admire locomotives – he wanted to master driving them. The development of rail networks had started in Russia in the early 1830s, with its first railway line – between St Petersburg and Tsarskoe Selo – built in 1837. It was only 17 kilometres long and has been described as a 'toy' railway, as it seems to have been mainly for the convenience of the Tsar. It was on this railway that Tadeusz learned to drive a locomotive, first as an assistant/fireman ('engine driver's mate') whilst at the gymnasium school, but later getting his full licence when at University in St Petersburg. Władisław, recalls:

> Tadeusz had a great love of trains and would go to look at them whenever he could. At Tsarskoe Selo where he completed grammar school, he spent all his free time at the railway station. He got to know all the train drivers and they let him climb into the engine room with them. They taught him about the trains, how to apply the brakes, and even how to drive them. He became so skilled he took the exams as an engine driver's assistant and was then allowed to drive them unaccompanied between Tsarskoe Selo and Witebsk, and from Tsarskoe Selo and St Petersburg. When he continued at the university he went on train journeys for practice but also because he loved the engines so much. It was only a short time before he achieved a full engine driver's licence. His interest in trains was noticed at university where they put him in charge of the engine room.

Subsequently Tadeusz held the certificate of the 'Technical Railway of Moscow, Vilna and Rybin'. The locomotives of the day would have been somewhat dangerous. Tadeusz was involved in accidents in this early, unregulated period of train travel. While at the university and driving a train, a jet of steam hit him in the face and he was in hospital for three weeks, fortunately not scarred. His father writes:

> Later he had many accidents, knocking over cattle and horses and sometimes even people who blocked the line. He was mortified by the accidents, which were not considered his fault. One time the assistant train driver died while looking out of the window to admire the view and was hit by the side of the tunnel. One time Tadeusz stopped the train in the middle of the countryside. The passengers came to the front and asked why they had stopped. He told them that he didn't know, it was just instinctive. Then they found out that a bridge over the river had fallen in and his braking earlier in the track had saved a lethal crash.

This involvement by privileged youth in manual activity was a relatively new phenomenon in the early 1900s; previously this would have been looked down on by the upper social classes. Marie Curie's biographer notes that there was an: 'inherited aristocratic contempt for the merchant and manufacturer, to say nothing of the shopkeeper or mechanic' (Quin, 1995, p. 29). Yet in Marie Curie's family a few decades earlier, the same new orientation is noted. For example, her mother learned to make shoes for her children and then started selling them in a small shop. Marie's brother Josef comments: 'it shows my parents' true democratic nature – they didn't resent any physical work, even such a low occupation as a cobbler' (*op cit*, p. 29). Tadeusz too wanted practical involvement as an engineer with the machines he loved. Therefore to drive trains and later physically to undertake car mechanics would prove a useful skill both in the army and in providing for his family during a period of exile. This is perhaps another indication of a modern identity linked to new technology, and a sign of increased personal autonomy.

Resisting Russification

Despite Russification and studying in Russia, Tadeusz seems to have retained his Polish identity and sensibilities. As was usual at the time, the family always spoke Polish at home. Władysław describes an incident which is illustrative of his patriotic fervour. While at the military academy, after he had left university and during a grand banquet, another Russian cadet loudly insulted General Tadeusz Koscuiszko, a historical Polish hero from the previous century and someone revered by Tadeusz. Kosciuszko was a military general and engineer who found fame in the American War of Independence owing to his engineering brilliance. He was also a national hero of the Polish 1794 insurrection against Russia and later a key figure in American independence. It is not difficult to see how the young Tadeusz would be inspired by such a heroic Polish character and to identify with him, both as a budding engineer and potential leader. Kosciuszko would be a rallying call for Poles wanting their independence in the 1900s. Anyway, on hearing the insult, Tadeusz slapped the face of the cadet and challenged him to a duel with pistols. The duel took place, Tadeusz emerged as victor, fortunately only wounding the other cadet, but with his Polish honour intact. Tadeusz, in his early to mid-twenties, risked not only his life but also his career by breaking academy rules, for which he got punished. It tells us about his character – his values, pride, fearlessness – and he had a good aim with a pistol! He clearly had no caution about his political views being known amongst his Russian peers.

But as well as being such a man of action, lover of mechanics and speed, and highly principled, it is evident that Tadeusz had sensitivity and that all the pressures of the era and his situation as a foreigner in the heart of the Russian empire took its toll on his psychological state. He fell into some form of malaise, diagnosed as 'neurasthenia' by 'Dr Ochryni in Warsaw'. His father attributed it to the various accidents he had in his train driving. However, it is likely to have had a deeper foundation, possibly due to his early school separation from his family and his conflicting loyalties with the political scene around him. The diagnosis, around 1904, was made at a time of the early development of psychology, psychiatry and – more specifically – psychoanalysis.

As a clinical term, neurasthenia was first used by a psychiatrist called Beard in the USA in 1869, to denote a condition with symptoms of fatigue, anxiety, headache, heart palpitations, high blood pressure, neuralgia and depressed mood (Beard, 1869). It gained popularity as a diagnostic label into the early twentieth century, being considered to occur more among the upper classes and particularly commonly diagnosed in Americans. It was later recognised as a combat disorder in the First World War. It was explained as exhaustion of the central nervous system's reserves. It would now more commonly be diagnosed as depression, anxiety or even chronic fatigue syndrome. Initially badged as a female disorder, it was subsequently known to similarly affect men. Common characteristics of sufferers were overactivity, anxiety, drive to succeed and overwork. Sufferers were mainly white-collar workers, businessmen, civil servants, teachers and students. Neurasthenia was also linked to stress in those at the frontiers of technology – telephone operators, typesetters, railway workers, engineers and factory workers handling fast machines. One German doctor called it 'the pathological signature of the time in which we are living'. In Russia, psychological research was advanced and active and many were fascinated by neurasthenia. We only know that Taduesz had an episode of neurasthenia, which seems to have been treated successfully. There is no sign that it recurred.

So what of Tadeusz's character? He was active and athletic, practical, self-sufficient and a keen patriot. He seems to have put himself in dangerous situations and survived various near-miss accidents. There are incidents described to show he was popular with his peers at school, and something of a ringleader – for instance, betting other youth on feats of physical prowess. He responded hotly to any criticism of his country. But he had sensitivities, and there was a psychological toll on his state of mind. Although he seems to have soon recovered from this disorder, episodes of anxiety, particularly panic, are seen in later generations.

We know rather less of my grandmother, Maria, at that time. She was from a large and close family who had suffered the adversity of a number of child losses. Julia and Maria were the only daughters and, after Julia left to become a nun, Maria was the only daughter at home in a house full of boys. It is likely she was much loved and admired by her parents. She also married for love, had a good education and was skilled in languages. Like Tadeusz, she would have been fluent in Russian as well as their native Polish, and French and German. She was a woman with a methodical approach to tasks – neat, tidy and a good administrator. She was well educated and saw herself as an independent woman. She had firm opinions, was devoutly religious and later loyal to friends and family. She was devoted to Tadeusz and achieved enduring closeness with her new family and sister-in-law, Grazyna.

The new century

My grandparents would have been 14 years old at the time of the turn of the century. It is described both as a time of decadence and cynicism, as well as romanticism and idealism. Certainly it was a time of great social and technological change. The rapid changes already described in transport, with new designs for cars and trains, were matched by increased munition production of grenades, Gatling guns, early tanks and armoured vehicles. All required steel and increased mining production. 'The Vertigo years' – the first 14 years of twentieth-century Europe – are described in detail by Philip Blom (Blom, 2008). The themes sound very modern – terrorism, globalisation, immigration, consumerism, the collapse of moral values and the rivalry of superpowers. Cities grew following the culmination of the Industrial Revolution, science created new possibilities, while education and mass-produced items changed people's daily life and outlook. This resulted in industrial labourers and women demanding a share of political power. 'Futurism' was labelled in Italy in 1909 by Marinetti, and was devoted to speed and the worship of cars, velocity and technology, as well as violence. It praised danger, energy and fearlessness; courage, audacity and aggressive action. Marinetti stated: 'Time and Space died yesterday. We live in the absolute, because we have created eternal, omnipresent speed' (Blom, 2008, p. 262). This was a young man's movement, freeing itself of 'professors and antiquarians' but also glorifying war.

The scientific revolutions in this period included Marie Curie and her husband Pierre seeking to discover the properties of X-rays and uranium, and discovering radiation. Marie Curie's doctoral thesis identifying this new element caused a sensation in scientific circles, and she and her husband Pierre subsequently won the Nobel prize for Physics in 1903. After Pierre's untimely death, Marie continued in the field and was awarded a second Nobel prize in 1911 for her research into radioactivity. There must have been delight in Poland to have one of their female scientists win these awards, a recognition of the success of the secret education organised so effectively.

Einstein was similarly active in this period, publishing in 1905 the *Special Theory of Relativity*. He effectively 'emancipated space and time from human experience, from old ways of understanding the world. He had chosen logical consistency over perception' (Blom, 2008, p. 82). Around the same time, Freud was developing psychoanalysis, based on the hypothesis that a destructive conflict between conscious values and subconscious desires was fought out through dreams. In the space of the first decade of the twentieth century, key publications by Curie, Einstein and Freud were to make seismic changes to our understanding of science. Such advances must also have reached the ears of an increasingly scientifically informed public.

There were two directives towards peace instituted in these years. The Nobel Peace prize, the second of these, occurred due to the failure of the International Peace Conference held in The Hague in 1907. Baroness Suttner, then aged 64, who had witnessed soldiers suffering in the Russo-Turkish War 1877, resolved to spend her life dedicated to peace. She became a close friend to Alfred Nobel, who on his death bequeathed his fortune to a foundation to award prizes in peace as well as in science and literature. In 1905 the Baroness herself was a recipient, with her stated fear of a cataclysmic war where: 'Every village will be a holocaust and every city a pile of rubble, every field a field of corpses and the war will rage on' (Blom, 2008, p. 193).

Prior to this, another peace initiative was started in Geneva to form what was to become the International Committee of the Red Cross in 1863, by Henry Dunant and five influential Swiss families.[3] His book *Solferino* described suffering in the Franco-Austrian War, and his aim was to create national voluntary relief organisations to help nurse wounded soldiers in the case of war. A conference was held in 1863, with official delegates from thirteen countries or states attending. The resolutions results included: the foundation of national relief societies for wounded soldiers; neutrality and protection for wounded soldiers; the utilisation of volunteer forces for relief assistance on the battlefield; the organisation of additional conferences to enact these concepts in legally binding international treaties; and the introduction of a common distinctive protection symbol for medical personnel in the field, namely a white armlet bearing a red cross. On 22 August 1864, the conference adopted the first Geneva Convention 'for the Amelioration of the Condition of the Wounded in Armies in the Field'. Representatives of twelve states and kingdoms signed the convention, excluding Russia and Austria. Dunant and Passy, a noted pacifist, were awarded the Nobel Peace prize in 1901. By 1914 there were forty-five national Red Cross relief societies internationally.

The lead-up to war and marriage

For Poles, the repression after the January uprising 1864 had left permanent scars. A whole generation of Poles were deprived of their careers and expectations of advancement. Thousands of Poles, those most educated, were sent to Siberia, and most never returned. There was no amnesty even 25 years later. Tension arose in

East Europe: there was upheaval caused by the 1904 Japanese attack on the Russian fleet in Manchuria and the Bosnian crisis of 1908. Political parties grew up in Poland and there was a deteriorating economic situation due to the Japanese block on markets and increased political militancy. One hundred thousand Polish workers were made unemployed and many other workers took a pay cut.

In early 1905, the Bloody Sunday massacre of civilians in St Petersburg by Tsarist Cossack cavalry was paralleled by a school strike in Poland, which lasted 3 years. The Russian University in Warsaw was deserted. The same month saw a general strike of 400,000 workers for four weeks, which in the following year rose to include 1.3 million people. The political conflict led to fatalities in the three major cities of Warsaw, Łódz and Częstochowa. The general strike deteriorated into open hostilities. When barricades were thrown up the Tsar declared a state of war, with further Polish casualties resulting. The troubles in Poland were soon joined by more widespread disturbance in Russia.

Tsar Nicholas was required to make concessions but did not lessen his autocracy. There was still a rule of terror, police raids, lockouts and reprisals. Workers were starved and bullied into submission. By the end of 1906 all factories in Łódz were closed indefinitely until workers agreed conditions. Thousands were deported to their villages of origin, with 104 prisoners summarily executed. The Polish national movement was hindered by feuds and schisms. It was in this political atmosphere that Tadeusz changed from his planned career as an engineer, to military officer. Tadeusz and Maria also decided to marry in this period of uncertainty and set the date for September 1911. Marriage of trainee officers was prohibited at the Russian military college, so Tadeusz knowingly broke the rules and travelled back home to Płock for the ceremony. The priests and officials in Płock would not conduct the wedding so the family had to apply for permits to go to Prussian-occupied Poland, outside Russian jurisdiction. The Czechowski and Cygler family members thus went together from Płock to the town of Rypin, 70 kilometres away, presumably by train, and then by horse to the small village of Siedziebna. St Bartholomew's, an elegant white-stone Baroque building, was its only church. It was still proving difficult to find a priest willing to marry the couple who were not local, but they finally found Father Snekienski, a priest related to the Cygler family, who conducted the wedding Mass. Władisław describes it as a happy occasion and very festive. Their determination won out and the marriage was happily celebrated by both families. The formal wedding photograph is taken by a Płock photographer and the couple look beautiful, holding hands, to start their married life together.

Tadeusz and Maria began their married life initially separated for several months while Tadeusz completed his officer training in St Petersburg, and Maria remained with her family in Płock. He was then offered a position in the 2nd Battalion of Military Engineers in Warsaw, based in Mokotow just south of the city centre. The Mokotow area of Warsaw is now known for its foreign embassies and green areas and parks. Taduesz also became interested in law and served as an official in the Committee of Justice. His main role, however, was as head of an engineering corps responsible for the army cars and armoured vehicles in the Russian army. His father, Władysław reports that Tadeusz was a popular officer with his soldiers because he was practical and an excellent engineer himself. He would roll his sleeves up and get involved in the mechanical repairs. Meanwhile Tadeusz's parents and siblings had also moved to Warsaw, to Bednarska Street not far from the river. This winding street going down to the Wisła was one of stucco-fronted, terraced villas in a narrow, cobbled street; number 22 was a large stone, three-storey house in a terrace. Photographs of the family at that time show happy family life. There are pictures of Maria and Tadeusz sitting together on a sofa, Tadeusz at the piano, friends gathering to eat. Holiday pictures show them by a large lake, picnicking in the open air and with large family gatherings posing for pictures on the porch. They seem happy occasions.

Maria fell pregnant with Jurek early in 1913. She travelled back home to her parents in Płock for the birth. A healthy baby boy was born to the proud parents on 16 October 1913, and named Jerzy (Jurek) Tadeusz. There are pictures of Jurek as an infant on holiday, and a number of the young family. Tadeusz is always in uniform, Maria elegant in her ankle-length gowns and Jurek typically in little sailor outfits. He is fair-haired and round-faced and looks directly at the camera. His father and mother hold his hand or have an arm around him. The photographs also show larger family gatherings, often at the country houses. Here Jurek is often seen with his cousin Staś just a year older. The two little boys appear much loved at these family gatherings.

Discussion

In thinking of autonomy and willpower as the theme of the chapter, Tadeusz emerges having both, and as a headstrong and determined young man. He was clearly ambitious and a high achiever, but he didn't follow rules blindly. When he decided to marry Maria, nothing held him back. He broke the rules of his college – the couple had to travel to a different national territory to get the necessary papers and search for a priest. Maria also showed determination in marrying Tadeusz, complying with their adventurous ceremony and was clearly in love with this dashing young officer. Her life was to change dramatically as she followed him in his military career.

My grandparents seemed clear about their identity as Poles, as Catholics, as educated and upper-class young adults. But there were social and political barriers imposed. A theme developed throughout this account will be about hidden identity and subterfuge. Under Russification, there were no Poles recognised, only Russians. Whilst Tadeusz did have some Russian blood on his mother's side, his sense of identity was fully Polish. Similarly with Maria, her possible Jewish roots would have also set up barriers in some upper-class groups, but she seems to have been confident in her Polish Catholicism. No doubt both would have spoken Polish to each other and at home, despite the language being illegal. Jurek recalled only being allowed to speak Polish at home, never Russian as a young child, but actually

46 Poland: the first generation

he learned Russian from the servants. His parents would have been proficient linguists. It would be common for people of their class to speak three or four languages well and in that sense to be Europeans (Figure 2.5).

In terms of attachment, the families described were all close. Tadeusz, whilst enduring separation during his schooling, seems to have retained independence and autonomy. His bout of neurasthenia is the only sign that the pressure may have been too high. The family marriages described seem stable, the children looked after lovingly and the wider family meeting up regularly. Is the family portrayed as too perfect? All families have points of dissension, conflict, dissatisfaction and unmet need. There is little personal information about how my grandparents felt during this period and there are no personal letters or diaries from them, so it is difficult to surmise. Specifically I have no information about Tadeusz's mother, Maria-Victoria, often described as the matriarch of the family, both warm and strong. I wish I knew more of her. There is no outward sign of family conflict or dissension.

Maybe the family imposed too much autonomy on the growing Tadeusz – the distance at which he was schooled, his numerous sporting and rail-related accidents for which he sought no support. Yet this was probably typical of eldest sons of the time. There is a suggestion that the Czechowski family may have looked down on the Cygler family. But this was firmly nipped in the bud by Władysław as head of the family, and it is clear from later events that Maria is very much accepted

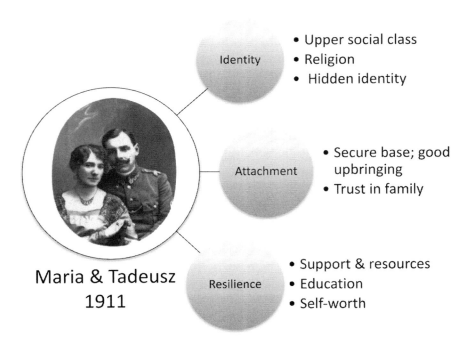

FIGURE 2.5 Summary of the themes in Chapter 2

into the family and she and Grazyna become very close lifelong friends. There were clearly separations, which must have caused anguish – Maria-Victoria from her teenage son, Maria and Tadeusz when first married, Jurek when his father was away – but the family seems to have coped with these.

How do I reflect on my grandparents lives at this time? They seems rather distant to me, something of history more than memory. The imagery is of *Dr Zhivago*, of upper-class life, of political tension and intrigue. Both my parents sound like upright people – I like the extent to which Tadeusz seems like a modern and practical man. I have been surprised at their elevated social class, not something I really understood from family stories. This chapter has served to set the scene; the following will be the test of my grandparent's fortitude as the First World War begins.

Thus with strong identity and secure attachment, there is a high likelihood of resilience. At this point it is not tested by serious adversity. Tadeusz showed some signs of neurosis, but this did not inhibit his actions, his marriage or his career success and is not described as recurring. He had built up the self-confidence, self-determination and competencies he would need in the challenging next phase of his life.

Notes

1 http://lubimyczytac.pl/autor/4345/maria-rodziewiczowna
2 www.polish-railways.com/history/
3 https://en.m.wikipedia.org/wiki/International_Committee_of_the_Red_Cross

Photographs section 1

FIGURE 2.6
Maria-Victoria with baby Tadeusz, 1886

FIGURE 2.7
Władisław Czechowski

FIGURE 2.8
Felicija Cygler, with daughter Maria

FIGURE 2.9
Maria and Tadeusz marry, 1911

FIGURE 2.10
Tadeusz, Maria and Jurek, 1918

FIGURE 2.11
Stas and mother Julia

FIGURE 2.12
Grazyna and Maria, defence of Warsaw, 1920

FIGURE 2.13
Maria and Jurek, 1923

FIGURE 2.14
Maria and Jurek in Warsaw, 1931

FIGURE 2.15
Jurek at University, Warsaw 1932

FIGURE 2.16
Myszka and Jurek marry, Warsaw 1938

3
INITIATIVE

Fighting on the Eastern Front (1914–20)

> A man's conflicts represent what he 'really' is.
>
> Erik Erikson

Introduction

This chapter has the theme of initiative. In Erikson's scheme, it adds action to autonomy: it includes undertaking, planning and attacking a task. Initiative is thus the operational side of autonomy. In the case of development, the growing child enjoys increasing locomotor and mental powers and these lead to developing the further adult stages. A conflict over initiative may be expressed as 'Denial', with emotional paralysis and inhibition resulting. The virtue said to be associated with this stage is 'Purpose'. In the story unfolding, initiative refers to actions in war, resisting oppression and seeking political independence – in particular, my grandfather Tadeusz's military action in fighting for his country, and at a time of personal threat, for his family. He was strong in purpose, in competence and his ultimate level of sacrifice, as for many of his generation, was very high. In terms of the Polish nation, the critical taking of initiative, when a void appeared following the German and Austrian retreat and Russian preoccupation with Revolution, left a space for Polish initiative for independence.

In this chapter identity is no longer hidden, as in the last, but asserts itself. However, national or cultural identity was at odds in the first conflict, where Poles were fighting in different armies, against each other. Attachments were disrupted by war, with separation and loss resulting and lack of a safe haven when flight was necessary for survival. Resilience was required under extreme duress from the scale of the political conflicts involved.

Maria and Tadeusz in Warsaw

In the summer of 1914, Maria and Tadeusz were living with their baby son Jurek in Mokotow, Warsaw. Tadeusz was stationed there as a military officer and head of an engineering corps. This Polish division, was part of the Tsarist Russian army. Tadeusz's parents and younger siblings were living nearby, the family having moved from Płock to the capital, Warsaw. Maria, now in her late twenties, had developed a very close sisterly friendship with her young sister-in-law Grazyna who, at eighteen, was still living at home. She was godmother to Jurek and no doubt doted on him as the first grandchild.

War was expected. The first crisis occurred in East Europe, when on 28 June 1914 the Archduke Franz Ferdinand, heir to the Austro-Hungarian throne, was assassinated at the hands of a Serbian nationalist. This caused Austria-Hungary to declare war on the Kingdom of Serbia, resulting in a domino effect as prior treaties and alliances were honoured. Russia, allied to Serbia, declared war on Austria-Hungary, whilst a Russian–French allegiance held. The Triple Alliance (Germany, Austria, Italy) was triggered in opposition, although Italy subsequently moved against Austria. A tripwire for a European war was in place when Germany invaded Luxembourg and Belgium, and Britain intervened.

In its origins, the First World War had nothing to do with Polish issues of independence but it gave fresh impetus to the 'Polish Question'. For the first time since 1762, the two major partitioning powers of Poland were at war – Berlin with St Petersburg. Polish lands, being at the nexus of the three powers, became an international battleground. Fighting affected areas close to the Czechowski family – the Eastern borderlands of Polesie near Rudzk, and Warsaw itself. Poles were in the direct line of conflict. The scale of war was to be larger than ever before, with European mass conscript armies raised by the heads of the four empires – all of them with royalty descended from the British Queen Victoria. Recent mechanisation, through use of rail travel, enabled soldiers to be moved to battle lines in unprecedented numbers. There were great demands on the civilian population. The central powers competed for the loyalty and fighting capacity of their Polish subjects, who found themselves on three different sides in the conflict. It was not a patriotic war for the Poles. There was the certainty of fratricidal slaughter with tens of thousands of Poles in each of the armies on opposing sides being at risk.

When war broke out, Tadeusz's battalion formed part of the Russian 2nd Army. It was an army-level command of the Imperial Russian Army, formed just prior to the outbreak of hostilities from the units of the Warsaw Military District. It was mobilised in August 1914. On the outbreak of war, the Russian army positioned itself to cross the German border into East Prussia to the north east of Poland on the Baltic. Tadeusz missed the immediate call to arms: he was involved in an accident, having been badly trampled by a horse, presumably on military duties, and so was unable to join the soldiers on the Eastern Front for three weeks. He stayed instead, close to the Front, with his maternal grandfather, Bolesław

Rodziewicz, nearby in Suwałki. Tadeusz wrote to Maria saying how unhappy he was, being left behind while the other soldiers were fighting. However, it was not long before he joined the army and was immediately involved in combat with the Germans in East Prussia. Władisław narrates:

> Near the town of Koenigsburg in East Prussia he was ordered to destroy a German gun battery which had caused great loss of life to the Russian troops. To do this he had to climb a rope to a high tower, unprotected from gunfire, and use binoculars to pinpoint the gun battery. He managed this, and the gun battery was then shot down by his own troops successfully.

The Battle of Tannenberg resulted, fought between Russia and Germany in August 1914. This led to the almost complete destruction of the Russian Second Army, of which Tadeusz was a part. In follow-up battles, at the First Masurian Lakes, the First Army was destroyed. The Russians were being defeated. Tadeusz then moved with the army to Łódź (south west of Warsaw) in the freezing winter. The Battle of Łódź, at the end of 1914, was fought between the German Ninth Army and the Russian First, Second (in which Tadeusz was an officer) and Fifth armies, in harsh winter conditions. The transition to mechanised vehicles from cavalry and horse-drawn wagons was just emerging in this war. The Russians were at a disadvantage, having no armoured cars, something for which Tadeusz as an engineering officer would have been involved. Eventually these arrived from England from the Austin Motor Company, shipped through the Russian port of Archangel and transported to Tadeusz's division in Pabianice (outside Łódź), Central Poland. In 1914, forty-nine 'Austin First Series' were ordered and delivered to the Russian Front from England.[1] Pictures show these to be strange-looking vehicles, not much more than van-sized, and boxed in steel. These were uncomfortable to travel in, dangerously unstable and vulnerable to sustained firepower. Tadeusz volunteered to travel in an armoured car behind enemy lines, knowing there was an element of surprise – the Germans were unaware the Russians had imported armoured cars. Władisław writes:

> The authorities asked Tadeusz if he would agree to take part in an expedition of these (armoured) cars to the centre of the German trenches, which lay across the road from Pabianice. They asked him (*rather than ordered*) because he did not belong to this section of armoured cars. He was very happy with the proposition. Four cars went down this road between the enemy trenches. The Germans did not fire as they thought the Russians had no armoured cars, and as the cars fired into the German trenches many Germans were killed. As a result the Germans were humiliated. In his car all the officers were wounded except Tadeusz.

But the Russians were outgunned, and Tadeusz became concerned for his life. According to his father it was the only time he lost faith in his survival. He narrates:

Near Dunska, Łódź the Russian army was surrounded by the Germans. He was in the thick of the fighting continually repairing machines which were damaged. He feared his death was coming, so he told a junior soldier to send a parting telegram to his wife Maria. The letter arrived two months later. You can imagine her despair. The stupid soldier had forgotten to send a letter later to say Tadeusz was still alive.

The Russian army, with disastrous leadership from Tsar Nicolas II, became demoralised. Tadeusz witnessed the near desertion in the Russian ranks. Władysław writes:

> He came across a group of soldiers led, not by an officer, but by a sergeant. Tadeusz stopped and asked him where they were going. The sergeant answered that the Germans had won a victory and the Russian army had panicked and run. Tadeusz ordered them back, but the sergeant attacked him on horseback so Tadeusz took out his gun and killed the man. In this way he stopped, for the time being, the panic and desertion in the army.

In 1915, the Tsarist army were retreating in chaos. The railways had an important function with many roads impassable, so there was high demand for Tadeusz's division's mechanical expertise. Władysław continues:

> During fighting at Łódź a train driver was wounded, so Tadeusz took over the job as driver and transported Russian soldiers, until Łódź was lost. During this time he transported 22,000 soldiers. One evening during incessant gunfire, the staff caring for the wounded were very frightened. Not only the women, including Lady Guczkowa the wife of a Russian agent, but also the men and doctors. The head doctor ordered the train to be stopped. Lady Guczkowa fainted and the fearful doctor asked Tadeusz to take the train back to Łódź. He replied he could not do that, because he had been ordered to take the wounded to Andrzejow (60 km south of Łódź). The doctor said 'I order you to go back' and Tadeusz answered, looking at his watch, 'Doctor, I will give you two minutes to return to your place then I will go to Andrzejow', and he returned to the engine. The doctor returned to his seat.
>
> When Tadeusz was returning from Andrzejow to Łódź he was very tired and hungry, and was walking down the street to a restaurant for dinner. He saw ahead of him two Sisters of Charity. Suddenly a grenade roared overhead and killed the two nuns. Their blood and brains splattered over him. You can imagine how it affected him. He went straight to the restaurant and had two stiff drinks.

The Russians withdrew, and Tadeusz went to Warsaw to join his family. The withdrawing Russian army was using scorched earth tactics. They burnt down villages on Polish soil as they retreated. The German troops started pursuing the Tsarist Russian army to join up with the Austro-Hungarian army. A letter from a young German soldier, Hans Petras, on 20 July 1915 describes the German advance and Russian retreat:

> We passed on through a mass of ruins. Everywhere there are Russian supplies and ammunition. Obviously they must have evacuated the place rapidly. But where are the Russians?. . . . And so we press on, from farm to farm, from forest to forest, picking up prisoners, young fellows who don't want to fight anymore and who are glad to turn over their guns to us. The peasants seem friendly. . . .
> And then suddenly we see the Russian method of fighting flaring on the horizon—huge pillars of smoke, as one by one they proceed to burn down the farm buildings, and even whole villages, driving out the people and the animals. Day and night we follow in pursuit. . . . And everywhere we find only fires and ruins. Fires which the Russians have set in their own land! What nonsense! What valuable things they are destroying! Without in the slightest fashion hindering our advance. . . . Now finally we can once again become cavalry! The Russians are destroying the bridges, and point out their line of retreat by flames, the whole horizon seems to be on fire. We are now pursuing them closer than ever in the direction of Warsaw.
>
> Heineman, 1994, p. 294

Tadeusz was assigned the role of chief of electro-lighting in Pruszkow, an outer suburb west of Warsaw. The family moved there, Maria and Jurek joining him. Pruszkow was a major station on the Vienna–Warsaw railway and had factories in rail wagon repair. It had only acquired electricity in 1913, and by 1914 it began operating a makeshift electronic plant. There was already significant damage to Pruszkow from German artillery. Churches were seriously damaged, as was the railway station, and the factory buildings, including the porcelain factory and the Majeski factory. Władysław narrates further:

> In Pruszkow near Warsaw, Tadeusz was the Chief of Electro-lighting. His job was to light up the German positions. Usually a heavy vehicle carried a light to do this. One time Tadeusz could not see the Germans with the use of the light, since they were obscured by buildings. Then he had the idea of taking the light off the car and putting it high up on the Majeski factory. He quickly found the German positions. He thought it amusing as the Germans could not find out where the light was coming from. They fired near the ground instead of high up.

Pruszkow was, however, abandoned as the Russian army retreated. We know nothing from Władysław's account of battle conditions, but some of the horror is described in an English eye-witness account from the letters of an orderly, Robert Scotland Liddell, a British reporter and photographer for *The Sphere* newspaper. He covered the events on the Russian Front in the spring of 1915 and soon moved to Warsaw, where he served as a member of the Group of Polish Red Cross Volunteers with the Russian army. He writes in his diary (Scotland Lidell, 1915):

> 4 August 1915, Warsaw: We left Pruszkow two nights ago at a little after nine o'clock. We left it, I ought to say, on fire. The flames were eating up the place as we streamed slowly out. We stopped for a while outside Warsaw. Behind us was the glare of the burning town; in front of us was a fine crescent moon, the lights of Warsaw, and to the north was a great patch of dull red in the sky that marked the destruction of another village. The Russians burn all they leave behind. The Germans will find nothing at all, but cinders and blackened stones. 'So when they get there, they'll find the place bare and so the poor dogs'll get none.' (Heaven knows what made me think of that wretched rhyme just now).
>
> 18 August 1915: Heaven only knows when this retreat will stop. I suppose it'll come to an end sometime, but at present we are still on the run. I think we will move from here any day now, perhaps any minute. To tell you the truth, I'm so absolutely tired of all the horror and tragedy that I don't much care whether we go away or remain. Can you understand the tiredness that leads to utter indifference? . . . Oh Lord, what sights I have seen today! It's horrible—horrible—horrible! I am often afraid that the tragedies I see will haunt me all my life; that my dreams will be blood-red and that armies of wrecked men will parade before me as I sleep. Ugh! I thought I was hardened. I'm as sensitive as a little convent girl of seventeen. Of course I do not cry. But, Heaven knows, I could—and I don't know why I don't. . . . Today we've had hundreds, the crop of yesterday's battle. They've come in carts, in wagons and motor ambulances. Some of the poor devils have limped their way here, leaning on each other and on rough branches. Two died in one wagon. I hear the death rattle in their throats now. One of them had half his head taken away with shrapnel. The other had his back torn open to the lungs. They lay breathing in great breaths of air and breathing out with a rattling gurgling sound that signals coming death. . . . Grey-faced men, splashed with blood.

The Germans occupied Pruszkow in 1915, at which point the railway workshops, factories, metal products and files were all evacuated to Russia together with the railwaymen. This led to total desolation in many homes. The hospital in nearby Tworkowski was evacuated to Russia. Taduesz moved around the country. Władysław notes: 'We were very worried about him, we often heard nothing from him for a long time. Sometimes I unexpectedly met him in Warsaw'.

Then by October 1917 the Russians withdrew, the country was in revolution. The casualties on the Eastern Front in the First World War were catastrophic. Almost 15 million served in the Russian army, including Poles, Lithuanians, Ukrainians and Jews. Casualties totalled an estimated 1.8 million killed, 2.8 million wounded and 2.4 million taken prisoner. It effectively ended in defeat as the Russians withdrew.

Taduesz's heroism during the First World War was rewarded with several medals. Photographs from 1918 show him wearing the Order of St Stanislaus, II class (commander) with swords and ribbons, worn at the neck of his Russian uniform. Other awards included the order of St. Vladimir IV Class and St. Anna III Class with swords 'for courage'. None of these is in the possession of the family today.

Revolution and escape

Tadeusz, Maria and Jurek were still living in Pruszkow when the Russian Revolution broke out October 1917. As an officer and member of the upper classes, Tadeusz and his family were in danger from the Bolsheviks. Officers and aristocrats were being killed indiscriminately. Tadeusz managed to escape with his family in one of his division's military cars, posing as the military chauffeur for the wife and son of a Bolshevik commissioner. It was Maria and Jurek he was transporting. Władysław writes:

> He saw one of his servants was in danger from the gunfire so he went to take him to safety. The man said: 'Sir, take care of yourself, this is a very dangerous place and I can do nothing to help you'. After the outbreak of Revolution in Russia, in the first days of the Bolshevik threat, the family of three were in great danger as the Bolsheviks were catching Russian officers and killing them. Tadeusz warned friendly soldiers, and pretended loyalty to the Bolshevik authorities, and managed to get a car and took Maria and Jurek, and escaped. He was driving slowly, and suddenly turned into a field travelling at great speed to cross the Romanian border. It was a heart-stopping journey, as they did not know the route. Before reaching the field they met with a Bolshevik patrol. Tadeusz had a rifle in case of danger. The patrol stopped the car and asked where you were going. Tadeusz told him he was just a driver and was driving the wife and son of a Bolshevik Commissar. It was a nerve-racking time and he did not want to betray them by showing how frightened he was. The patrol believed him and wished him: 'Good journey, Comrade' and went away. Tadeusz was very relieved.

The family found themselves living in Romania. By 1918 the family had settled and Tadeusz had opened a garage and was selling cars with success, even exporting these to nearby Ukraine. Jurek was by then five years old, his parents in their early 30s. The family was separated from the rest of the Czechowski family in Warsaw. The country house at Rudzk had been plundered by Bolshevik toops, with Tadeusz's uncle Justyn and cousin Julia (Stas's mother) escaping to Warsaw. Meanwhile Tadeusz and his family had to move once again go to Ukraine. Wladislaw writes:

> In Romania he got along very well. He found a car workshop and made a good trade in cars, selling them abroad to the Ukraine. In Romania, like everywhere at that time, there was an atmosphere of great uncertainty, things

tolerated one day, were not the next. A new authority came into power which did not look on Tadeusz in a friendly way. In the end they decided to arrest him. As in the escape from the Bolsheviks, he pretended to be loyal, but took Jurek and Maria by car to the Ukraine. He did not tell Maria that this was an escape. After travelling they came to a bridge half in Romania and half in the Ukraine. Romanian guards stopped them and asked to look at Tadeusz's papers. When Tadeusz showed them faked papers, they waved them through, being unable to read. It was a good thing Maria knew nothing about it. That is how the family travelled to the Ukraine.

The family, with the young Jurek, set up home in the Ukraine. This was to be a brief stay since there was now a call for Poles to return to their own country in its fight for independence, as the First World War was ending in 1918. They would return to Warsaw.

Warsaw, 1918

Warsaw was still suffering after its German occupation since 1915. Conditions were difficult, with more and more homeless on the streets coming into the city from other war-torn districts and the city shelters full to bursting (Olczak-Ronnier, 2004). Ration cards appeared for bread and other food products, with long queues outside shops. The currency had changed to German marks, which led to raging inflation while the previous Tsarist currency became valueless. Political debate of Bolshevik, socialist and capitalist ideals was rife: 'There were endless stubborn arguments about ideology, as political factions, parties programmes and slogans multiplied like mushrooms after rain' (Olczak-Ronnier, 2004, p. 137).

Retreating Russians had wilfully destroyed Warsaw's bridges, stations and metal production works. Nationalist sentiment against the occupying Germans was shown, with the first celebration for fifty years of Polish National day on 3 May 1916. The University of Warsaw was back in Polish hands and the Polish Legions entered the city. In 1917 there were repeated strikes, economic distress and the arrest of Joseph Piłsudski, a socialist and highly respected military leader. He was then released in November 1918 and arrived at Warsaw station where he took over as Commander-in-Chief on Western Armistice day. He told the German Command to lay down their arms and leave before civil uprising. They agreed, and Warsaw was free of an occupying force. Piłsudski took control of Polish political affairs. Neither the Allies nor the Soviets had any part in his appointment. He had found power 'lying in the streets' (Davies, 2005, p. 289). The citizens were delighted:

> It is impossible to describe the rapture, the frenzy of joy that overcame the Polish population at that moment. After 120 years the bonds were broken . . . Liberty! Independence! Unification! Our own state . . . Four generations had waited in vain for this moment, and the fifth had lived to see it.
>
> Olczak-Ronnier, 2004, p. 140

On 11 November 1918, the war ended for Austria-Hungary with a complete military loss. The Treaty of Versailles, signed on 28 June 1919, was debated between Great Britain, France, USA and their allies and the defeated Germany. Russia was not invited to join. The documents fixed the new borders and redrew the political map of central Europe. It offered Polish independence, thus separating Germany from Russia and similarly bringing other East European states to independence. A 'buffer zone' was created between communist Russia and Western Europe. Russia did not accept these terms. The Polish Republic came into being in November 1918, created in the void left by the collapse of the three Partitioning powers and nominally by the Treaty of Versailles. But it proved not to be a puppet of the West as envisaged, nor a Russian 'Red Bridge' to Germany, but to follow its own agenda and take its own initiative (Davies, 2005).

Fighting for independence

Tadeusz and his family returned to Warsaw and joined the Czechowski family. Władysław and Maria-Victoria were living with Grazyna in Bednarska Street, with Władysław working as Head of Department at the Ministry of Public Works. The University of Warsaw was opened, with a call for new undergraduate students. Tadeusz and his younger brother, Olgierd, both enrolled in the School of Politics. Tadeusz was seeing a new career for himself in political circles if independence could be achieved. Then the new Polish government summoned all men with military experience to form a Polish army to secure the new-found independence. Both Tadeusz and Olgierd joined the new Polish army, with Tadeusz given the position of major. He was dispatched to Częstochowa, with his young family, in the South of Poland where the government was based. Olgierd, also a hero in the First World War, had been awarded medals for bravery and in 1918 he joined the Polish cavalry as second lieutenant. He later followed in his brother's footsteps, training in the Officers Automobile School in Krakow where he was promoted to captain. Władysław writes about his eldest son, Tadeusz:

> Tadeusz quickly became acknowledged by the Polish authorities. He was ordered to organise the Kielce district of the army, with the seat of government at Częstochowa and was pleased with this. As Chief of that district and Director of the automotive workshops he was well liked by subordinate officers who acknowledged his official and social advantages, and by the workers for his good treatment of them. Also in the workshop, he did not limit himself to supervision, as most Specialist Chiefs did, but inspected all the work himself because of his technical knowledge. He often taught the workers himself, and this limited mistakes. Officers and workers were impressed by his knowledge.

When German troops retreated in 1918, Russian Bolsheviks took their place. Their aim was to export Bolshevik revolution to Europe. First, they had to get through Poland but this proved more difficult than they expected. The Poles' memories of domination by the Russian Tsar were too recent. Their struggles had worked through all social classes and ethnicities and they proved immune to the Bolshevik class warfare propaganda.

But Poland itself was in a catastrophic condition following the hardship of the First World War. A US relief mission led by Herbert Hoover described Poland at that time:

> Here were about 28 million people who had for four years been ravaged by four separate invasions during this one war, where battles and retreating armies had destroyed and destroyed again ... in parts seven invasions and seven destructive defeats. Many thousands died of starvation. The homes of millions destroyed and people there living in hovels. Their agricultural implements had been depleted, their animals taken by armies, their crops only partially harvested. Industry in the cities was dead from lack of materials. The people were unemployed and millions destitute. They had been flooded with roubles and kronen, all of which were now valueless. The railroads were barely functioning. The cities were almost without food; typhus and other diseases raged over whole provinces.
> Herbert Hoover, Relief Mission, 1919; Hoover, 1951, p. 356

In the summer of 1920, the Russian Red army swept through Poland to bring revolution to Germany and impose Bolshevism across Europe. For a few weeks in the summer of 1920 the future of Europe was determined by two of its least mature states – a new Poland and the newly formed communist Bolshevik Russia – the former led by a self-taught general (Piłsudski), the latter by a Russian nobleman aged only 27 (Tukhachevsky). Officers in both armies were young; Tadeusz was a major aged only 31.

Both armies were in a state of disarray – the new Polish army cobbled together an ill-equipped band of soldiers from three different empires. The Red Army, having shot its Tsarist officers in the Revolution, was also in disarray, and ill-equipped. Both armies were exhausted by war, and the Bolsheviks were simultaneously fighting an ideological civil war with the White Russians. The army of the Russian Bolsheviks (the Red Army) and the new Polish regiments must have been the most curious in modern times. Depleted, without uniform or provisions, both had gone through strange transformations and emerged as some sort of post-apocalyptic hybrid force (Zamoyski, 2008/2014). The Red Army, formed from the previous Tsarist force, had been decimated by the government-dictated shooting of its Tsarist officers and by the desertion of its peasant soldiers. Trotsky, appointed to overhaul the army, reinstated the Tsarist officers (redesignated from 'enemies of the people' to 'specialists'). Trotsky gave each officer a 'guardian angel' in the shape of a political commissar to protect him from the troops and keep him in line politically. This had the effect of not only creating barriers to military efficiency but also ensuring systemic mistrust.

The Red Army comprised idealists, criminals, professional soldiers, mutineers, students, workers and every nationality of the former Russian Empire. Trotsky disbanded all existing units and placed the men piecemeal into new formations, each of which contained a communist cell loyal to the party. This left the troops disorientated and having to build new loyalties. The resulting army was shabby and its equipment haphazard. Its uniform comprised remnants of Imperial army uniform embellished with red or yellow breeches, captured cartridge cases and sword belts and a variety of headgear, including fur hats, Tartar bonnets, peaked or pointed soviet caps and the odd French helmet taken from dead White Russian soldiers (Zamoyski, 2008/2014). The Red Army cavalry's strength was mainly in its savage reputation as a Mongol horde. It had speed of movement, cohesion and strong tactical sense when it came to fighting.

In contrast, the fledgling Polish army was born of a tradition forged in the nineteenth century insurgencies. It started with just 9,000 men, Piłsudski's own Polish Legion, with some assorted cavalry and cadets. These were soon joined by demobilised Polish units from the Austro-Hungarian, German and Russian armies. These all had different military training and approaches to fighting. They included emigrés from other parts of the world, including an American and Canadian flying corps. They were a mix of professional soldiers, students, peasants, aristocrats and socialists and included many ethnicities. The Allies provided a small French military mission under General Paul Henry, accompanied by a young major called Charles de Gaulle. The total numbers in the Polish army were just under one million in 1920, less than a fifth of the Russian force. The emerging six divisions of the Polish army were described as being like 'children of different fathers and the same mother' (Zamoyski, 2008, 2014). For example, from the Austrian tradition, the fighters (Lancers) had good discipline, were smartly attired and lordly in appearance. Those trained by Russians were in scruffy uniforms but riding thoroughbred horses, led by a 28-year-old colonel whom they addressed by his first name. The Legions, well disciplined and ordered, still had equipment and armaments from Germany with stylish uniforms – and rode heavy horses overloaded with kit, which rattled and clanked when they were on the move like a company of knights. It was a motley crew.

The Polish officer corps, mainly men in their 30s like Tadeusz, was similarly diverse having trained in Russian, Austrian, German, French armies or in the Polish Legion. There were some of amazing talent – not only Piłsudski, but also Sikorski, Komorowski and Anders, all to have later fame in subsequent conflict. There were differences to overcome within the army, in language, education and style, and in strategic and tactical approaches including different usage of technical and military terms. There was also a shortage of horses; many had been lost in the First World War, but also fewer had been trained, considered outmoded by motorisation. Polish weapons were those they had inherited, captured or imported, with Polish infantry rifles from half a dozen countries. So a makeshift army, with no period for consolidation or joint training exercises, was forced to take on the Red Army, several times its size. One of its greatest assets was its commander-in-chief, General Piłsudski. He was loved and trusted by the rank-and-file soldiers.

Given that much of the fighting of the First World War had been in Poland, the roads and communication infrastructure were breaking down. There was a problem with rail travel because of the different gauges across the country, as well as the fact the defeated Germans pulled up railway lines when retreating. Roads were in disrepair due to shelling and similar rearguard German action in deserting the cities. Tadeusz was inventive, adapting motor cars to run on the railway lines – the only way to cross long distances. Władisław describes the dangers:

> In Częstochowa at that time, he had two terrible accidents and it was a miracle he escaped alive. Once he was going by military car on the railway tracks. The track ran over a bridge and in between the two tracks there was just empty space. He was driving very fast when suddenly the car skidded and fell through the gap between the tracks and hung there with the wheels hooked onto the track. I do not recall the cause of the accident and who helped him out.
>
> When Tadeusz's subordinates heard of the accident they were very concerned. Later they were relieved when they knew he was not hurt. The officers and workers gave him beautiful presents with fine inscriptions. With his mother and sister Grazyna and I staying with them in Częstochowa we saw with what respect Tadeusz was held, and it made us happy and proud.

Tadeusz's skills as both a trained officer and effective mechanical engineer were in demand. He was called to a meeting with General Sosnkowski who, in 1920, commanded the northern front and had become responsible overall for supply, logistics and organisation (he was later Minister of Military Affairs). After the meeting he received orders also from General Szeptycki, who commanded the Polish Northeast Front and the 4th Army. Władislaw notes:

> At that time the Army Commanders decided to move Tadeusz from Kielce to Łódź for the war against the Bolsheviks. Minister Sosnkowski called for him and told him help was needed at the Front and they had asked for him to go and organise a car division in cooperation with the Polish Army. Tadeusz answered, 'Minister, I have already been ordered to organise the Łódź car division for the army'. The minister replied: 'It seems you are very useful, let them help themselves at the Front!' Tadeusz left Warsaw but later Minister Sosnkowski recalled him and said: 'General Szeptycki sent a telegram, you must leave everything and go to the Front'.

The Battle for Warsaw

When the Red Army advanced on Warsaw, Joseph Piłsudski proved to be the man of the hour. He was then aged 51: 'rough-hewn, solid and gritty. He wore the simple grey tunic of a ranker of the Legion. His distinctive features – pale face, high broad forehead, drooping moustache and intense eyes – gave him a memorable and theatrical look' (Zamoyski, 2008/2014, p. 5). He had immense popularity in Poland.

Having been set free from prison in Germany, he arrived in Warsaw on 11 November 1918, the day the armistice was signed in the West. Members of his Polish Legion returned from hiding, disarmed the German garrison in Warsaw and proclaimed the resurrection of the Polish Republic under Piłsudski's leadership. The Allies were less happy about Piłsudski taking control, and they persuaded the famous pianist Ignacy Jan Paderewski, who had promoted the cause of Poland abroad, to leave Paris and take over as titular head of state and commander-in-chief. Thus Paderewski ran the day-to-day policy, while Piłsudski directed the overall strategy, and more importantly the new Polish army. Another 'man of the moment' was Władysław Sikorski, promoted to general, who had been allied with Piłsudski for more than twelve years. He was in his thirties and had been a civil engineer by profession. In 1919 he was given command of the 9th Infantry Division, and in 1920 the Polesie group in East Poland. He is described as having military brilliance:

> His efficiency and success made him the immediate choice for all the special assignments during the rest of the war. His business like habits and original, independent mind recommended him to the politicians as one of the few men who could speak to Piłsudski on equal terms.
>
> Davies, 1972/2003, p. 195

Under threat from the advancing Red Army, Warsaw was noted to be calm although preparations for defence were being made. The population had no sympathies for the advancing communist Bolshevik army. In the civil defence, class divisions were forgotten. The Workers Battalions with staffs and scythes joined with the middle-class citizen's watch, who had paraded 'in boaters and wing collars' (Davies, 2005, p. 294). Civilians were prepared for combat. There was a Women's Shock Brigade – a picture of Maria and Grazyna, both in military uniform, presumably as part of such defence in Warsaw. Volunteers were from the intelligentsia and the bourgeoisie. Many were students, 'whose intelligence, enthusiasm and education acted like a blood-transfusion to regiments which had hitherto consisted of illiterate and apathetic peasant conscripts' (Davies, 1972/2003, p. 194). The church rallied against the communist approach. Volunteers signed up by the thousand and formed their own army under General Haller.

On 13 August the diplomatic corps decamped to Poznan, their safety no longer guaranteed in Warsaw. An Italian delegation and papal emissaries stayed in the city. Sosnkowski, Deputy Minister of Military Affairs, made pleas for national unity. Lord D'Abernon, the British Ambassador in Berlin, witnessed the preparations and was amazed at the calm: 'The insouciance of the people here is beyond belief. One could imagine the Bolsheviks a thousand miles away and the country in no danger' (D'Abernon, 1931, 1977).

On 5 August 1920, General Piłsudski was in Warsaw staying in the Royal Belvedere Palace as he pondered his strategy, while the Red Army was advancing on Warsaw. He decided to disengage his armies further east on the River Bug and transfer them to Warsaw. Between 13 and 16 August, a battle raged in and around

Warsaw between Polish and Bolshevik forces. The Red Army commanders made a tactical error when a large part of their force diverted north of Warsaw in order to cut Polish supply lines from the Baltic Sea. Piłsudski had set a trap, leaving a small force in Warsaw whilst himself taking the army north to strike across the flank of the Red Army. He sprung it, taking full advantage of the Russian error. The result was that the diverted Red Army force itself became cut off from its supply line, and the remaining Red Army force was decimated. General Sikorski commanded a force along with civilian volunteers to defend the city of Warsaw. This turn in the tide was regarded by many as a miracle, and became known as the 'Miracle on the Vistula' (Wisła). Commentators have long argued over whether it was the strategic brilliance of Piłsudski or the failings of Tukhachevsky. Piłsudski himself called it a 'brawl' and referred to the 'nonsense of the situation' and 'the excessive risk, contrary to all logic and sound military principles' (Davies, 1972/2003, p. 297).

Władysław and his family did not leave the city. He recalls being with his wife Maria-Victoria, his daughter-in-law Maria and grandson Jurek while Tadeusz was involved in the fighting. The family heard the advancing battle: 'We were standing on the balcony of our apartment in Warsaw when we heard the guns and saw the flashes of gunfire in the distance'.

Wounded at the Battle of Grodno

The fighting then moved with the retreating Soviet Russian army to the north east of Poland at Grodno, on the Niemen river. This was near the Polesie region from where Taduesz's family originated. The Red Army under Tukachevsky were defeated, and forced to withdraw by the Polish cavalry led by Captain Tadeusz Komorowski and the Polish Lancers on 25 August 1920. A renowned cavalryman and one-time Olympian show-jumper, Komorowski had been promoted to head of the Grudziadz cavalry school and he was to take a prominent part in Poland's later conflicts.

Piłsudski was to tie down Tukachevsky's main Red Army force around Grodno with a strong frontal assault, with diversionary attacks on nearby Wołkowysk and Pinsk and across the Niemen river. The attack began on the 21 September, taking the Russian Red Army by surprise. There was a fierce battle, with the Polish attack coming to a standstill as the Russians threw in more and more troops. Tadeusz was by then chief of all the Polish army transportation. He was ordered to Grodno to arrange cars for the army in pursuit of the retreating Bolsheviks. His commander, General Narwido-Naigebau, ordered him to take the cars nearer to Grodno, across the river Niemen. He went first with some officers to check out the bridge, where he saw the retreating Bolsheviks. The colonel then ordered Tadeusz to defend the bridge to halt the retreating Bolsheviks. During this defence, Tadeusz was hit by enemy gunfire, a bullet entered his temple and left ear. His officers brought him back by car to Augustow, not far from where his mother's family were living in Suwałki.

Initiative: fighting on the Eastern front

The action had stopped the Bolsheviks destroying the bridge, an action noted in the military attaches subsequently recommending Tadeusz's heroic actions. On 25 September, the defence of Grodno by the Russians began to slacken. Piłsudski's advance into the city was successful. The Russian army began a retreat, which turned into a disorganised flight.

Wladislaw recounts of Tadeusz:

> He was in a safer position that he had been during the Great War, but he seemed more unhappy, as if he did not have the same faith in his safety. The commander, General Narwido-Naigebaum, ordered him to move his division of cars near Grodno across the river. He went with a few officers and a machine gun to examine the river crossing. A short distance from the bridge he saw the Bolsheviks approach it to burn it and prevent the Polish Army pursuing them. Tadeusz decided at that moment to bring over a nearby infantry regiment to save the bridge. The Colonel said the regiment would come immediately and he asked Tadeusz to take some officers and defend the bridge before they got there. So he began to fire his machine gun towards the opposite bank to drive the Bolsheviks away from the bridge. One of the officers nearby (as he later told me in Grodno) caught hold of Tadeusz, and said 'Major you must not be in view' as the Bolsheviks were firing back. Then came a terrible moment when a bullet hit him in the left temple, exiting through his right ear. He jumped and fell down the river bank but he was stopped before he reached the river. The officers quickly took him to the car and brought him to Augustow. The Bolsheviks had been stopped from destroying the bridge.

Władysław continues:

> Olgierd was immediately informed of the accident and without telling us what happened, went directly to Augustow. Next day I learned by telephone from one of the officers that Tadeusz was dangerously wounded. I sent a telegram to Maria who was in Płock and after her return and a pass to allow us to travel in army trains we both went to Augustow. We found Tadeusz with his head bandaged so we could only see part of his mouth and one good eye. He recognised us, and said some words, which were scarcely audible. When they had brought him to Augustow he was unconscious and they thought he was dead, so no one put a bandage on his head until a doctor arrived. The doctor said he must be taken to hospital, so everyone went in two cars to Białystok. Olgierd and I made Tadeusz a straw mattress so he would be more comfortable. He was conscious the whole time, especially after a night's rest at Grajewo. Tadeusz enquired about the towns we passed through, and remembered them. In Grajewo where we stopped for the night, Maria stayed with him in a small provisional army hospital. Olgierd and I stayed at the home of Bolesław Rodziewicz (maternal grandfather) who was

a district engineer. In the night, Tadeusz had a fever and Maria was afraid so she sent a servant for Olgierd. In the morning he was better and at midday we went on our way. In Białystok the doctor told us to take Tadeusz to Warsaw, as what we wanted him to do was impossible, as first he must have an operation to remove the damaged eye. Tadeusz was feeling well and had no fever. He talked to us the whole time, and told us what had happened. He dictated a letter to Maria for General Narwid and asked me to give it to him personally, recounting the events. After staying some days in Białystok, Tadeusz did not seem to be in any danger. The operation of taking out the damaged eye and putting in a glass one, was not a serious one. I went back to Warsaw since my leave was over.

Tadeusz was brought to the military hospital of the Red Cross, previously Warsaw City Hospital; this had been re-designated a Red Cross hospital shortly before, on 18 January 1919, with the backing of Helena Paderewski, wife of the famous pianist Ignacy, and prime minister. The large, red brick Victorian-style building with beds for 500 patients was in grounds that included a park, two medical schools and four hospital buildings. Wladislaw writes:

> After three weeks, Maria and Olgierd brought Tadeusz to Warsaw to the military hospital of the Red Cross. He felt well and the day before the operation in the evening we all went with Jurek to see him. Two officers from his division went with us and he spoke to them freely as though he was quite healthy. He said that after the operation he would leave the army as he could not work properly with one eye. The two officers planned to take their leave of Tadeusz. He said to them: 'Good hunting – remember to bring me a wolf skin!' We stayed with him for some hours as we forgot we were in hospital. He seemed like a healthy man. He said to us 'Tomorrow, my dears, come and see me after the operation'. He picked Jurek up and kissed him and although I do not remember the exact words, the sense was that because of the two wars he had been very active and it had been impossible for him to take care of Jurek as he had wanted to, and to be with him more often. But now everything was alright as Jurek will always have him near, and after he left hospital he would buy such a present (as the child) had never dreamed of. Nobody guessed it would be the last time he would speak to us. He felt well and what was important was that he did not have a fever. He was not afraid, as the operation was an easy one. Doctor Alexander Mecierze from Płock who was then in Warsaw visited Tadeusz. I met him in the street and he told me it was a simple operation and usually had no complications.
>
> On 17 October Tadeusz was taken to Warsaw and on the morning of the 20th at about 11 o'clock he was operated on. After it he felt very weak and complained of head pain, and in the evening he lost consciousness and

never regained it until he died. I had believed everything was alright and I did not think his state after the operation to be very dangerous.

Olgierd rang me on 22 October telling me to come immediately to the hospital. I thought he called me to see Tadeusz with a different dressing or something. Immediately after that I left home and arrived at the hospital. Poor Tadeusz, after talking earlier about life, was dead. I could not believe it. After what the doctor had said, I thought everything would be alright, but it was the end. I came back home with one of his subordinate officers Lt Dzieciekowski, who was very attached to Tadeusz and took the biggest part with Olgierd in the funeral arrangements. He told me what a good commander Tadeusz had been, and friend, and how all the soldiers and workers loved him.

We mourned him, the best of Polish officers and cursed fate that such men died while mediocre good-for-nothings lived. Tadeusz was a far from average man and if he had lived would have taken a leading position in society.

Tadeusz was awarded the Virtuti Militari – Poland's highest military decoration, for heroism and courage in the face of the enemy at war. The family has a copy of the large funeral notice posted up across Warsaw. After his name in large letters it reads:

> Tadeusz Czechowski: Major and Leader of the 2nd and 4th field Squadron, the head of the Division of Automobiles and Leader of the Car Troops O.G. Kielce. Presented with the order of Virtuti Militari, badly injured at the conquest of Grodno in September. The funeral is at the Garrison Church (Długiej Stree). He died 22 October 1920, aged 33. Immersed in deep grief are his wife, son, parents, sister, brother and family who invite you, relatives, friends, colleagues and those who knew him, to this devotional funeral in the Church of the Garrison (Długiej Street) on Tuesday 26 at 10 in the morning, and after, the body will be taken to the Powązki cemetery to the family grave.

The Garrison Cathedral was the seat of a Polish bishop and a military church. The rebuilt church is still in Krasinski Square, close to the Old Town of Warsaw. Peace was finally signed between Poland and Russia at Riga on 18 March 1921.

Discussion

The theme of the chapter has been initiative, the relative virtue being willpower. Such was shown by my grandfather Tadeusz, but also by the Polish population that took up the challenge of fighting for independence against the Bolsheviks. Although many in the West are unaware of this war, it is described as one of the 18 most significant battles in history (D'Abernon, 1931, 1977):

Had Piłsudski and Weygand failed to arrest the triumphant advance of the Soviet Army at the Battle of Warsaw, not only would Christianity have experienced a dangerous reverse but the very existence of western civilisation would have been imperilled.

p. 49

Before Tadeusz died, it is likely he had the satisfaction of knowing that the Poles had won the war, that Poland had finally regained her independence and that his efforts had not been in vain. He secured for his son a happy childhood for the next 19 years, free from the totalitarian regimes of fascism or communism. It was a time of renaissance for Poland. There were tremendous difficulties to overcome, but the dream of independence was finally made a reality. The initiative had been taken by the Poles to regain independence for their country when the surrounding powers were looking elsewhere. The willpower required was substantial given the devastation and exhaustion following the First World War. The Polish–Soviet war changed the power and politics of the period. The benefits were clear to a generation brought up in Poland at that time. Democracy was installed and the mass deportations, murders and genocide of its powerful neighbours (Germany and Soviet Russia) averted. It bought my father's childhood. The themes in this chapter are summarised in Figure 3.1.

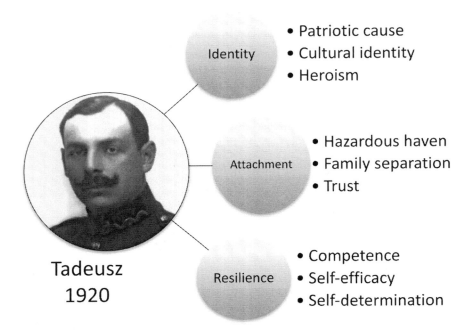

FIGURE 3.1 Summary of the themes in Chapter 3

In terms of identity, the themes for Tadeusz are patriotism, cultural identity and heroism, particularly in the Polish–Soviet war for independence. This also affected the civilian population in Warsaw, who were in readiness if the Red Army invaded. The picture of Maria with Grazyna in military uniform looks as though they would have agreed to pitch in.

Heroism is defined as a type of autonomy involving personal action and extreme risk to the self in order to protect others, individually or in a group, or in common or personal ideals, but without an awareness of personal gain (Becker and Eagly, 2004). Eight traits have been identified – smart, strong, resilient, selfless, caring, charismatic, reliable and inspiring – with most heroes having a majority of these (Allison and Goethals, 2011). Tadeusz would appear to have had most. The issue of helping others is central: 'Heroism consists of actions undertaken to help others, despite the possibility that they may result in the helper's death or injury' (Becker and Eagly, 2004). It is interesting that despite his history of neurasthenia, Tadeusz was able to rise to the challenge. There is no description of him suffering traumatic stress, but maybe if he had lived he would have shown such symptoms later as many of his generation did.

Geraldine Thomas, a psychotherapist friend, argues that the concept of heroism can be usefully adapted as an intervention in school or with youth. Expecting young people to take a stand and be brave, altruistic and protective to peers or siblings may help with alleviating bullying or other harms in school. It may also increase young people's sense of responsibility. The fact that a military hero such as Tadeusz had also suffered emotional disorder may provide a heartening message in terms of the range of individuals who can be heroic.

In terms of attachment, the war represented a 'hazard' and not a safe haven. Tadeusz was separated from his family, and during the last conflict he wasn't even sure of their safety as Warsaw was threatened. He himself was in constant jeopardy. However, the attachments themselves were strong – he could send telegrams to Maria, and would do so when he feared being lost in the conflict. There was trust in comrades, something much noted by soldiers in war, and likely to have been more a feature of the Polish army than in the parallel Red Army given its composition. Trust was a means of cohesion. The Red Army functioned on mistrust – party officials were to report on military officers, divisions were split and redistributed which lowered morale – Tsarist officers were hounded out, often shot, but then the survivors lured back because of their expertise. It is difficult to imagine a more treacherous environment in which to be fighting. The Polish army while, beset by being made up from three different national armies and all that entailed, had unity of purpose which was pervasive. Also the Poles had great luck in their leaders – not just Piłsudski, but emerging talent from Sikorski, Komorowski and Anders who were to lead the Poles twenty years later. Tadeusz may well have been added to this list if he had survived. It is strange for me to think he could have taken part in the Second World War only twenty years later if he had survived and could possibly, although unlikely given the latter conflict, have lived to an old age. As it is, he was for ever aged 33. His younger brother survived until the 1950s, also heroic, but much scarred from his later experience. Yet the family seem to remember Tadeusz particularly as the hero in the family. His parents mourned with the old lament common to parents of soldiers lost in battle – thousands of hours of caring to bring up a child, lost in a matter of hours, or days, of war.

Jurek lost his father when only just seven – one week after his birthday. Later in life he remembered his father in hospital, recalling he was given an apple and a promise to take him to the circus when his father was well. He remembers being kissed. Tadeusz had been away fighting for much of Jurek's early years, with only intermittent contact and Maria in constant anxiety for his welfare. The family had been uprooted, around Poland and in Romania and Ukraine. Tadeusz had regret for not having spent more time with his son. Yet, the relationship was affectionate and Tadeusz would write and send gifts to his young son. A brief letter in neat childish writing from six-year old Jurek in Płock, 10 May 1920 reads:

> Dear Daddy! I write to you, Daddy, in my own hand. Thank you for the chocolates and for your printed letter, because I could read it myself and I hid it as a souvenir of you. I very much want to be with you and Mummy together. I kiss you Daddy, your face and hands. Jurek

Many men of Jurek's generation lost their fathers due to war. No doubt it had psychological effects on him, but these were mitigated perhaps by the amount of care from his loving mother, grandparents and aunt Grazyna, with the help of wider family in Warsaw and Płock. The image of his father dying as a hero may well have been an abiding ideal to look up to. It is a consolation that the family had a formal funeral and burial, attended by many and with full military honours. Many soldiers who died in the wars of the last century did not have this recognition, and when their bodies were not found the mourning process would have been much harder.

The resilience theme lies in the fact that the very aspects that had made Poland weak (being dominated by three huge and disparate powers; having unsuccessful insurrections; having fought in three different armies in the First World War) all proved to provide strength to their ultimate purpose. They had the knowledge, fighting skills, strategy and insight needed about their enemy to utilise into their common cause. Their long history of resistance had taught them not only perseverance but also cohesion and organisation under pressure. It also provided them with a pool of skills such as in encryption and radio jamming which they used to good effect. (This was later to come to the fore when cracking Second World War codes and Enigma.) They had also learned flexibility and resourcefulness under pressure. Whilst they had some of the technology of the time – they used cars and armoured cars, trains and armoured trains – when required, they were equally adept at fighting on horseback and improvising weapons.

Tadeusz had the right combination of knowledge, mechanical expertise, skills and leadership to be the man of the hour. He showed bravery and ingenuity in both conflicts and was awarded medals for bravery. The cost was that he was fighting for most of the first seven years of his son Jurek's life, and spent little settled time with his wife Maria. Where possible they moved to where he was stationed, and during the escape from the Russian Revolution all travelled together to Romania and Ukraine. Although under pressure there, maybe there were happier times together. It is likely that Tadeusz knew the war had been successful; he died with his family around him and was optimistic to the last that he would move into a new role in politics in the emerging, newborn Poland.

There were other men of the hour. Piłsudski went on to lead, and younger military leaders like Sikorski, Komorowski and Anders were to hone their skills for their key roles in the next conflict. Indeed it could be argued that Charles de Gaulle as an observer learned a more flexible and creative approach to combat than his French military seniors. Whilst this stage ended in sadness for the family, it started a period of hope and flourishing for the fledgling state, allowing a period of democracy and liberalism at a time when its powerful neighbours were moving to fascism and more oppressive communism. Tadeusz, and others like him, bought twenty years of peace and relative freedom for their families and their nation.

Notes

1   www.militaryfactory.com/armor/detail-page-2.asp?armor_id=724

4

INDUSTRIOUSNESS

Life in independent Warsaw (1921–39)

> Farms and in castles, in homes, studies, and cloisters – where sensible people manage to live relatively lusty and decent lives, as moral as they must be, as free as they may be, and as masterly as they can be. If we only knew it, this elusive arrangement is happiness.
>
> Erik Erikson

Introduction

Erikson identifies 'industry' or 'creativity' in early adolescence as an active and positive phase focused on developing productivity in the growing youth. In this stage the growing young person can complete tasks previously only undertaken as play. Here the fundamentals of technology and artistic endeavour are developed. The young person chooses whether to conform to others' expectations or to lead their own industry in a creative way. The associated virtue is 'competence'. In this family narrative, industriousness and creativity refer to Jurek's upbringing, education and early adulthood. It also describes a period of Polish independence when the nation was beginning to assert itself and find the practical resources and competence to unite the country and try to develop a liberal political agenda. It was a time indeed of great industry when the young nation state had to overcome huge social, economic and political disadvantage in unifying the country. There was a need to bring the three separate partitioned territories into one, unified through common currency, language and legal codes. In the nearly twenty years following, Poland made great advances in a liberal and democratic agenda and in social and economic domains but was hampered by the world depression in the 1930s and the extremely polarised politics internationally.

It is at this point I introduce my Anglo-Irish family in England, my mother's parents. They have links to both academia and industry and they also visited, and wrote about, the newly independent Poland.

The focus is on the growing Jurek and his cousin, Stas. The themes developed are around developing a confident sense of cultural and personal identity, a secure base in terms of upbringing and the groundwork for future resilience in terms of competencies and developing self-worth.

Independent Poland

The year 1920 saw the creation of the Second Polish Republic and a new period of independence. Whilst this engendered hope and optimism following the achievement of this very long-held objective, it was also a time when the country, and indeed continent, was exhausted by war. The countryside and agriculture was decimated, a million Polish men had been killed and the country faced influenza epidemics, economic crisis and major changes in the way people saw the world (Davies, 2005). The first problem was one of integration. The populations, institutions and traditions of the three partitions had to be welded into one new entity. Everything was disparate: there were six currencies, five regions maintaining separate administrations, four languages of command in the army, three legal codes and eighteen registered political parties, all of which vied for power.

The new republic had high ideals. It aimed for a liberal democracy modelled on France's Third Republic, but with greater attention to social welfare. It advocated universal suffrage, legal equality and protection by the state of all citizens irrespective of nationality, race, language or religion (Davies, 2005; Zamoyski, 2008, 2014). It espoused the right of free expression, freedom of the press, freedom of assembly, conscience and religious practice. The state also aimed for benefits to those unemployed or sick, protection against abuse (for children, women and employees), free education and retention by minorities of their nationality, language and character. There was abolition of hereditary and class privileges, and with the right to private farm ownership, a new class of landowners was created, and lands provided for the legionnaires and others for their loyalty in the war of independence. Many of these were in eastern Poland, and this was to have particular and dire future consequences for these new landowners being in the path of invaders. However, in general, all the elements proposed are those we would expect in a modern liberal state in our own century. Attempting this in 1920 was both challenging and against the tide of non-democratic movements in the neighbouring states of Russia and Germany.

Two-thirds of the population of the new Poland were ethnic Poles, the rest mainly Ukrainians, Lithuanians and Jews. The three million Jews in the new Poland suffered more from economic difficulties and discrimination and were increasing in numbers (Olczak-Ronnier, 2004). This appears not to have been institutionalised discrimination, and in the twenty years of independence many spheres of Jewish life in Poland experienced a period of well-being (Davies, 2005). The Polish leader, Piłsudski, was not anti-Semitic. Jewish schools flourished and the Jewish press, theatre, film-makers and centres of cultural life all did well. Jewish politicians operated freely and had more places is the Sejm parliament of 1922 than the socialists.

Jewish social bodies were formed, including hospitals, orphanages, sports clubs, musical societies as well as insurance and cooperative societies. There were 200,000 Jewish writers of Yiddish and Hebrew literature in Łódź alone. Jews were an integral part of the entertainment industry, working in publishing, photography, motion pictures, music and arts. In addition, three-quarters of retail was Jewish owned and operated, half of this devoted to the clothing industry. As elsewhere, Jews were very prominent in banking as well as many modes of transportation, including railroads, and such businesses appeared to prosper during this period.

However, not all Jews identified with the new state or welcomed such independence. In tracing his own family background, Jonathan Wittenberg describes the family experience as Jews, first in Moravia and then in western Poland in Poznan (or Posen), which was in the German partition (Wittenberg, 2016). In 1914 his great-grandfather, Jacob Freimann, was called to the rabbinic seat in Posen, which had a high standing in the Jewish community. However, the family affiliation was more with Germany than Poland. He says:

> ... most of the city's Jews who spoke German, identified with German culture, and who felt threatened by the rising anti-Semitic tones of Polish nationalism backed by major elements of the Catholic church, left to live in the Reich.
>
> Wittenberg, 2016, p. 38

Joanna Olczak-Ronnier, from an assimilated Jewish family in Warsaw, notes anti-Semitism in this generation (Olczak-Ronnier, 2004). Her great-uncle, Maks Horowitz, was co-founder of the Polish Communist Party and at one time close to Piłsudski (who had been a witness at his wedding), whilst her uncle Gustav had fought in the Polish Legions in the First World War. Maks had been brought up an assimilated Jew, but found even then his identity was invisible:

> You had to make every effort to hide everything that made you psychologically, intellectually and culturally different and pretend to be someone else, to become completely Polish, to a point of illusion.
>
> Olczak-Ronnier, 2004, p. 111

The more Polonised Jews became a target for anti-Semitism, with a charge that they were not being true to their origins. The increased Jewish-Polish intelligentsia was not automatically accepted into the Polish sphere, this apparently less so than for those of an earlier generation. Joanna Olczak-Ronnier was herself born between the wars; she writes:

> At home I never heard anyone mention trouble with anti-Semitism, which must after all have affected my family in the inter-war years, just as it affected other assimilated Jews, but there were the *numerus clausus* (a ceiling on the number of Jews admitted to institutions), the segregation of Jewish students,

who were obliged to sit in a separate area of university halls, and open insults by colleagues at the university. Attacks by the extreme right wing were always in the same, all-too-familiar tone: The Jews are everywhere. The Jews are a threat to national unity. The Jews are scheming.

Olczak-Ronnier, 2004, p. 169

But in her family reminiscence, after the Second World War experience during the 'gloom of the communist regime, the years 1918–39, despite their shadows, seemed like a lost paradise' (Olczak-Ronnier, 2004, p. 169).

The task of reintegrating Polish society into a coherent whole began as soon as this Second Republic started. The task was formidable, with few material resources and little time. Three-quarters of the population lived in the countryside – most were agricultural peasants and a third were manual workers. Industrialisation continued at a modest pace. Between 1919 and 1938 over one-fifth of the landed estates of the Church, the state and private landowners were given to peasants and a large number of new holdings started. Rural poverty remained, the population was quickly increasing and the rural economy fell into decline. Farm prices halved and peasant income dropped to a third. Unemployment in the countryside reached 45 per cent. Credit was eventually suspended and investment in machinery stopped. Poland was not alone in this suffering – it was in the context of a world recession. However, lack of state funding to ameliorate the effects made its impact worse than in Western Europe. Social ills multiplied. The first strike broke out in Krakow and spread to Warsaw. There was a general strike of railwaymen as early as 1921, with subsequent militarisation of the railways, followed in 1922–3 with more strikes and hyperinflation.

However, much was achieved by the industrious population and government. An eight-hour work day was introduced, safety precautions at work implemented and living conditions improved. With the entire economic system started from nothing, the budget could not be balanced until 1926. Bank Polski and the 'złoty' (currency) was introduced in 1924. Whilst initially industrially underdeveloped, by the late 1930s Poland was more productive than Belgium or France. Foreign loans were negotiated, particularly from France. However, Poland did not join the 'Little Entente' with France in subsequent foreign policy, having been disillusioned by its lack of support in the Polish–Soviet war.

The government was, however, unstable. There was violence, with the assassination of the first constitutional president in 1922, and the Soviet ambassador in 1927. Parliamentary politics were characterised by squabbling and factionalism, with disenchantment growing on all sides. When the government was threatened with take-over from the Right in 1926, the Left feared for its future and Piłsudski emerged from retirement to stage the successful May coup (Davies, 2005). For the remaining nine years of his life, Piłsudski was the effective ruler of Poland and of the *Sanjaca* period, named after its slogan of the 'Sanitation' of politics. Piłsudski supporters (such as former Legionary officers) had considerable influence and dominated the Republic. Its democratic principles waned and its opposition weakened.

A challenge from the opposition with a Convention of People's Rights was met with military response, its leaders escaping abroad or sentenced to three years' imprisonment. There was concern by previous prominent figures such as Paderewski, Sikorski and Haller, but the Sejm (Parliament) survived even after Piłsudski's death in 1935. In the 1930s tensions between state authorities and the masses grew, and between Poles and ethnic minorities.

The Great Depression, arising from the US stock market crash on 4 September 1929, lasted through much of the 1930s. The entire decade was marked by widespread unemployment and poverty. Economic interventionist policies increased in popularity. In the Western world, Keynesianism replaced classical economic theory. In an effort to reduce unemployment the government created work – for example, by maintaining national parks and building roads. In the USA this included large projects such as the Hoover Dam, constructed between 1931 and 1936. Drought conditions in Oklahoma and Texas in the USA caused the 'dust bowl', which forced tens of thousands of families to abandon their farms and seek employment elsewhere.

In the Soviet Union, agricultural collectivisation and rapid industrialisation were taking place. Millions died in the 1932–3 famine in the Ukraine. This is termed the *Holodomor* ('Extermination by hunger'), believed to be deliberately planned by Stalin to eliminate the Ukrainian independence movement. The Soviets rejected outside aid, confiscated all household foodstuffs and restricted population movement. It was, however, part of the wider Soviet famine, which affected the major grain-producing areas of the country and caused 25 million people to migrate to cities in the Soviet Union. The 'Great Purge', Stalin's slaughter of old Bolsheviks from the Communist Party in 1936–8, resulted in hundreds of thousands of Russians being killed. The victims of the purge were scapegoats for the massive drop in grain production caused by the new and ineffective collective farming. So starvation was accompanied by mass slaughter.

The First World War produced an economic outcome disastrous for all parties, not just for the defeated Germany. The heavy war reparations imposed upon Germany at the Treaty of Versailles failed to fuel French economic recovery, but also greatly damaged Germany, which might have become France's leading trade and industrial development partner. American proposals, known as the Dawes Plan of 1924 and the Young Plan of 1929, succeeded in stabilising reparation payments. Germany was virtually bankrupt by 1931, and all payments were suspended. Poland's neighbours were having an even worse time.

Maria and Jurek in Warsaw

Maria and Jurek had settled in Warsaw, first living with her parents-in-law Władysław and Maria-Victoria in Bednarska Street but then moving to a newly developed area in the north of Warsaw, Zoliborz. Its name comes from the French *Joli bord* (pretty bank), on the side of the Wisła river. It also became identified as an area where military officers and their families settled (Figure 4.1). So 'Zoliborz

Industriousness: life in independent Warsaw   **77**

Oficerski' in Krasinski Street, became their home around 1925, and to other members of the family for the next few decades. Maria managed to get her own apartment near to her parents-in-law in the same block. She lived on an army pension provided for the widows of army officers, and later became personal assistant to a prominent general who lived in this officer district. Krasinski Street, on which they lived, was a long avenue perpendicular to the Wisła river ending at the Pawązki cemetery where Tadeusz was buried, and where subsequent family members were all laid to rest. The Zoliborz large apartment blocks were surrounded by greenery and gardens. Maria and Jurek lived in apartment block 21, apartment 21. This was near to the Convent of the Sisters of the Resurrection at number 31. The Church of St John Campius was next to the convent and likely to be where the family went to church, with a school and kindergarten on site, possibly where Jurek was sent for a time. Maria was still a young woman of 34, and her life now focused on her son, supported by the wider family. There were Cygler family members nearby – Maria's brother Jan and his wife Jadwiga, and her youngest brother Wacek and his wife Mira were in Warsaw. There is every indication of happy times, particularly during holidays in the country houses during the summer.

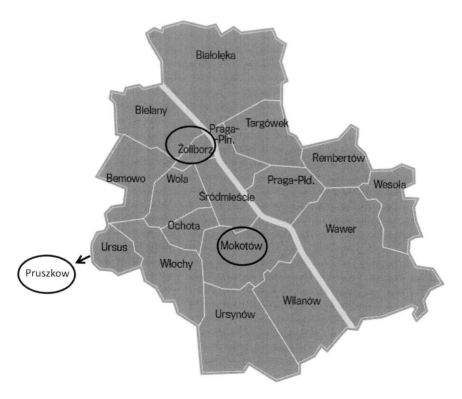

FIGURE 4.1 Plan of Warsaw

Jurek's cousin, Stas, was only one year older and they seem to have been as close as brothers and spent holiday times together at Rudzk. Stas had also lost his father early in the war and was looked after by his mother, Julia. As a young adult she had returned to live at the country house at Rudzk where she helped with the cheese production. Julia then married a neighbour, Kazimierz Leinweber, who, having been trained as an agricultural engineer and involved in farming, later became interested in managing an experimental school in Kalisz, western Poland. Stas, their only son, was born in 1912 and was only two when his father was killed early in the First World War. Julia returned from Kalisz to Rudzk with her young son. When the house and estate was plundered by the Bolsheviks in 1919, Julia moved with Stas to Warsaw to Puławska Street, south of Mokotow. In 1922 she remarried a distant relative with the same surname, Kazimierz Czechowski, and went to live on his estate in Pinsk near Rudzk. In 1925, when Stas was aged 13, Julia moved with her son to an apartment in Warsaw, leaving her husband, accompanied by her sister Zosia. Julia studied home economics and worked as a cooking instructor and conducted cooking classes. She published a recipe book for vegetarians, as well as a number of articles on food and nutrition.

In 1925, there were just over one million people in Warsaw and the city's wealth would double in the next five years. Building work took place, new broad boulevards were constructed and a new airport built in 1921, situated first in Mokotow, near to where Tadeusz had been stationed in the army, but then moving to the neighbouring Okęcie, its permanent location and where it still remains, just south of the city centre. The city government worked out plans for a metro system, but this was only part constructed in the 1930s, to be completed only in recent times.

Employment in the city was largely in state enterprises. Despite unemployment, immigration to the city (from the countryside or outside the borders) continued. The outer suburbs of Warsaw spread to accommodate the increased population. Zoliborz was one of those extended by a model housing settlement, positioned to link to the army cemetery of Pawązki. The new area was planned for four groups of the population: workers in a housing association, writers and journalists, civil servants and army officers. There was much rebuilding throughout the city, with the centre having new monumental architecture. There was also a restoration movement with palaces restored, these given largely to state officials. Patriotic monuments were also created, commemorating Chopin, Poniatowski and the 'unknown soldier' to commemorate the two recent wars.

The architecture of the city benefited from a range of historical influences. Gothic architecture from the fifteenth century was represented in St John's Cathedral and the Royal Castle; seventeenth-century Baroque, influenced by a distinct Warsaw style, was exemplified in Wilanow and Krasinski Palaces. Later Baroque style utilised Italianate suburban villas and grand buildings with side towers and extensive wings. Rococo architecture was also seen in the Czapski Palace and the Visitation Church. Neoclassical architecture was also common with Palladian patterns – for example, the beautiful Łasienki Palace (Palace on the Lake). In the 1920s and 1930s new building work for housing workers and 'villa' housing estates was undertaken. There were also some skyscrapers – that built by the Polish Telegraph company in 1908 was 51 metres high; the Prudential Insurance company high-rise was to follow in 1934, at 66 metres.

Jurek at school

The education system in Poland required reconstruction. By 1919 compulsory school attendance of children from ages 7 to 14 was in place. Schools were free of charge and accessible to all children. Common education was intensively developed, especially between 1922 and 1929, but provision could not match need.[1] During the first three years the schools were comprehensive, teaching all students at the same level. During the following five years, students were grouped into specialised areas of study for part of their schooling. The school diploma opened up the prospect of further studies. There were also independent grammar schools, with many secondary and high schools demanding tuition fees.

There was a major focus on education. By 1928 nearly all young children were in primary school, and global illiteracy dramatically reduced. By 1938 there were 25 universities, upper schools and polytechnic schools. There were also new military schools opened, as well as specialist schools for art and technical subjects. It was a time when ideas in education were changing, influenced, for example, by Janusz Korczak. Originally called Henryk Goldszmit, of Jewish origin, he was a paediatrician who had opened a home for Jewish orphans in 1911. In the new Republic he opened 'Nasz Dom' (Our House) for orphans. He created the 'Children's Republic' involving self-governing structures in schools, the forerunner of social pedagogy (Eichsteller, 2009). It was a new concept of childcare, moving from the Victorian model of children as workers and economic units to children as worthy persons to be valued for who they were. He noted that this was already the case in upper-class Polish homes (Eichsteller, 2009, p. 380).

Maria, with advice from her parents-in-law, searched for suitable schooling for Jurek, who would have been around ten years old when they went to live in Zoliborz. First she sent him to a monastery school, but Jurek decided this was not for him and repeatedly ran away. He wanted to go to military school, probably influenced by his father as a war hero. Maria was at first shocked at the idea – she had suffered enough from the military life, but eventually acceded to him. The Czechowski family were in favour, since it would 'make a man' of him. They worried that, with only his mother to look after him, he might become a 'mummy's boy'. So Jurek was sent to a newly opened military school in North Poland. The Korpus Kadet school in Chełmno was a boarding school. Newly opened in the Second Republic, it echoed an ancient tradition of training officers in chivalric principles. Its purpose was the training of young men to become the military leaders of the future. Its location was in a previously Prussian dominated area, and the city of Chełmno was part of the famous Hanseatic League along the Baltic. This medieval city had five Gothic churches and a beautiful Renaissance town hall in the middle of its market square.

Jurek would have probably gone to the cadet boarding school aged eleven or so, around 1924. We have his identity card from 1929. We don't know how his education was paid for – maybe as the son of a war hero he was given a free place, or possibly Jurek's grandparents paid for him. Having insisted on going to this cadet school, Jurek was then terribly homesick for the first term. He missed his mother and family and found the regime harsh. In winter at dawn, the boys would wash in ice-cold water; they slept in dormitories and the discipline was rigid. However, gradually he became accustomed to it, made friends and did well at his studies and at the physical sports and weapons training. Later documents showed he trained in fencing, jujitsu, boxing and shooting. He learned to march, to load and fire a rifle and was presumably schooled in military tactics and strategy. He was not, however, a very dedicated cadet. He recalls one early morning when the boys all had to go out on a march of several miles. Half asleep, they returned to the cadet college with all their rifles having been taken. None of them knew how this had happened. Jurek much preferred dancing in the local town and would regularly leave the school premises, often without permission. On one such venture he went dancing even though unwell, developed an ear infection which proved quite serious and was confined to the sick room. However, his boyish charm soon got round the school nurse and he left again to go into town as soon as he could.

Jurek returned to Warsaw for holidays, as well as to the family country houses in Rudzk and Mohylew for the summers. As an only child he was close to male cousins his age – Stas in particular, but also Henryk, actually an uncle but only a few years older. The teenage boys hung around together. There is a fine picture taken in 1930 at Rudzk, of Stas and Henryk standing protectively on either side of 16-year-old Jurek, ready for tennis. Rudzk, with its forest and lake for fishing and swimming, and tennis courts and stables, was ideal for young men interested in sport. There are also photographs of picnics and the family lounging in the garden. Later in life Jurek would remember eating honey directly from the honeycomb. Stas was a keen photographer and took a number of photographs in the summer of 1930. These still remain in their original photograph albums, carefully displayed and hand-labelled, in my cousin Piotr's possession. They show happy summers in the country.

In 1922 Stas began studying at the National Gymnasium in Warsaw, matriculating in 1933. He was an active scout (in the Warsaw Fellowship of Scouting, called the 'Wildcats'). He loved outdoor pursuits and went with the scouts to riding camps, hiking, cycling and skiing in the winter. He also played volleyball, joining the Academic Sports Association (AZS) where he was the team representative and lead Polish volleyball player, travelling abroad to matches. In 1932 and 1937, his team won the silver medal at the Polish Championships and in 1935 the gold medal. Stas also played basketball, handball and tennis. He studied at Warsaw Agricultural University in 1933, joined the Reserve Officers School of Artillery and was appointed reserve lieutenant and assigned to the 30 Artillery Regiment stationed in Brest. He graduated in 1938 and the following year he married a fellow student, Janina (Inka) Idzwikowska.

Photographs and film of Warsaw in the 1930s show it to be a thriving capital city. The streets were busy with trams, cars and horse-drawn buggies. Its avenues appear clean and wide, with flower vendors, traffic police and children playing in the streets. Workmen can be seen repairing roads. People look smartly dressed. There are pictures of beggars or poor street musicians, but no more than in any other capital city in the 1930s. Cafés and restaurants were lively and by night the streets were lit, with music and dancing widespread at the opulent hotels – the Bristol, the Europa and the Café George. Photographs of the famous Oasis restaurant show diners with table telephones available to ring other diners. The restaurant Dom Polski is still a white art deco building with fine dining and garden tables for eating al fresco. Café Adria was a very fashionable nightspot; a surviving film shows the orchestra Jerzego Lederman and the Corda duet of 1933 playing the foxtrot. The Café Adria had an elegant hallway, art deco dining room, grand ballroom and room for the orchestra. Pictures show elegant customers – men in white tie or smart suits, some in officer uniform, women in evening dress and fur wraps. People are eating, drinking, dancing and posing for photographs. The final picture shows people leaving at dawn into snowy weather.

Ordinary life in Warsaw continued. Photographs of the time show a new diesel train at a station, young men riding bicycles, motorbikes and even a light aircraft in evidence. Other pictures show boys putting firecrackers on tramlines for fun, people gathering for football matches and climbing trees to see the action for free. Sport became popular, with basketball starting in the Warsaw Military Academy in the early 1930s. However, football was paramount, and starting a league was one of the first actions of the new state in 1919, with as many as 30 football teams emerging in Warsaw alone. In 1921 the first league tournament was held, with Cracovia winning and Polonia Warszawa in second place. Warsaw hosted the first football international in June 1928, where Poland tied 3–3 with the USA, the game played in the army stadium in Warsaw. In *Boys Own* fashion, Poland were losing 3–2 until the 89th minute when they were awarded a penalty kick, and the only one offering to take the kick was Zygmunt Steuermann, a forward from a Jewish-minority team in Lwów, who then scored the equalising goal.

There are various photographs of Jurek in his cadet uniform, and one with his mother as a young teenager. Although still a beautiful woman, the effect on Maria of being widowed can be seen. There is a photograph of Jurek, in his teens and in full cadet uniform walking down the central Marszalkowska Street in Warsaw, with his mother when on leave from the Kadet Korps. Maria, then aged about 45, is elegant in her tailored suit, gloves and hat. They made a striking pair, with Jurek now over six feet in height. When Jurek finally graduated from the cadets, he came back to Warsaw and enrolled at the Warsaw Technical University aged 20.

Among the educational accomplishments of the inter-war period was the establishment of Polish state universities, in Warsaw and in four other major cities. These were paralleled by the universities of technology, which taught science. The student numbers in Warsaw had doubled to 4,673 by 1939. Jurek decided to enrol in the Technology University in Warsaw (where his father had briefly attended) to study business and economics. The university building had been completed in 1902 and was notable for its architecture built in the academic renaissance style, with a four-cloistered courtyard covered with a glass roof (this has been refurbished and is still in evidence today). It became the most important scientific centre of engineering in Poland and gained international prestige. Jurek, however, did not have the same interest in engineering held by his father, or architecture by his grandfather, but chose business studies.

It was clear that Jurek enjoyed his university days, making many friends and becoming close to a young student, Maria Janiszewska, whose nickname was 'Myszka' or mouse. (She was petite, only just over five feet tall, but with her forceful and outgoing personality the nickname is probably ironic.) Jurek loved being back in Warsaw; it was a time of energy and optimism, particularly amongst the young, who enjoyed the café society and the music, arts and free expression. Jurek is known to have enjoyed playing the piano, writing song lyrics, being popular with his peers, playing endless bridge and always short of money. After leaving his home in Zoliborz, he found an apartment in the city and attended the university.

Marriage

In February 1938, at the age of 24, Jurek married Myszka aged 21. There are two photographs surviving – the newly married couple outside the church in traditional wedding outfits in the freezing cold, Jurek in a fur-collared coat over his white tie and evening suit and Myska in her long, white dress engulfed in a white wrap and veils. They are smiling, happy and make a very handsome couple. The families were all present. Jurek's mother Maria and his other family members attended, although his grandparents Władysław and Maria-Victoria had died a few years earlier. Jurek now had two younger female cousins aged around ten: Danuta, Olgierd's daughter and Marysia, Grazyna's daughter, who also attended. The wedding feast was held in Myszka's aunt's large apartment. Myszka came from a wealthy family who owned sugar factories in Lublin and had a large country house in Kebel. Her parents and younger sister Dzidia (aged nine) were present. Petite, pretty and dark-haired, Myszka was lively and outgoing. The couple moved into an apartment in the City Centre district, near the Technical University, bought for them by her uncle Pawel. The building still stands on Mokotowska Street, with shops and cafés leading to the church of Christ the Saviour, the tall, white, double-spired church standing dramatically in a square where roads and tramlines meet, ringed with cafés. It is only a few minutes walk to the University. Łasienki Palace and its lakes and grounds are nearby for Sunday walks – a wonderful city location.

The couple employed a maid, took on two red setter dogs and enjoyed eighteen months of happily married life. When Jurek was called up for military service in December 1938, he was allowed to take a civilian-style job at the airfield at Okęcie near his apartment. This (together with his tardiness) delayed his final undergraduate dissertation, so his bachelor degree was never awarded. A rare, small black-and-white photograph shows him in the office looking rather bored, chin in hand, smoking and looking up at the camera. A relatively easy way to undertake military service and life was good, with studying and intellectual discussion, membership of the local sports club (we have his enrolment card), plenty of culture and entertainment in this capital city, student friends, young love and the independence of their own apartment. A keen card player, he became adept at bridge, a lifelong hobby.

My family only learned these details of Myszka recently when her nephew Peter unexpectedly emailed my sister Joanna from Warsaw in 2015. He is the son of Myszka's younger sister Dzidiza, born after the war, his mother now in her 80s. He sent the two wedding pictures, talked about his uncle Jurek and described their marriage:

> Your grandmother (Maria) was present at the wedding and reception but I don't have any photos. Most photos were lost during the war. The wedding took place in Aunt Nata's apartment. After the wedding they lived in a comfortable apartment on the borders of Mokotow and Okęcie. This apartment was probably bought for them by Uncle Pawel who was a factory owner (of sugar refineries and yeast factories in Lublin). They had two dogs which were red setters and Jurek worked in an office linked with the air force. I don't have any photos of the factories but I do have photos of the family palace in Kebel. Now it is a school and a residential home for orphans. We have not tried to recover this property although my mother is the rightful heir.

At the time of the wedding, the young couple must have been aware of impending war, signs of which had been steadily building during the 1930s. Whilst Jurek was enjoying young adult life in the busy capital, my mother Christine, 13 years younger, was growing up in the English Midlands.

Christine in England

In 1926 in Manchester, England, Christine Elizabeth was born, the first child to Hugh and Barbara O'Neill. It was 19 November, just six months after the birth of the royal Princess Elizabeth. Christine's father, Hugh, had an academic post at Manchester University at the time, having moved there from Sheffield where both he and Barbara were born. He was third-generation Irish, his family having settled in Sheffield in the mid-1800s. In his autobiography he writes about the Sheffield Irish community and the steel industry in which he became involved:

> This was the setting in which my Irish emigrant grandfather established himself after the Great Famine of 1846, and my upbringing was largely amongst Irish exiles, but as they proved to be incurably cheerful, nostalgia does not seem worthwhile . . .

> The domestic steel industry still survived and 'little mesters' forged their blades by hand and the file cutters tapped away. Nor must I forget Sheffield's other products – silverplate and Britannia metal – or that my maternal grandfather was a respected silversmith. Most Saturday mornings, *en route* to watch my father's blacksmith or to seek the occasional single-driver locomotive at the Midland Station, I generally paused at a backstreet gateway for a distant view of the movements of men in steaming rags in the flashing light of furnaces. One day, unseen hands propelled me forward to gain a close-up of this casting of liquid crucible steel. My father asked from behind me whether I liked it, and perhaps it was then that I fancied metallurgical work.
>
> O'Neill, 1967, p. 139

The O'Neill family came to England during the Irish potato famine, where 1.5 million Irish people died and another million emigrated. Hugh's grandfather, Daniel O'Neill, was born in County Derry around 1820. In the famine he stowed away with cattle being transported on a boat bound for England. As a stonemason he soon got work in Durham, in the north of England, and then on the developing railway network, and finally with the John Brown steel firm in Sheffield. In 1855, Daniel O'Neill married Louisa Graysmark whose mother, also Louisa, was born in Bruges and had been married to a French officer, General Depienne. Her uncle was said to be 'head copper plate writer' to Napoleon. Louisa's maternal grandfather was Dutch (or *Deutsch*, German as the family believed). Louisa's family had settled near Arundel Castle, West Sussex, but then moved to Sheffield where she became a lady's maid and seems to have also been a nurse. Daniel and Louisa met when an accident at work led to him breaking his leg. A large man, his workers took down the door of a room and carried him upon it to Sheffield infirmary where Louisa nursed him to health, 'applying fomentations in the continental fashion to avoid an amputation' (O'Neill, 1995, p. 1). In 1856 Daniel started his own building firm, D. O'Neill and Son. An energetic and lively man, he obtained a loan from the bank, completed several substantial buildings in Sheffield in his lifetime and became a respected citizen with a social conscience who aided the poor.

His son Aloysuis, 'Young Dan' and father to Hugh, was born in 1865, joined the family business to become director, and married Lucy Cunningham in 1898. She was Anglo-Irish. Her Irish grandfather had joined the British Army and became Troop Sergeant Major of the 9th Queen's Royal Lancers and married an Englishwoman, Elizabeth Tilley, of Winchester. Their son James Cunningham, Lucy's father, born in 1839, lived with his parents in India until 1850 and then returned to England. At the age of 15 he became apprenticed to the Sheffield silversmiths James Dixon and Sons, where he became general manager. The involvement with metals continued with three of his sons and three grandsons. Of James's ten children by two marriages, Hugh writes: 'only my mother (Lucy Cunningham O'Neill) retained the religious faith of her fathers and taught it to her children' (O'Neill, 1995, p. 2). Hugh and his siblings were raised as Catholics.

Industriousness: life in independent Warsaw

Hugh was born to Aloysius and Lucy in 1899, and grandfather Daniel 'insisted I be called simply Hugh, after the great Earl of Tyrone, King of Ulster (1540–1616) from whom by tradition we were descended'. There was even talk of unclaimed possessions in Spain following the 'flight of the earls' when defeated by the Tudors, and in Portugal where the head of the O'Neill clan still resides. The claim was never realised and, whilst never rich, the family prospered. The Irish community in Sheffield included many who were poor, Hugh recalls:

> As in so many British towns during the Industrial revolution the Irish immigrants crowded together in ghettos and in 1851 comprised about 4 per cent of the population of Sheffield. At church and school, poor and better off mixed freely and amongst the few with top hats there would be a few with shawls, clogs and even bare feet . . . My father for 50 years was a member of the St Vincent de Paul Society founded by a Professor at the Sorbonne in 1833, for laymen to engage in works of charity. Frequently he would take me with him to help the poor in our Sheffield slums so that I had an early acquaintance with poverty – and drunkenness.

Hugh's father had successfully created a family building company in Sheffield responsible for many civic buildings:

> The family firm was specialising in erecting fine stone buildings, such as the beautiful Edgar Allen library of the university, which was opened by the Prince of Wales (George V) in 1909. Also the tower of St Vincent's which was blessed by Cardinal Logue in 1911. . . . In the same year my father was converting a disused orphanage founded by nuns in 1871 on the bleak Kirk Edge hill outside the city, for use as a Carmelite convent.
>
> O'Neill, 1995, p.4

Hugh, like other boys born in the Victorian era and like my other grandfather Tadeusz, also took an interest in steam trains:

> My father liked us to visit his buildings and plant and I also remember a trip to Liverpool to see the Lusitania, the largest ship in the world. The journey was by old railway coaches having the vacuum brake alarm operated by a cord running along the outside above the doors, whilst lighting was by gas jets ignited individually by a man walking along the roof. Many trains were heated in winter by hot metal containers holding sodium acetate placed by porters under the carriage seats. We had happy times at home with a great interest in hobbies like model railways and engines, the new 'Meccano' and fretwork.

The O'Neill family tree is shown in Figure 4.2.

86 Poland: the first generation

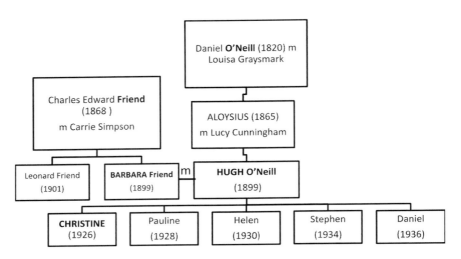

FIGURE 4.2 The O'Neill family tree

By 1910, Hugh was at the Central Secondary School in Sheffield, winning a free place, and his father had built the family a new house in Crookesmoor, which included a stained-glass window featuring the 'Red Hand of Ulster' (the O'Neill coat of arms) on the staircase. Hugh's younger brothers, Bernard and Daniel, attended the same school, with Bernard leaving early to be trained as an electrical engineer at a local steelworks and Daniel remaining in the family building firm. Daniel became managing director, and much later, Lord Mayor of Sheffield. Bernard came in time, to own his own steelworks. Hugh became an academic and researcher into metals. Too young to enlist for military service at the beginning of the First World War, the age limit was reduced in 1918 and, aged 17, he was conscripted. He underwent training and, due to his interest in wireless sets (he had built his own), was sent to the Signal Corps at Bedford to learn telegraphy. After training, and a bout of Spanish flu where he was extremely ill, the war ended, and in 1919 the army 'dispensed of my services'. He was pleased to return to Sheffield, attended a university dancing class and met Barbara Friend, his future wife and my grandmother.

Barbara came from a middle-class English family; her father, Charles Edward Friend, a cabinet-maker and company director, was married to Carrie Simpson, an intellectual and activist. They had two children – Barbara had a younger brother, Leonard. Their religious upbringing was Unitarian, her grandfather Frederick having been a Methodist minister who preached around the country; he married Mary Coop, their five children all born in different cities. Charles Edward was the second, born in Cheadle, Staffordshire. He later settled in Sheffield, where he met Carrie

Simpson and their two children were born. Charles Edward was a keen rower and sporting man, and he and Carrie both enjoyed walking on the Yorkshire moors. He was a man of firm beliefs, and he did not approve of his daughter marrying a Roman Catholic.

Nevertheless, Barbara married Hugh and followed him to Birmingham where he took up his first lectureship after graduation at the Technical College. This course was for ex-serviceman and senior students who worked in industry and attended lectures and laboratory classes in the evening. From there Hugh was invited by Professor Thompson to become assistant lecturer at Manchester University, which he accepted before moving up to more senior positions. Hugh was an ardent Catholic and took up voluntary work, prison visiting (later Amnesty International) as well as helping the university Catholic movement to grow, along with its international wing – Pax Romana – whose aim was to encourage peace in Europe. He writes in his memoire:

> That we might be truly men-of-the-world, I took hundreds of students and graduates abroad, and especially remember a Budapest congress of 1924 with the Danube journey and the gypsy music. We often met foreign statesmen e.g. Minister Sramek in new Czechoslovakia (1922) who became Premier of the exiled government in London after the war and was eventually imprisoned by the communists. Also Chancellor Seipel of anxious Austria after he had escaped assassination. In 1927 a Regent of renewed Poland received us in his house in Warsaw, from where we travelled to zinc and iron works near Katowice and saw hardy workmen loading coke in bare feet....

The year after Christine was born, Hugh again travelled to Poland for the 7th Pax Romana conference in 1927, taking a party of 27 delegates. He boarded the Berlin express from the Hook of Holland on 9 August and then changed to the Nord Express for Warsaw. He writes:

> At dawn the train was crossing the plain of old Russian Poland with its hardy barefoot peasants and wood cabins and the plots marked out by small white stones. After 43 hours continuous travel we were welcomed at Warsaw station and conducted to student hostels. My room must have been occupied by a warlike youth, for the doorframe was tattooed with a pattern of small bullets. Breakfast was served by Polish ladies at their HQ in the city and the other meals were provided in the splendid *Casino de Officiers* where rooms were available for socials and dancing.
>
> High Mass at the University Church, and the opening of the sessions in the University Great Hall with speeches broadcast on national radio (and a walk out by the Czechoslovak delegation), were followed by an unexpected event in a circus hall in the city. Some of us had been informed that the Diaghilev ballet *en route* to Moscow had broken its journey to give a special

performance for which we could obtain tickets. I therefore literally had a ring-side view and the ballet was greeted with immense enthusiasm by the Warsaw audience. There was also a visit to the Presidential Palace (even to Piłsudski's apartments, with a bottle of medicine standing on his bedside table), and an Anglo-Polish singsong in a famous old wine tavern in the historic Market Place, and a trip to the Wilanow (Palace) home of (King) John Sobieski with its portrait of Bonny Prince Charlie who married one of the family. . . .

On walking through the streets one was struck by the large number of Jews, recognisable by their long black caftans, black caps, beards and long hair with ringlets. They comprised about 30 per cent of the Warsaw population and I wandered through that ghetto. . . .

Hugh spent two days visiting steel and zinc works in Upper Silesia and then got the train to Poznan, and from there to Berlin and on to The Hague before returning to England.

When Christine was aged eight, the O'Neill family, with her younger sisters Pauline and Helen and baby brother Stephen, moved to Derby in the English Midlands, where Hugh was offered research work for the London Midland and Scottish Railway (LMS). Derby was a centre for railways, the site of Rolls-Royce aero-engines and a thriving industrial town. It is the site of the world's first factory, the 'Silk Mill', which in the 1700s had produced silk by the side of the River Derwent. The town then developed a fabric industry through a number of cotton mills. It was also well located on the edge of the Peak District National Park, a good town in which to bring up a family. The youngest child, Daniel, was born there. All the children attended St Mary's Catholic Primary school, a convent school attached to St Mary's Church, not far from the old Silk Mill and the river. There was a fairly large Irish community in the town, which had pooled its resources in the early days to build the Victorian church of St Mary's. After first renting a house, Hugh bought a plot of land in Highfield Road and had a large detached house built, surrounded by a wide garden. He had the foresight to build a bomb shelter attached to the cellar. The family prospered. Hugh writes:

> It was a great break to leave Manchester and our home in Withington and we now had four children. But Derby appealed to me as a town to live in and we rented a suitable house in Highfield Road and moved there during August 1934. The day arrived when I reported at the old Locomotive works – behind the station built by Robert Stephenson – where the grotesque metallurgical lab was situated . . .
>
> . . . the family settled down well in Derby and we now had a fifth child so I considered a more convenient house to live in. It was a fortunate coincidence that my old friend C.H. Aslin who had made the drawings for our Manchester house was now the borough architect of Derby and he supported the idea of building a new residence. I bought a portion of the

kitchen garden off the nearby Highfield House, planned the new building and one of Aslin's assistants made the formal drawings, ... it was a pleasure to move into this new home during 1936.

O'Neill, 1995, p. 30

The railway work involved travelling around the UK to major factories at Glasgow, Horwich, Crewe and Wolverton, electric power stations in Lancashire and near London, and marine stations in England and Wales. Hugh's work involved visiting sites where there was corrosion in tunnels and at water troughs where the tracks were damaged. It involved walking along the track with a 'platelayer', who knew each length of track, and with gas lamps to provide light. On one occasion they found a 'refuge' in the tunnel only seconds before a train sped by. Not long after joining the LMS, Hugh's work took him to Germany in 1936:

> Germany was rather on show that year and acted as host to the Olympic Games, the International Foundry Congress and the autumn meeting of the British Iron and Steel Institute. I was asked to attend the latter . . . Dusseldorf, with its 'brown shirts' and parades of singing Hitler youth and torchlight processions at night, so people almost automatically left the cafes to line the footpaths and give the Nazi salute. More work visits followed and sometimes an individual guide who would yell 'Heil Hitler' at any workman he met, and expect a return of his salute. . . . The many works visits made some of the British foundry men remark they were getting tired of 'riding round the ruddy Ruhr' . . .

O'Neill, 1995, p. 32

The run-up to war

The lead-up to the Second World War saw Jozef Beck as Polish foreign minister from 1932–9, trying to protect Poland's national and strategic interests in the face of Nazi aggression. When Chamberlain (from Britain) and Daladier (from France) tried appeasement, Beck refused to make concessions to either Germany or the Soviet Union. He resisted both Goering and Ribbentrop of Germany as much as Litvinov and Molotov of Soviet Russia. Czechoslovakia followed the appeasement views of the Allies and fell to the advancing Germans. Beck put his trust in the Allies' (Britain and France's) guarantees of support.

All attempts by Berlin to draw Poland into closer collaboration were resisted. As soon as Nazi propaganda turned on German claims for Danzig (*Gdansk*) and the 'Polish corridor' to the Baltic, it was clear that Poland was at the same risk as Czechoslovakia. On 31 March 1939, Chamberlain proffered an unconditional guarantee that Britain would do everything possible to resist an attack by Germany on Poland's independence. In fact, he could offer nothing practical – British forces did not have the means available, but this was an attempt to deter Hitler.

On 28 April, Hitler renounced the Polish–German pact of non-aggression. French and British chiefs of staff gave assurances of their proposed action against any German aggression. Both governments believed in a common peace front with the Soviet Union, on the assumption they could make a pact with Stalin. The Soviets installed Molotov as Foreign Commissioner. The most accurate assessment of Poland's position came from Mussolini's foreign minister and son-in-law (Ciano, 1945), who had spoken with the German high command and made brief notes of his impressions, which proved prophetic:

> Conversations with Goering . . . struck by the tone in which he described relations with Poland . . . as with Czechoslovakia and Austria. The Germans are mistaken if they think they can carry on in the same manner. The Poles will be beaten; but they will not lay down their arms without a fierce and bloody struggle . . . The Germans should not imagine that they are simply going to hold a victory parade in Poland. If the Poles are attacked they will fight . . . Conversation with Wienawia (retiring Polish ambassador in Rome). Urged him to show greatest moderation. Whatever happens Poland will pay the cost of the conflict. No Franco-British assistance will be forthcoming, at least not in the first phase of the war. Poland would be quickly turned into a pile of ruins.
>
> Ciano, 1945, p. 320

In Soviet Russia between 1935 and 1938, Tukhachevsky and most of the other military leaders had been murdered in Stalin's purges. In some cases this included their wives, considered 'enemies of the people' (Zamoyski, 2008/2014). The Polish–Soviet war had been considered a humiliation for Soviet Russia, revealing its frailty and limited power. Stalin was shown to have performed badly in the war, guilty of insubordination and failing to obey orders, which cost them heavily in the south of the country. He was not to forget this humiliation. The new Soviet state began to see the world as ranged against them, leading to a siege mentality, isolation and the 'communism in one country' policy. It was viewed by the outside world as both defensive and aggressive. Such isolation aided Stalin's rise to power and his subsequent reign of terror. He gave up trying to convert Poland to communism.

In Germany the Treaty of Versailles had left the country poor and bankrupt. It was plagued by huge war reparations of $32 billion. The German Weimar Republic, a liberal government, allowed the president to rule by decree, which led to protests and attempted coups from both Left and Right. Hyper-inflation and the Great Depression blocked attempts to rebuild the economy. The currency was revalued. The Dawes Plan with the USA allowed for a refinancing of reparations in 1924 to pay the war debt to France. Germany joined the League of Nations in 1925. However, the Nationalsozialistische Deutsche Arbeiterpartei (Nazi) Party rose in the early 1930s and gained strength when unemployment increased after tariffs were imposed. This had closed foreign markets. Hitler, emerging as a leader, stressed that Germany was a victim of the Treaty of Versailles and promoted the return to a glorious past as the Greater Germany. His speeches insisted on the superiority of the German culture and people.

Hitler became German Chancellor in 1933, and the Reichstag fire the following month was blamed on the communists. Martial law was imposed, which remained in effect until May 1945. Hitler's key men were Josef Goebbels (head of propaganda), Hermann Goering (Vice-Chancellor and head of the Luftwaffe) and Heinrich Himmler (head of the Interior and the SS (Schutzstaffel, the paramilitary organisation responsible for enforcing the racial laws). The Nuremberg Laws were imposed in 1935, ousting Jews from mainstream German life, repressing and expelling them from Germany. From that time, Jews could not be German citizens, had no vote and could not occupy public office. In 1938 the shooting of a German diplomat by a Jew in Paris triggered 'Kristallnacht', used by the Nazis to incite riots against Jews across Germany. These were carefully orchestrated by the SS, under Himmler and Heidrich. Nearly a hundred Jews were killed and 30,000 arrested and placed in concentration camps. Over a thousand synagogues were burned and 7,000 businesses destroyed. Thousands of homes were ransacked. Jews were then charged 1 billion Deutschmarks for the cost to the government to 'restore peace' and repair damage. Jews finally started to escape from Germany.

Hitler challenged the Versailles Treaty, and Europe was reluctant to challenge him through fear of another war. This led to a policy of appeasement by Western nations, who turned a blind eye to German rearmament. In 1935, Hitler rebuilt the German airforce, the Luftwaffe; in 1936 he reoccupied and militarised the Rhineland; and in 1938 he created the *Anschluss*, effectively taking over Austria. The Munich Pact gave Germany the German-speaking Sudetenland bordering Czechoslovakia. Chamberlain began appeasement talks with 'peace in our time', just as Germany invaded Czechoslovakia. In August 1939 Hitler signed a non-aggression pact with Stalin, an unforeseen fascist–communist alliance. The writing was on the wall for Poland with its historic enemies in surprise alliance.

Discussion

This chapter is entitled 'industry', to show the hard work and efforts the citizens of Poland made to create a new and successful independent state. Whilst there were social problems, it seems to have been a time of optimism and relative stability. It provided Jurek with a happy childhood and his transition through school and university to adulthood. In many ways it was a creative time for him, as well as his city and his country. The Anglo-Irish family of the O'Neills are introduced in England, with my grandfather Hugh also having numerous links to industry and engineering. Hugh travelled to Poland in the 1930s, involved in student trips but also in the emerging metal industries. There were ties of religion, and developing industrial knowledge, but I think also a great admiration for the Poles, which was to continue through later years. It also indicates that the two countries had more interchange and contact than is perhaps generally admitted.

In terms of the theme of 'industry or creativity', Jurek's early education in military college gave him all the strategic, leadership and fighting skills which would equip him for the next phase of his life. However, as a young adult he found his natural tendency was both creative and entrepreneurial. He had musical and artistic flair, as well as being a keen sportsman, and his chosen subject at university was business and economics. Thus competence relates to all the skills he learned for survival, not least his personal charm, social skills and capacity for attachment and forming enduring bonds with others. Figure 4.3 summarises the themes of this chapter.

The years 1920–39 were optimistic ones for Poland, and for Jurek and his family. The 100-year search for independence was achieved and Warsaw in particular experienced a resurgence in culture and creativity. Although it is easy to see this past shadowed by later events, in hindsight it was a good period for Jurek to grow up in. In terms of the themes of attachment and identity, both seem positive for the growing young man. It is clear he had a close and loving family. Although his mother was widowed, she had frequent contact with her relatives and in-laws and had made a career for herself. She had a good apartment in an affluent suburb and summer holidays were spent in the Czechowski or Rodziewicz country houses. Maria was particularly close to her sister-in-law Grazyna, who had a daughter Marysia ten years younger than Jurek. Maria's parents-in-law were very involved with Jurek their first grandchild. Being sent away to boarding school was probably

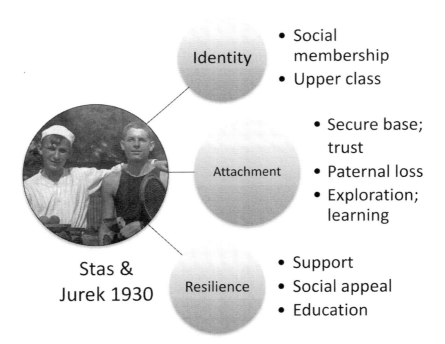

FIGURE 4.3 Summary of the themes in Chapter 4

a challenging and upsetting time for Jurek when he first went, but he seems to have adapted and had friends there. He was also close to his cousins (particularly Stas), and seems to have been surrounded by loving family and is likely to have had a positive attachment experience. Both Jurek and Stas seem to have had a good teenage and early adulthood. In terms of identity, this is not described explicitly, but we know that both considered themselves very Polish and were very patriotic. Unlike his father, Jurek had few military leanings and although learning the skills required of an officer at military school, he left that behind to pursue academic studies. He then seems to have enjoyed life in a very vibrant Warsaw, and found love and happiness in his first marriage. Stas also married and received a university education, in addition to excelling as a sportsman. These are the building blocks for resilience. This was to be seriously challenged for Jurek, for Stas and their family in Poland in 1939.

Note

1 Poland – History Background – Schools, Education, School and Polish – StateUniversity.com http://education.stateuniversity.com/pages/1209/Poland-HISTORY-BACKGROUND.html#ixzz44JAdGJwF

SECTION II
Poland and England
The second generation

This second section reflects the adult aspects of Erikson's development stages (Figure 5.1), and in terms of the family narrative takes place in both Poland and England. All of this section takes place during the Second World War and focuses on two generations: my grandmother, Maria and her son Jurek and his first wife,

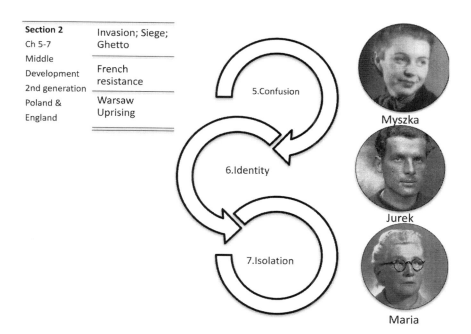

FIGURE 5.1 Erikson's phases of development, midpoint

Myszka. This looks at how these individuals, and family members, coped with war and separation in the family. It deals with hidden identities and the subterfuge needed for survival, but also hope for reunion and of a better life to come. It covers both 'fight' and 'flight' experiences in response to adversity.

5

CONFUSION

Nazi occupation of Warsaw (1939–43)

> You can actively flee, then, and you can actively stay put.
>
> Erik Erikson

Introduction

Erikson's next stage of development involves the onset of a sense of identity. This begins in adolescence and leads into early adulthood. Social roles become important, as does a sense of belonging to a group to help develop social identity. The associated virtue identified by Erikson is 'Fidelity', the negative aspect, 'Confusion'. The latter is highlighted in this chapter, given the confusion of the political events that occur. This describes Poland being invaded at the start of the Second World War. Myszka and Maria are separated from Jurek, and Warsaw is put under extreme siege and threat of destruction. The Nazi ideology insists on the Polish population as being subhuman and their treatment is dehumanising. The Jews are segregated by the Nazis, and knowledge of their mass extermination leads to the Warsaw Ghetto Uprising. This is seen as part of the striving of Jews for public expression of identity. The focus is on Myszka and her response to the invasion of her country and threat to her city.

The family documents for this chapter are mainly in the forms of letters from both Maria and Myszka to Jurek, who is then abroad in France, continuing the struggle there.

Double invasion

At 6am on 1 September 1939, Warsaw was struck by the first of a succession of bombing raids. Simultaneously, 62 German divisions supported by 1,300 aircraft invaded by air, and bombed the Polish airforce at its base (Lightbody, 2004).

The Luftwaffe heavily bombed all road and rail junctions. Army barracks were also bombed. Towns and villages, and their civilian population, were deliberately targeted. A fleeing mass of terror-stricken people blocked the roads, hampering the flow of Polish military reinforcements to the Front at the German border. At 8am, Poland requested immediate military assistance from its allies France and Britain. There was a delay until noon on 3 September, when Britain declared war on Germany, followed by France's declaration at 5pm. The delay reflected the vain hope that Hitler would respond to demands to end the invasion. The West was unprepared for war.

By 8 September the leading Panzer German tanks were on the outskirts of Warsaw, having covered 140 miles in only eight days. Two days later, all Polish forces were ordered to fall back and regroup in eastern Poland for a last stand. The Poles pinned their hopes on a major French and British offensive in the west to relieve the pressure. However, despite French assurances, all military action on the Western Front ended on 13 September. French troops fell back behind the security of the Maginot line of fortified defences. Warsaw was surrounded by the German army on 15 September and suffered punishing bombing raids, without any offer of relief.

Many Poles, as soldiers, fled across the border into Romania, and later reached the West to continue the fight as the Free Polish Forces. Warsaw bravely held out until 27 September, only surrendering after enduring 18 days of continuous bombardment. The German army gained a swift victory. Poland had become the first battleground of the Second World War. The new 'blitzkrieg' form of war was relentless. It was massively mechanised (tanks and bomber aircraft, seen in their thousands for the first time ever) with a gruelling marching schedule for foot soldiers. We now know this was achieved through the soldiers' drugged-induced highs from Pervitin, a version of crystal meth given to troops (Ohler, 2016). This gave them a sense of invulnerability, reduced sensitivity to pain or hunger, and reduced the need for sleep. Side effects included reduced moral sensibility and greater violence, and mistreatment of subordinates or other victims of war. This type of war had never been seen before, and had a dehumanising effect – for the perpetrators as well as the victims.

Worse was to come. On 17 September, the Soviet Red Army crossed the Polish border in the east, a result of the secret Nazi–Soviet Pact. As with the German invasion, there was no formal declaration of war. The invasion lasted for 20 days, ending on 6 October 1939 with the two-way division and annexation of the entire territory of the Second Polish Republic by both Germany and the Soviet Union. Both powers held the same antagonism and destructive intent towards Poland. The Red Army, which vastly outnumbered the Polish defenders, achieved its targets by deception. Some 230,000 Polish prisoners of war were captured by the Soviet Russians. The Poles could not know the Soviets were secretly allied to the German Nazis. The campaign of mass persecution in East Poland began immediately. Some 13.5 million Polish citizens fell under this military occupation and became new Soviet subjects following mock elections conducted by the NKVD (communist secret police, precursor to the KGB) in an atmosphere of terror. The Soviet campaign of ethnic/political cleansing began immediately with a wave of arrests and summary executions of officers, policemen and priests. Over the next year and a half, the Soviet NKVD sent hundreds of thousands of people – including families with children – from eastern Poland to Siberia. Their ideological 'crime' was owning land, this freely granted after Polish independence. During the Red Army's rapid advance, about 7,000 Polish soldiers died in the fighting and 300,000 were taken prisoner. The Soviets promised them freedom after surrender, but immediately reneged on this, arresting or killing those who laid down their arms. There was no observance of the Geneva Convention – the Soviets were not signatories.

Warsaw siege

Meanwhile in Warsaw, the siege lasted 17 gruelling days following the population repelling the first German attacks. It was fought between the Polish Warsaw Army (*Armia Warszawa*) entrenched in the capital and the invading German army. It lasted until 28 September, when the Polish garrison commander officially capitulated. The following day, approximately 140,000 Polish soldiers and troops left the city and were taken as prisoners of war by the Germans. On 1 October, the German *Wehrmacht* army entered Warsaw, starting a period of German occupation to last for five years. During the 17 days of the siege around 18,000 civilians were killed by air bombardments, 10 per cent of the city's buildings were entirely destroyed and a further 40 per cent were heavily damaged – this in just one month. On 10 September, more than 70 German bombers were seen above Warsaw. During that single day, named 'Bloody Sunday', there were 17 consecutive bombing raids. Two entire German air fleets took part in the air raids against both civilian and military targets. This *blitzkrieg* was a great shock to Warsaw and the world. No one would have experienced aerial bombardment before, its only trial by the German's being in the Spanish Civil War. Tank-to-air radio communication was newly invented to coordinate the attacks. Thousands of machines were ranged against human beings, most of them civilians. On 'Black Monday', 25 September, as many as 1,200 German aircraft hurled an artillery and air bombardment (Davies, 2004). An eye witness account from ten-year-old Wira, living in the city, describes it:

> Bombs were hurled down on us for the whole day and night without a break. It was too dangerous to stay in our apartment and our building didn't have a proper basement so we had to look for better shelter. Outside was chaos. Fires burned all around, buildings tumbled and people ran in panic in all directions. We searched for somewhere to hide as the bombs rained down. I recall being too scared to look up.
>
> Szhlachetko, 2015, p. 9

Julien Bryan, one of the last US reporters in Poland in September 1939, filmed *Siege*, a ten-minute black-and-white production that recorded the horror and confusion of Warsaw during the German attack.[1] It shows German fighters targeting hospitals and churches from the air, while German planes strafed refugee columns flooding out of the city to the east, without regard for the lives of women and children. The Warsaw population filmed are calm, organised and helping others to survive. For two weeks Bryan stayed in Warsaw filming and photographing the German bombardment and its impact on the people of the city. He left during a brief truce for citizens of neutral countries and took his films out secretly to New York. Bryan actively promoted the story, film and pictures on lecture tours and to the American press, including the President and his wife.

Capitulation and surrender

The situation for civilian inhabitants in Warsaw became increasingly tragic. Constant bombardment and lack of food and medical supplies resulted in heavy casualties among the city's population. The water supply was destroyed by German bombers, and all Warsaw boroughs experienced a lack of water for drinking and extinguishing the fires caused by the bombing. The inaction and lack of support from Western allies, and the Soviet Union's betrayal, made the defence of the city seem pointless and heavily demotivated the volunteers in continuing. On 26 September, capitulation talks were held with the German commander. On 27 September at 12pm, a ceasefire agreement was signed, and all fighting halted. Two days later the garrison of Warsaw started to hide or destroy their heavy armaments, some used later during the Warsaw Uprising. On 30 September, the Polish forces were evacuated to German prisoner-of-war camps and German units entered the capital for a victory parade.

The Polish September Campaign was the first ever experience of 'total war' (*blitzkrieg*) with vast numbers of civilian casualties. This was called *Operation Tannenberg* and it was part of Hitler's Master Plan for the East (*Generalplan Ost*). From the start, the Luftwaffe airforce attacked civilian targets and columns of refugees to wreak havoc, disrupt communications and undermine Polish morale. Tens of thousands of Polish civilians were killed in the very earliest stages. The policy of *Lebensraum* (living space for Germans) together with the *Drang nach Osten* (Drive towards the East) required the takeover of the whole country, and destruction of the population. This was not a fight between armies. The Nazi ideology was to create a pan-German racial state, with supremacy of the Aryan-Nordic 'master race'. It required massive territorial expansion into Eastern Europe, which was to be colonised with German settlers. It also meant the physical annihilation of the Jews and others considered to be 'unworthy of life'. It required the extermination, expulsion or enslavement of most of the Slavic peoples, with a particular focus on the Poles, regarded as racially inferior (Gumkowski and Leszcynski, 1961).

The Nazi's allocated 85 per cent of the Polish nation to be either exterminated or removed to camps. Targeted shootings were conducted, with the use of proscription lists compiled by the Gestapo in the two years before the 1939 attack. These top-secret lists identified more than 61,000 members of the Polish elite including activists, academics and scholars, actors, former officers and others, who were the first to be interned or shot. Members of the German minority living in Poland (*Volkesdeutsch*, about 20,000) had collaborated and assisted in preparing the lists. This group were to continue to be German collaborators throughout the war in return for greater food rations and other favours. Much despised by the bulk of the population, they were nevertheless Polish citizens. There were many others of German ancestry who rejected the label and collaborationist role.

Intelligenzaktion, a second phase of the Nazi plan, lasted until January 1940 whereby 100,000 professionals including teachers, doctors, priests and community leaders were killed. Most were massacred in remote locations and buried in hidden grave-pits. A selected few were publicly executed to inflict terror on the population. Ten thousand academics were sent to concentration camps (Davies, 2005). Nazi officials took over the administration and government of occupied Poland. The term 'politicide' is used for the mass killing of an identified group who are potential threats to the conquering state, rather than an ethnic group that constitutes genocide (Harff and Gurr, 1988). The groups concerned fitted both criteria given they were despised Slavs. The programme of executions also involved the mass killing of hospital patients by mid-1940. There were 6,000 killed by order of Commandant Lange alone. These provided a testing for the gas van experiments later used in concentration camps. Nazi propaganda convinced the German people that both Jews and Slavs were *Untermenschen* (subhumans). This programme of dehumanisation led to widespread slaughter, even before the round-up and annihilation of Polish Jews.

On 5 October 1939, Hitler made his first and only visit to Warsaw. He took the salute of his army in a victory parade with a two-hour march past. He visited Belvedere Palace before returning to Berlin. On 23 August, Hitler told his commanders[2] (Lukas, 2001):

> The destruction of Poland is our goal. The first objective is to liquidate the enemy forces. Be brutal, not merciful. Might is right. Hence, I've ordered my SS units to kill Polish men, women and children without hesitation. . . . All Poles will disappear from the world. . . . It is essential that the great German people should consider it as its major task to destroy all Poles.

Jurek and Myszka

July and August 1939 had been a very hot summer, temperatures reaching 31°C and the harvest began earlier than usual in the fields around Warsaw. Schools were on holiday and many families had gone to the countryside. Jurek had enjoyed a canoe trip with his cousin, Tadek Cygler, along the River Wisła. By 13 August, the mobilisation of the Polish army began in secret and by 24 August included 75 per cent of all men who could be mobilised. By 30 August, Polish battleships were ordered to leave for Britain, the MS *Stefan Batory* already having been taken into service earlier in July. The Polish Navy and merchant marine vessels were operated from French and British ports and were able to deliver supplies through Romania.

The first day of September was the first day back at school after the summer holidays, so families had returned to the city. Jurek watched the sky fill with bombers from his flat in the centre of Warsaw. He could see the thousand enemy planes overhead and the tanks moving across the fields of Mokotow approaching the town centre. Jurek had been mobilised into the army and, as directed, left Warsaw as soon as Nazi troops invaded. There had been time for him and Myszka to have a 'last supper' with family at her family's country house at Kebel, and then he was evacuated with other soldiers and officials out of the city using whatever transport was available. He headed with all the others for the Romanian border, following a hasty plan constructed in the few preceding days. They were tasked to join the armed forces in France, where General Sikorski was rallying Polish troops. Myszka could not leave because she had her ageing mother and younger sister to look after. Also the evacuation was primarily military – most of the Warsaw population had to stay. Up to 120,000 Polish troops withdrew to neutral Romania, Hungary and Yugoslavia and from there to France or England. Jurek left for the border and wept at leaving Poland, taking a little Polish earth with him as a memento.

Stas goes to war

Jurek's cousin Stas was also part of the emergency mobilisation. Policemen secretly delivered slips of paper house to house, demanding mobilisation and orders to leave Warsaw and join the regiments (Karski, 1944, 2012).[3] On 24 August, hundreds of thousands of soldiers and officers congregated at the railway stations. Stas joined the other soldiers to be transported by train, in carriages that were packed to overflowing. The mood was described as confident (Karski, 1944, 2012). The initial German attack had happened while soldiers were asleep and army barracks destroyed. This was a chance to fight back. Parts of the railway track had been destroyed and soldiers had to disembark and wait for hours in the hot sun while it was repaired. Eventually they arrived at Krakow in the south. Continuing their journey, early the next day, the train was hit by aircraft fire with more than half the carriages hit, survivors having to leave the train and collectively continue their journey on foot. News was relayed that the major Polish cities were occupied. After two weeks of marching, the troops reached Tarnopol where they were met by Russian soldiers. Radio transmitters in Russian and Polish relayed that the Russian soldiers had come as friends and liberators to 'protect . . . and to unite the Slavic people'. Loudspeakers demanded the troops board the Soviet trains, and soldiers were ordered to assemble into formation. Many were unarmed and all were from different units or detachments. They were told that the Polish high command and government was gone following the German invasion, and the Soviet Union had come to the aid of the Poles. A lone soldier sobbed that this was 'the fourth partition of Poland', and shot himself. This caused pandemonium, and officers went among the men telling them to lay down their weapons (Karski, 1944, 2012).

Then Soviet tanks and guns were trained on the Polish soldiers and they were made to give up their weapons and march towards Tarnopol as prisoners of the

Red Army. In the morning, a freight train with 60 freight wagons arrived. These were filled over a two-hour period with 60 Polish soldiers to each wagon. These had iron stoves and containers with water and food, and were fitted for a long journey east. It took over four days and four nights before the train stopped in Russian territory. Finally, in the cold autumn weather the men alighted and were forced to march uphill over bleak terrain for several hours. They arrived at a group of wooden buildings. The ordinary soldiers were given the better buildings and provisions. The officers, such as Stas, were assigned to the wooden barns, 400 to each of ten barracks, and forced to labour, cutting wood in the forest and loading it into trains. The officers were required to undertake menial tasks, such as cleaning the cooking pots for the regular soldiers. The latter were then loaded back into trains going to Germany for slave labour, an exchange undertaken with the Nazis for captured Ukrainians and White Russians. It was by then November 1939 and the Polish officers were kept in the Russian prison camp. Stas remained with the many thousands of Polish officers in Katyn Russia, 12 miles west of Smolensk. The area is not far from Polesie, near to where Stas's mother's family, the Czechowski, originated and where he spent his summers.

Reports later tell of how the army officers were apportioned to three separate camps. Starobelsk took eight generals, over 100 colonels, 250 majors, 1,000 captains, 2,500 subalterns, 30 cadets and 50 civilians. There were also 380 doctors and many university professors. Kozelsk took 5,000 prisoners, most of whom were army officers. Ostashkov had 6,570 prisoners including 380 officers, politicians, professionals and clergy (Maresch, 2010). All remained in these Soviet prison camps for over six months, Stas amongst them. All were held in secret, unknown to the rest of the world. It was not until 1943 when the Germans were fighting the Soviets in this region that the mass graves of these officers were uncovered. All 22,000 men had been executed individually, by a shot to the back of the head. They were laid in the graves, head to toe, in layers 20 or more deep. They still had their identity cards, Russian newspapers, letters and diaries with them, although all watches had been removed. Fir trees had been planted on top of the mass graves to hide them.

Stas was shot on 13 April 1940, his 28th birthday. He is listed on the website for Katyn victims, where his photograph is shown with a brief biography.[4] He is now buried on the territory of the present Polish military cemetery in Katyn (id number 2563). He was identified by the personal possessions left on his body – his identity card, driving licence, university id, notebook and pocket diary. His name appears on the Katyn memorials in Pawązki cemetery and in the Garrison Cathedral, Warsaw. His family were not to know of his death for six or seven years. The aftermath and political ramifications of the Katyn massacre were to reverberate for the next 75 years.

Maria in Warsaw

Maria was still living in her apartment in Zoliborz, north of the city centre, when the Germans invaded. Aged 53, she had been working as a personal assistant to an army general, so was probably aware of the political and military situation coming to a head. Zoliborz was affected, like other areas, by ground and aerial bombardment with individual buildings hit. There were a number of Czechowski family members in Warsaw during the invasion: Tadeusz's sister Grazyna and her husband Wacław, with their young daughter Marysia; Tadeusz's brother Olgierd and his wife Olenka with their young daughter Danuta, as well as Julia (Stas's mother) and her sister Zosia. There were also Cygler family members in Warsaw – Maria's brother Jan and his wife Jadwiga, and her youngest brother Wacek and his wife Mira. Myszka was now living alone, but she went to join Maria for a while after Jurek left the city. A letter from Maria received by Jurek two years later describes some of the hardship. Her reference to things 'being better in the spring' was a common phrase of hope and is repeated in other witness accounts:

> My dear son,
>
> Not long ago I wrote to you with Christmas greetings and already it is after the holidays, but we have no communication from you for months at a time. Maybe that is why Myszka's health is often poor because she is sad, upset and worried and this affects her frame of mind and the state of her health. Has your aversion to writing letters grown to such an extent? Nothing much has changed here. Winter is fully here with all its attributes. My apartment, as you know, has never been a warm one, in spite of intensive heating. So you can imagine the temperature now when we don't heat it at all and with such severe winters as we've been having recently. That's why my handwriting is so bad because I can't feel the pen in my fingers and my hand is going numb. Even with all this my health is fine, it hasn't let me down in times of trial and has passed the endurance test. The hope of spring being near is keeping me warm. My thoughts are always with you. I would so like to know; how you are feeling? What you are doing? What you are thinking now and about the future? What do you look like? Are your studies giving good results? Is this separation erasing your memories of those closest to you who live only thinking about you? I am ending now by commending you to God's care, as I do every day.

Life under occupation

Daily life in Warsaw was hard. The whole population was individually ascribed a racial category affirmed by a 'Certificate of Racial Origin', as well as an identity card and a ration card. The food ration was determined by the hierarchy of racial superiority. For Reich Germans transported into Poland, and for *Volksdeutsch* or ethnic Germans, the ration was 2,613 calories per day. For non-German Aryans (suitable for Germanisation or mixed race) it was 669 calories. For the rest of the population it was 184 calories a day (equivalent to a bowl of cornflakes and milk). This would have been the allocation each for Maria, Myszka and their families.

There was little fuel for heating, this becoming ever more scarce as the war progressed, so people felt the bitter cold, with winters in Warsaw reaching as low as −30°C. The city was filled with *Werhmacht* soldiers and *Waffen SS* (*SchutzStaffel*) officers, the military wing of the Nazi party. These were responsible for terrorising the population. They were under orders to inflict hardship, deportation and death on the civilian population. The emerging resistance led to the bombing of homes, the shooting of Poles and random round-ups of people to be hanged, this to instil fear and hopelessness. The Pawiak prison in Warsaw became filled with prisoners who were shot or sent on to Auschwitz concentration camp in the south of Poland.

Myszka remained in Warsaw. She spent some time with Maria in Zoliborz, but also in her flat in the centre of town. She enrolled with the Polish Red Cross hospital, in central Warsaw (Smolna Street), where she did administrative work and later undertook voluntary work in two other hospitals as well. The Red Cross Hospital (where Tadeusz had died 20 years earlier) had been assigned for injured Polish soldiers during the Warsaw Siege. The hospital school survived occupation under dangerous conditions becoming for a time a 'safe haven' for the home army soldiers, who received help, shelter, care and concealment. The connection enabled Myszka to write to Jurek through Red Cross couriers going to France. Myszka wrote to Jurek while he was in France from 1940 through to 1942. It had been through the Red Cross that Jurek at that time was registered at the University of Grenoble, and so was part of the network. Myszka describes her day-to-day life to Jurek in November 1940, a year after invasion:

Dearest Jurek,

I have got rid of my flat and am living with Mother, but I dream of having my own place. I would like a tiny room, but my own, somewhere where I can be in my own place. I remember our apartment and those past times with great affection. I think I wasted that happiness a bit. I will try to make up for this when we are together again. I am working at the moment as a clerk for the Red Cross. Financially this is not very profitable. I am trying to find a job as a waitress in some respectable café, maybe this will improve my finances. Think about how wonderful it will be when the two of us will be together again. We will have our own apartment, we'll have a dog and later we will have a son. He will have his own room and will look like you. He will have fair, curly hair and will, one day, be a lot taller than me!

In my last letter I wrote a little about our friends. There aren't many of us left. From time to time I see Maciek. From the whole group, only he remains. He often gives me great help as a friend. He helped me to get rid of the rest of my possessions. Otherwise I manage by myself, as usual. Janek and the rest of the company are no longer here. My old office has revived somewhat, but the staff has only three directors, the manager of the office and Jadzia – a typist. Imagine, I can now type very well. I was able to practise at the Red Cross where I have a fantastic position: deputy manageress for medical reports for one of the larger sections of PSK [Polish Red Cross]. In spring, I traded a bit. I made clogs, fixing leather to a wooden base. Some of them were very nice. In other words I pretended to be a shoemaker. As well, I look after patients in the hospital.

In the next letter, ten months later, Myszka seems to have received at least one letter back from Jurek but complains there are no more. She writes again on 1 August 1941, nearly two years after invasion, where it is evident her health is suffering from the hardship, but where she is trying to keep her spirits high:

Dearest Jurek,

There is nothing of great interest here. This war luckily has moved away from us a bit, though we are now so used to various troubles, that there is little that can make any impact on us. It's raining cats and dogs and I have just decided to take a week's holiday in a few days' time. I am terribly tired, so although our holidays have been cancelled, I will be able to have a week as an exception. I have a huge problem with cigarettes. You can't get them! Don't worry, I won't learn to stop smoking! I'll smoke grass or the leaves of my geranium. Mother, although she is against smoking, on principle (she lets everyone else smoke as long as you don't) brings me a couple of cigarettes when she is able to. Also Wiktor Cy, who doesn't smoke himself, gives any he gets to me.

My dear, (I know you don't like writing letters) but make yourself write a long and proper letter. I can't help it if I feel lonely and abandoned. I really am alone, and really abandoned, you can't deny this. If we ever see each other again, you will be proud of me, I am stubborn and patient, somehow I have acquired these virtues. I found in a cupboard, in our home, your letters to me when I was away for Christmas. I read them yesterday and in number nine, one of many, I am still ambitious. I don't know whether this is a virtue, but anyway there was a time when my ambitions were deeply hidden, now from that memorable September, they have developed again. I am writing nonsense. I miss normal life. I suppose I won't die before your triumphal return and things will be good for us again. Anyway I would like to live with you again my dear. I'm sure I will be good and pleasant.

The letters tell of hardship, but also downplay the actual trauma and grind involved in day-to-day existence. Life was deprived of food, warmth, lighting and liberty. There was daily terror of shootings of friends, acquaintances, neighbours and other Warsaw citizens. Myszka tries to sound optimistic and sends her love across the war-stricken continent to Jurek living in Vichy France. She writes again at Christmas 1941, over two years after they separated:

I will try to have my photograph taken and send it to you. I have a couple of amateur photos of myself on the balcony at work. I have changed my dear. I have aged. I am writing to you at work, because I have the opportunity to send a letter today. It's just so happened that it is quiet for five minutes. There are no clients, the phone isn't ringing, so I am taking advantage and dealing with some personal matters. I am working on Smolna Street, my window has a view of Aleja 3ego Maja. I have a pleasant view of Poniatowski Bridge from my balcony. I am working very hard, but one has to, that way the time passes more quickly. However these last years will count as double, at least for me. Dzidzia [her sister] has grown a bit and naturally has become plainer. You can't say that the women of the Janiszewski family err on the side of beauty! At least for that sin we have less on our conscience. Mother is not feeling too good. They asked me to send you kisses.

Mother asks after you in every letter. I am staying in Warsaw for Christmas, I will spend it with Mother in Zoliborz. Jurek, you wanted to know something about our friends. Zbyszek has been very seriously ill. I haven't had any contact with him for quite a while. I haven't seen Maciek for over half a year. He has left, but I don't know where to. Everything is fine with Wanda and Tadeusz. We found out, not long ago, that Walek is alive. This is the first news of Walek since September 1939.

Only one thing is better where you are and that is the climate. It is cold here with snow storms. There is a lack of coal and warm clothes. Sometimes one doesn't want to live, but it isn't quite two years, thank God, that have passed and I miss you. It's sad that a third Christmas will be without you. I have a lot of work and am occupied for whole days, but even so I feel lonely. Mother is well and asks me to send you her best regards. My mother and Dzidzia are finding it hard. Soon I will send you a longer letter although nothing very interesting is happening here.

In January 1942 it seems Myszka has moved back to her flat in Mokotowska Street. She writes:

The carrier of the letter will be able to tell you something of our lives here. This time I am also sending you a couple of my photos. Jurek, just think, our fourth wedding anniversary is drawing near, how long have we been apart, how much longer will we be apart? Dear God, the best years have been taken from us. Remind yourself what your wife looks like and think of me. Jurek I will always love you and am waiting for you. I had a sad Christmas and a sad New Year. I am still living on Mokotowska Street with some very pleasant people who show me a lot of kindness and sympathy. We often play bridge. You were right that I should learn and that I would become crazy about bridge. I am a poor player but I am very enthusiastic. Unfortunately I don't have a lot of time, paid work nowadays takes up a lot of time. I am tired and often ill but I have to carry on working. Anyway, it's better because I don't have time to think. I have given you news of our friends. Nothing has changed. There's always somebody missing. The rest are bearing up as well as they can. Maciek lived for a while on Dzika Street, then he left. They say that he is seriously ill but unfortunately I'm not able to see him. He is with Zbyszek. Janek (remember him? 2 metres tall, and me 2 cm tall!) has gone somewhere. I've seen him twice. He was so thin, as always. We remembered good times, Christmas at S.G.A, my troubles and the like. Now he has also disappeared.

Do you really want me to come and join you? I believe that you only need to long for impossible things. Naturally this is quite difficult, I only have to know that this is what you really want. Before this I had several possibilities for travelling to you, but since you didn't write that you wanted to see me, I didn't set out. Your letter has given me great pleasure. I thought, at last, that you hadn't forgotten about me. Lately I have felt like a recruit being inspected without the command to march off. It would give me great happiness to see you but I must tell you that I have become uglier. I am wearing out what remains of my clothes and I don't feel too well. The carrier of this letter and photographs will tell you the rest about me. I love you, Jurek, and I want you to be happy with me. I would join you with great joy, only say that this is what you want.

I am living, like most people, in an improvised way. Concerning my office work: I am the assistant manager of the Department for the Protection of Welfare and Health. As well, I am a secretary in the Department for Health at the Polish Red Cross. One department comes under the jurisdiction of the other, so I can do both jobs. I have a lot of work, you could even say a great deal and the Red Cross pays me 225 zl monthly. Since a kilo of butter costs 70 zl and a pair of horrible stockings 100 zl, I have to do some other work as well to earn some more money. PCK is now on 17 Samotna Street and the windows of my room look out on Aleje 3ego Maja so I have a pleasant view. As well, I care for sick people, voluntarily, in Hallanski Hospital and in Ujazdowski Hospital. I was often in Hallanski Hospital. I often see our dear pre-war friends. For example Wanda and Tadeusz are still living on Saska Kepa. To make life even more pleasant as well as a lack of fuel there is a lack of light! A few weeks ago I didn't have any electricity for two weeks but from two days ago I again feel like a king because at least I have light. The bearer of this letter will be able to tell you a bit about our conditions.

Włodek Sylwestrowicz has been shot and dead for a year. Others are also in difficulties. These are not happy times! I dream of peace. I have made friends with the wife of Włodek. You have probably forgotten about everyone and everything but we carry on living. We think about you. Kurcjusz is somewhere abroad, but the news we get about him is not good. Przemek is where he was before the war. Jurek, you do understand what I am writing to you, that if I survive the war we will see each other? I am tired, I work a lot. It's just as well that I am obstinate and patient. Jurek pray for us.

Don't be surprised that I am writing that you chose the better path by going abroad. We live an eventful life. We dream about having a quiet night.

Another letter from Myszka, on 12 February 1942, was the last she was to write to him:

> In a week's time it will be our fourth wedding anniversary. Look inside your wedding ring and remember the date and me. I should give myself a wish that we will be able to spend our fifth anniversary together. You too I think. Remember; there will be bridge, home baked cakes and the dog will be bothering you. Now I don't have you, I don't have a home and the dog won't be bothering me. There won't be any guests or home baked cakes either. I will be thinking of you, and that by now we might have had a son who would be nearly two years old. I miss you, Jurek, and I'm afraid to think how many more anniversaries we will spend alone. I keep waiting for you and I love you. On this, our fourth anniversary I hope that all your wishes will come true. I wish that someday you will be happy with me.
>
> Your last letter of 15.7.41 gave me a lot of joy. I was happy to think (unrealistically) that I might one day join you. Although, I'm not sure that this is what you really want. Anyway it raised my spirits. I don't have anything interesting to write about myself. I was ill in a cold room which was unpleasant. I don't have any electricity, the candle is spluttering. This is very irritating. Still, I thank God, that I can heat the room every three days. For a couple of days it was warm (–6 degrees). Now a wave of cold weather has arrived. It is now between –10 and –20 degrees with lots of snow.
>
> I am looking for a job as a waitress. I want to carry on working for the Red Cross in the mornings and am looking to work in a respectable café in the afternoons, or possibly in a restaurant. Imagine me in a black dress and a white apron! Mother is well. She is bearing up in spite of the difficult conditions. She has lost a lot of weight and there is only half of her left.
>
> Dzidzia writes to me and in each letter she asks me to send you loving kisses. I've sent you a whole lot of photos, large and small. One of my friends takes excellent photos using a Leica camera. He is a professor of psychology but now he has a photographic studio and from small snaps he makes excellent prints. Before Christmas I went there to be photographed so I could send you a lot of photos. Have you received them? My dear, this time I am sending you one of the worst ones. I have already sent the best ones. I want you to be able to talk to me or at least to a photograph. It is difficult for me at the moment, not only materially but also mentally. I am completely alone. You realise, of course, what you have always meant to me. Consider how many years we were great friends before we got married. I miss you. I would like to see you as soon as possible. They say that nothing is impossible, so it wasn't necessary to invite me. I am enterprising and stubborn, so Jerzy till we meet again. All my best thoughts, my heart, are always with you. Myszka.

The Warsaw Resistance (AK)

The AK (*Armia Krajowa* or Home Army) was a branch of the regular Polish army and became the largest resistance movement in Europe. It fought the Germans in secret and was allied to the Polish Government in Exile (in London), taking its order from the Commander-in-Chief General Sikorski (Davies, 2004). Its aim was for a national uprising. The general population was involved, initially friends and families of serving officers, later extending to most of the civilian population. It included men, women and teenagers. In Warsaw it eventually involved over 40,000 people, most located in the city centre, as well as in Mokotow and Praga, but with smaller numbers in Zoliborz. As well as armed resistance it provided a determination to keep cultural life going – schools continued in secret, religious activity increased, architects and planners strove to find and hide plans of the city for after its likely destruction, and many people kept diaries of events. There was underground publishing, the printing presses continually being moved to evade detection. There was also training in firearms, and in evasion of capture, extended to children as young as twelve who were in the scouts or guides. Girls and women fought alongside boys and men. It was effectively a secret state with a secret army (Bor-Komorowski, 2010).

Accounts of daily life in Warsaw during the first years of the war describe hardship through lack of food and heating; lack of any freedom – of movement, of schooling, of speech; and cold and inadequate housing and infrastructure. It seems as though many of the citizens took part in the resistance movement, although always keeping this a secret from other family members. There were accidents in the dangerous bomb-damaged buildings. Wira describes her experience as a young teenager, going to school in secret, the curfews after dark, 'Germans only' signs in public areas and on public transport, German soldiers stopping local people at will. She felt nervous walking down the street. Given the number of men who had gone off to fight abroad, or taken away as prisoners or shot, women had to do much of the providing. There was no money and little in the shops. Wira's mother would take trips to the countryside to get food and return secretly after curfew. One time her mother was caught and the food confiscated, but fortunately she was released.

However, not everyone could be a combatant or courier for the underground movement. So for many older women, such as Maria, and mothers of young children, the days were spent searching for food, such as a bargain in bread or margarine, or taking long hikes into the countryside for flour, cereals or bacon. Most had sold nearly every article of value to pay for food for themselves and their family. Some bought tobacco from the peasants and manufactured cigarettes to sell on the black market. They lived in fear, waiting for a night-time call from the Gestapo. Yet when Jan Karski wrote of telling his landlady and her young son that he worked for the underground resistance, instead of fear and threats to expose him, they were full of praise and thanks and told him not to worry about any danger that would accrue to them (Karski, 1944, 2012).

Over 350,000 of the population had joined the AK by 1944. The Boy Scouts who joined were known as the Grey Ranks, while the Girl Scouts were called the Clover Society. Their numbers reached 5,000. They included Jurek's young cousins, Danuta and Marysia. Their experiences must have been like Wira's who trained in distributing propaganda, firearms skills, city orientation and medical aid. There was also training in how to respond if captured. The civilian population was aware of the underground movement, but family members kept their involvement secret from each other. People helped each other, but there was always an awareness of possible spies – the *Volkesdeutsch* – the collaborators who would report individuals to the Gestapo. Everyone was referred to by a pseudonym ('Wira' was a pseudonym). German soldiers were always watching their behaviour. There was less fear of the *Wehrmacht* regular soldiers than of the Gestapo, the latter identified by the red swastika armbands.

The underground became very well organised. It had its own publication – the Information Bulletin (BI) which ran to 317 issues. This circulated information for the underground army. It had its own Bureau for counter-intelligence. This was the direct successor of the pre-war Polish service, whose agents first broke the 'unbreakable' German Enigma system. It provided invaluable information to the Allies in London (Davies, 2004). The Bureau was responsible in late 1944 for discovering the German rocket programme and managed to get hold of the Germans' new weapon, the V2 rocket, disassemble it, take it to Warsaw, produce minute drawings of it and pack it for shipment. This was critical intelligence for the Western allies.

However, life became more and more difficult in the city. A new head of the German SS and Police, Franz Kutschera, arrived in Warsaw in 1943 and ordered mass street executions with random round-ups of civilians in *łapanki*, or traps. He began a new reign of terror. As many as forty or fifty Warsaw citizens would be rounded up and shot at a time. Jewish prisoners had to clear the dead bodies away and hose down the streets. Onlookers were ordered away, but later gathered for prayers and to light candles and lay flowers. Eventually Kutschera, much hated, was sentenced to death by the AK who intercepted his car and assassinated him. It led of course to reprisals and 100 Poles publicly executed.

The Warsaw ghetto

The Jewish quarter of Warsaw had been in Muranow, a poor area north east of the city centre. Jews, however, lived all over the city – nearly half of the population was Jewish in origin. From October 1940 the Germans herded all those identified by their ascribed 'Certificate of Racial Origin' as Jews into this district, which was then enclosed and turned by the Germans into a ghetto. Jews from other parts of Poland as well as those from other countries were taken to the ghetto. There was great overcrowding, and it became the largest Jewish ghetto created by the Nazis in East Europe. They enclosed it with walls, barbed wire and guards until there was little access to the rest of Warsaw, or to the outside world.

The conditions in the ghetto were dreadful. By October 1942 it became known locally that hundreds of thousands of Jews deported from the ghetto were being sent on to death camps. Heads of the Jewish community received demands from the Nazis for 10,000 people daily to report for 'work' – these were then sent for annihilation. In just two months, 300,000 Jews from the ghetto had been killed. Jan Karski, who worked for the AK, volunteered to go into the Jewish ghetto and then to the death camps as an eye-witness, and take this testimony to the Western Allies (Karski, 1944, 2012). He was briefed by two Jewish leaders (one head of the Zionist movement and another head of the Bunt Jewish Socialist movement) who were able to come in and out of the ghetto by secret means, usually through networks of cellars, to other parts of Warsaw.

Karski entered the ghetto through the secret tunnels linking cellars from outside. The houses were old and shabby, the streets narrow without pavements, with great gaps in the streets from bombings. A brick wall about eight feet high had been built around the entire area of the ghetto, from where all non-Jews had been evacuated. Conditions were appalling – there was a stench of rotting corpses, the living looked like walking skeletons. People were dying in the street and the corpses left naked where they had fallen. This was because of German burial taxes and because the clothes were precious to the living. The entire population was living in the streets with hardly a square yard of empty space. Shops or streets were labelled in Hebrew – the Germans had forbidden the use of any German or Polish writing in the ghetto. Many of the inhabitants, assimilated Jews who were Christians, couldn't read Hebrew.

The Polish underground movement worked in close cooperation with the Jewish leaders in the ghetto. The AK managed to smuggle in spies and follow some of the trucks and trains packed with Jews to Treblinka concentration camp 100 kilometres away, and thus found out about the exterminations. In 1942, the AK created the 'Council for the Rescue of Jews'. The decision was to protect Jewish children, providing false papers, hiding them in safe houses and passing them onto church networks (Davies, 2004). Around 100,000 Jews were saved by these actions. More Jews were killed in Poland by the Nazis than anywhere else in Europe, given the greater density of the Jewish population there, but thanks to the AK more Jews were also saved in Poland than in other country. Joanna Olczak-Ronnier describes the nuns in a convent school in Warsaw, who rescued her and other Jewish children and hid them. All were given a new identity. She writes:

> They were not just hiding Jewish children, but also teaching subjects banned by the Nazis. There were secret study groups for secondary school pupils, secret university lectures, a priesthood for Home Army soldiers, contacts with the Underground, help for prisoners and people deprived of a living, food for malnourished Jews who had escaped from the ghetto. . . . Courageous and composed, the nuns were only people after all and must sometimes have been terrified . . .
>
> Olczak-Ronnier, 2004, p. 254

It was essential for the AK to get the information about the reality of the ghetto and the exterminations to the West in order to try to prevent further deaths. Karski travelled undercover to Britain to provide an eye-witness account. He met with General Sikorski, who emphasised the need to co-opt the United Nations. He helped produce one of the earliest and most accurate accounts of the treatment of the Jews addressed to the UN in December 1942 (Karski, 1944, 2012). He was then sent to meet with US President Roosevelt in Washington. He says of the President:

> [his] questions were minute, detailed and directed squarely at important points. He enquired about our methods of education and our attempts to safeguard the children. He enquired about the Underground and the losses the Polish nation had suffered. He asked me how I explained the fact that Poland was the only country without a Qiusling (*collaborator*). He asked me to verify the stories told about the German practices against the Jews. He was anxious to learn the techniques for sabotage, diversion and partisan activities.
>
> Karski, 1944, 2012, p. 419

No action was taken on the basis of Karski's account; the Western allies chose not to believe or act on his account of the fate of the Jews.

There were *two* famous and fated uprisings in Warsaw during the German occupation. The first, described here, was the uprising in the Jewish Ghetto which broke out on 19 April 1943 and lasted for 27 days. The second was a year later and lasted for 63 days (see Chapter 7). The Jewish ghetto uprising was launched by two small groups of Jewish fighters who were aware of Hitler's plan for their collective annihilation. They wanted to resist actively and with courage, not to go as 'lambs to the slaughter'. The head of the Zionist movement in the ghetto declared to Jan Karski six months earlier:

> The ghetto is going to go up in flames. We are not going to die in slow torment, but fighting. We will declare war on Germany – the most hopeless declaration of war that has ever been made.
>
> Karski, 1944, 2012, p. 396

When the SS Brig Fhr Stroop entered the ghetto with 3,000 troops and police, he was met with a hail of grenades and bullets, provided by the AK outside the walls of the ghetto. The uprising was savagely supressed, despite a warren of hidden bunkers and invisible escape routes. In the end, instead of meeting such resistance, Stroop ordered his troops to turn off water, gas and electricity and torch the buildings, block by block. Over 20,000 people were killed. The Jewish resistance was quashed.

A codicil concerns Dr Janusz Korczak, mentioned earlier, who ran the Jewish orphanage in Warsaw along experimental lines involving social pedagogy. This included identifying the rights of the child: the right to die, the right to live for today and the right to be oneself. Whilst written before the invasion of Poland

and the ghetto, these seem prescient. He was forced into the Warsaw ghetto with the children he had taught. He refused earlier opportunities to escape, he would not leave the children and he finally accompanied them with his co-worker, Stefa Wilczynska, to Treblinka concentration camp. 'He died together with the children from the Jewish orphanage in Warsaw and he died for them, giving them hope in a situation of despair' (Eichsteller, 2009, p. 378). His work led to the UN 1989 Convention on the Rights of the Child, initiated in Poland.

Myszka's sacrifice

The population of Warsaw adapted to the network of conspiracy running throughout the city (Karski, 1944, 2012). There were so many people working in the underground that the rest of the population began to accept them and exercise discretion. Enormous numbers of people carried false documents or had something to conceal. Children carried pots of paint to hastily daub signs of resistance on walls over the city. (The emblem was a letter 'P' over an anchor, and meant 'fighting Poland'.) They became used to living in constant danger. The civilian liaison women had a particularly hard time – they provided a vital link in operations but were more exposed than the fighting men who were usually in hiding. General Bor-Komorowski, who led the Home Army in Warsaw, described their role in his influential memoire 'The Secret Army'. He writes:

> ... these women we constantly exposed to danger and lived in perpetual state of nervous strain. Theirs was, consequently, a most exhausting task. To be caught carrying mail was as grave an offence in German eyes as to be found in possession of a revolver, and several hundred liaison girls died soldiers' deaths.
>
> Bor-Komorowski, 2010, p. 60

The private apartment of a liaison woman was frequently placed at the disposal of the underground fighters. She could never be allowed to go out of sight, had to live where she could be found easily and was not allowed to change her name, or address, without permission. She could not go into hiding when working in liaison (Karski, 1944, 2012). Such women were in constant danger. The average life expectancy of a liaison woman was only a few months. If caught by the Gestapo she was unable to betray the underground because all names, addresses and contact would promptly be changed. If caught, she would be shot or sent to a concentration camp.

Myszka worked as a liaison worker for the AK, smuggling papers and undertaking other sabotage activities in secret against the Nazis. We do not know whether Maria or Myszka's own family knew, but it is more likely she kept it secret. Her nephew Peter, now still living in Warsaw, writes about Myszka:

> She was involved in the Resistance [AK]. In her work with the Red Cross she managed to get into contact with Jurek. In 1942, at a *łapanki* [random

round-up] she was stopped with false documents, and carrying false papers. She was transferred to the Gestapo, and sent to the Pawiak prison. Because our family was wealthy (before the war we owned a sugar factory) we tried to pay for her freedom. There was no chance, because she was considered enemy of the Reich No. 1, and a political prisoner. The only thing was to commute the death penalty to being sent to the concentration camp in Auschwitz. She was sent to the camp at the end of August 1942.

Myszka's family were to hear nothing of her until 1944. Then they learned that Myszka contracted typhus in Auschwitz and died on 10 January 1944. The German death certificate is a typed document with her name, maiden name, address, parents' and husband's name. It gives not only the date of death but also the hour (8.40). It is stamped with a German eagle and swastika. The Auschwitz death camp must have required millions of such documents. I wonder why this administration was required? Myszka was 27 years old. Neither Jurek nor his mother would know her fate until after the war.

Discussion

This chapter selects Myszka as its focus and her actions during the German occupation of her city, Warsaw. She shows great courage, but as a civilian this was recognised neither by military medals nor official personal recognition. She was one of tens of thousands of women who took the same action. She endured hardship and lived in hope of the end of the war and reunion with Jurek. Her letters show that she hoped for a future when he returned; they would return to their flat and have a baby boy. This was not to happen. She personified an 'everyday' heroism shown by women and teenagers. She would know that her chance of survival was low and lived under constant strain. A petite woman, with no military training, she was brave enough to resist the occupation of her city and used subterfuge to aid the resistance. She and Jurek were not to meet again. She was mourned by her family and by Jurek. My sisters and I knew nothing about Myszka, my father's first wife, when we were growing up. My mother insisted it be kept from us, her motives unclear, but I suspect jealousy and the feeling she could not live up to her sacrifice. It seems to me that Myszka has been excluded from the family story, her memory has been left frozen. She deserves honour and recognition. I hope this is now rectified. Figure 5.2 summarises the themes of this chapter.

The other sacrifice was by Stas. I do not know what happened to his young wife, but he was certainly mourned by his mother, aunts, uncles and cousins when the truth was known. He is now honoured, as other victims, on the Katyn website, and on stone memorials in Warsaw. His sacrifice is perhaps more poignant, resulting from political deception, before he or his peers had the chance to fight. His death and that of his comrades was kept secret for many years, and culpability denied. It represents a loss of such potential for each individual victim, for Stas a successful sportsman, agricultural student, officer, amateur photographer and newly

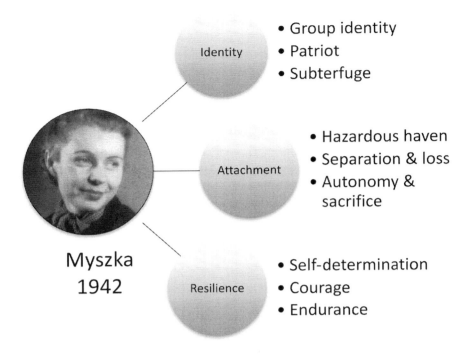

FIGURE 5.2 Summary of the themes in Chapter 5

married young man. Such waste. He was mourned in the family and by my father Jurek.

With the theme of 'Confusion', the negative lifestage associated with identity development, different elements are highlighted. In this account there is a direct affront to the cultural identity of both Jews and Slavs by Nazi ideology. A process of dehumanisation was invoked to both make groups appear less human and to reduce them to a level of existence which was subhuman, through denigration, deprivation of basic needs, brutality and violence. It failed in its aim with both groups. For the Slavic Poles the sense of Polish identity grew stronger when faced with this threat. It gave purpose to the resistance, the population retained a sense of purpose and they maintained high moral standards (for instance, in their benevolent treatment of German captives) and pride in their culture. Their opponents in contrast showed little humanity and nothing of culture or morality, the soldiers often terrorised by their own Gestapo.

Both German Nazi and Soviet Russian troops committed mass killings. They exercised forms of genocide under the terms of the UN Genocide Convention (Harff and Gurr, 1988). The first by the Germans on the Polish Jews and Jews of other nations with a view to extermination, the second on the Polish Slavs, which involved mass killings with a view to slave labour before extermination. Other forms of mass killings also occurred, are less easily classified and have been less openly acknowledged. These include those considered a threat to the state or 'politicides' (potential leaders or holders of culture and knowledge – academics, teachers, priests, judiciary and military officers) (Harff and Gurr, 1988); but also of hospital patients and those in psychiatric care. Many years later, when finally admitting responsibility for the Katyn massacre, communist apparatchiks claimed they didn't feel any shame since all the victims were from the upper class, and therefore enemies of the state and the proletariat. Their lives did not count in the ideological narrative (Maresch, 2010). When we exercise empathy for victims of massacre it is useful not to place them in the position of the 'other'. Any of us as professionals could be targeted in such ways.

Dehumanisation is a recognised basis for stigmatising and socially excluding groups, as a precursor or justification of violence (Moller and Deci, 2010). It is expressed by identifying others as being animal-like and divested of human dignity. It can be expressed linguistically, symbolically or physically (Haslam, Kashima, Loughnan, Shi and Suitner, 2008). It still happens. Dehumanisation hinders empathy or the proper understanding of a victimised or stigmatised group (Eberhardt, Williams and Jackson, 2008). This is the basis on which the Nazis justified their brutality, their creation of a slave class and the annihilation of millions. This was a period when identity was threatened both nationally and personally. It was living with the converse of that expectation – through resistance, through keeping high moral values, altruism, sacrifice and a strong cultural identity that proved the basis for resilience.

Notes

1   www.youtube.com/watch?v=nQ1VO3n-zR8
2   www.holocaustforgotten.com/poland.htm
3   The following account is taken from Jan Karski's experience of the same trip that Stas would have taken.
4   https://commons.wikimedia.org/wiki/File:Stanis%C5%82aw_Leinweber.JPG

6

IDENTITY

Resistance in France (1939–43)

> In the social jungle of human existence, there is no feeling of being alive without a sense of identity.
>
> Erik Erikson

Introduction

This chapter continues with the theme of identity as one of the developmental stages identified by Erikson. In this chapter, 'Identity' is used to consider issues of subterfuge and clandestine work, as Jurek leaves Poland to go to France to join the Allies and continue the fight against Nazism. This involves the conscious hiding of identity as a displaced Pole, without any authorised documents, travelling around France as a French Canadian and being active in the French Resistance. Jurek took on an assumed name, different national identity and even changed his birth year. It required a strong sense of self to be able to still retain purpose with a hidden identity. The documentary evidence for this section is mainly in the form of official papers: for example, Jurek's identity card from the French Army and papers for the Narwik engagement, his French demobilisation papers, his enrolment and identity card at the University of Grenoble and various papers associated with his imprisonment and release from forced labour in France and Spain. The time period covered overlaps with that of the last chapter, where the only letters surviving in this period from Maria and Myszka have been outlined.

Jurek leaves Warsaw

Jurek had left Poland following the invasion to make his way to France, directed to go through Ukraine, Romania and Yugoslavia (modern Croatia) as a soldier in the Polish army. On 14 September 1939, all Polish troops had been ordered to withdraw south east to the hills along the borders with Romania, known as the Romanian bridgehead. This retreat was initially defensive, a holding position until an expected French attack against the Germans in the west. The area has a rough terrain bounded by two rivers (Stryj and Dniestr), with valleys, hills and swamps which provided natural lines of defence against the German advance. The area also hid many ammunition dumps, weapons sent through the Romanian port of Constanta on the Black Sea coast to resupply the Polish troops. The Romanian Kingdom under Carol II was at first neutral in 1939, having fought with the Allies in the First World War. However, by summer 1940 it was to join the Axis alliance and support Germany, first when Britain and France failed to ensure its independence and borders, and second following the Allied major loss at Dunkirk. Once Germany invaded Poland, under pressure from the Soviet Union and Germany, the Romanians interned the escaping Polish government. The Romanian General Antonescu formed a fascist government, forcing the abdication of King Carol II. The new regime stiffened the already harsh anti-Semitic legislation and was explicitly anti-Slav. On 23 November 1940, Romania joined the Axis powers thus ranged against Poland, France and Britain.

While Romania was still neutral in September 1939, it received the treasury of the National Bank of Poland. The first part, 1,261 crates containing 82,403 kg of gold, was loaded aboard a commercial ship in the Romanian port of Constanta, and transported to western Europe. The Romanian navy guarded it against Soviet submarines in the Black Sea. The second part of the treasury was deposited in the Romanian National Bank and not returned to Poland until 1947. In his novel *The Polish Officer*, Alan Furst captures some of the atmosphere of those first days of the Warsaw invasion and the flight to Romania (Furst, 1995/2005). The hero, De Milja, and the crew of the small train endure a number of near misses as they successfully get their cargo to the Romanian border. This money was used by the Allies to help the war effort and to pay the Polish divisions fighting for them.

Up to 80,000 men from Polish units and isolated soldiers had escaped across the borders and were interned in Romania and Hungary. The French General Kleeberg organised their recovery in October, 1939. This enabled Poles such as Jurek to be released from internment camps, to be given civilian clothing, money and passports, together with a pass to get to France. Initially there was discreet collaboration of the countries concerned, but this ended in late November due to German pressure. So there was a relatively small period of escape. Nearly 32,000 Polish men were successfully evacuated at this time and eventually joined the Polish forces in France.

Jurek passed successfully through Ukraine, together with some other soldiers and with two friends, Przemek and Erwin, and on entering Romania lived in an internment camp. This was the second time he had escaped through Romania, previously as an infant in the back of a military car with his mother, when his father Tadeusz had driven off road and across the border to safety. This was a retracing of steps. He described the country as corrupt and full of bribery, which perhaps helped the Polish soldiers escape.

A fictionalised account, based on the actual experience of a Polish airman (Herbert) who lived in such camps, was published during the war and describes the main character reaching a Romanian internment camp in the winter of 1939:

> When we arrived at the camp, the situation seemed hopeless to me. A whole village of wooden huts, surrounded thickly with barbed wire stood in open snowed covered field. No light, no water, no drainage, no stoves! Here were six thousand Polish soldiers in rags, desperate or resigned, without officers, left to their fate under the guard of rough Romanian soldiers. We found a total lack of organisation, no medical care, miserable food supplied by crooked attendants, lack of even the most basic sanitary installations, lack of newspapers or books, no hope of improvement in their lot: in one word – misery.
>
> Herbert, 1944, pp. 89–90

However, the Poles managed to get organised in their usual entrepreneurial and energetic way, and after a time achieved more comfortable and hygenic conditions. It is likely that funds from Britain aided in improving conditions:

> We arranged and equipped nine canteens with tables and benches, stoves and lamps: with a library, a reading room, a wireless set, a set of games. We opened nine soldiers' shops with adequate equipment and large stocks. We organised a hospital of forty beds with an out-patient department for skin and infectious diseases as well as a surgery and dentistry; there was also a bath house with two bath tubs and a water heating installation. Attached to the hospital was a dispensary with stocks of medicine, a supply of linen, bandages and so on. One of the empty barracks was transformed into a chapel. The altar and the decorations for it were all made in the camp.
>
> Herbert, 1944, pp. 99–100

Herbert goes on to describe all the other positive changes in the camp effected by the Polish soldiers, including schools, a sports ground, newspapers, vegetable and fruit gardens and roads, funded by the British. Of the men held there about 3,000 escaped to join the Polish Forces in France. There are many escapes described in his book. These include escaping men being hidden in white sheets in the snow, escapes during outings to the public baths or from funerals, when half of those attending did not return to camp (Herbert, 1944). Other means of escape involved hiding in the boot of a Romanian officer's Buick car, and in one instance a Polish officer 'kidnapped' 120 of his men by marching his detachment on regular drill exercises, which finally culminated in a long march to the next town, with no return. All were given papers money, passports and rail tickets at predetermined evacuation posts.

Managing to leave Romania by similar means, Jurek reached Hungary by October 1939 and spent some months there. There was only a relatively short period of Hungarian neutrality before it too joined the Axis powers in November

1940. Hungarian politics and foreign policy became more stridently nationalistic and right wing, and they began to introduce anti-Jewish laws. Increasingly Poland was circled by fascist states, all with anti-Semitic policies.

There is a photograph of Jurek with fellow Poles in Hungary. He later remembered the Hungarians as kind and hospitable. He also received help there from the Red Cross. The escape from Hungary was nevertheless hazardous, involving procuring transport to the border with Yugoslavia (now Croatia) and crossing the border on foot near the village of Zákány. Nowadays the international border railway station lies in the centre of the village, with the River Drava also running nearby to the Danube forming most of its border with Hungary. Pictures show it to be a wide, flowing river with greenery on either bank. It was frozen during the winter of 1939 when Jurek and his friends needed to cross. Large numbers of Polish soldiers were fording the river, to get across the border, when the ice cracked and several following behind Jurek and his friends were drowned. The remainder, including Jurek, made their way to the Yugoslav coast at Split. Yugoslavia was at that time still at peace and striving for neutral status. Later, on 6 April 1941 the kingdom was swiftly conquered by Axis forces and the country partitioned between Germany, Italy, Hungary and Bulgaria.

The next photographs of Jurek, with friends Przemek and Erwin, show them in Split, Yugoslavia (Croatia). The weather was warm, so it was probably spring 1940. From Split they got the necessary papers and passports they needed to go by ship to Marseilles, France. Zenon Krzeptowski, a young Polish soldier, gives his account of a similar journey through Hungary in 1940:[1]

> I lodged with an old lady in a small village outside Barc called Erdecheconia. We had to stay for three weeks as the ice on the border river had started to crack. She asked me when I was going to France. I had been told to say I was going nowhere and was with her until the war ended. She opened a drawer and showed me four letters from previous boys that stayed with her that were now in France. That was the end of my cover. . . We reached the town of Virovatica. They put us in the town hall and although we were individually questioned, we all said we wanted to go to France. We were split into groups and I went to Zagreb with mine. We stayed in a small hotel and hospitality was great. We were given free tickets to theatres, swimming pools etc. A pleasant surprise. Then we were given free rail tickets to the town of Split. Another small hotel. Next morning we were surprised by the briefing we went to, as it was in a big hall full of young volunteers, regular officers and even generals. We were told we had just missed a ship for France and would have to spend Easter in Split. I sent a postcard to my Hungarian landlady. . . . After Easter, we boarded an old ship called the Warshawa and off we went. The weather was rough and most of us were seasick.

The ship *Warshawa* (*sic*) was a merchant ship, built in Sunderland, England in 1916 with a home port in Gdynia, Poland. When war had broken out September 1939 she had loaded arms intended for the Polish army at Le Havre, but was unable to deliver them. From November 1939 to June 1940, the ship transported 5,418 Polish soldiers and refugees in ten voyages from Greece and Yugoslavia to France and Syria. She was then interned by the Vichy French authorities at Beirut, but was soon taken to Haifa and used to transport 3,520 Polish refugees from Turkey to Palestine in seven voyages. In January 1941, the *Warshawa* was used to transport Australian troops from Alexandria to Tobruk and then carried war material to Greece and Crete. In 1941 she was damaged in a collision in the harbour of Alexandria and finally sunk there at the end of the war. Another lively story of a wartime ship. I am beginning to think that ships too can be heroic.

Jurek and his two friends sailed with other Polish soldiers on the *Warshawa* for Marseilles in the spring of 1940, over six months after leaving home. He too recalls that the sea was very rough and his friends Przemek and Erwin suffered badly from seasickness. Przemek wanted to stop the boat so he could get off. Jurek was unaffected, and since the others couldn't eat, he ate their rations as well as his own. Jozef Hartley, a Pole also travelling in France (he took his wife's Scottish name), describes the reception when these troops got to Marseilles:[2]

> It took us 6 nights and 7 days to reach Marseille on the 2nd of April. We were taken to a very big camp in the hills above. General Sikorski came to welcome us. A few days later we were moved by train to Bressiere where we were separated into different units. At the next town of Parthaney we had medicals and were given uniforms. From there to Versailles, where a French signals regiment had one Polish company attached, including some from my battalion from Krakow. We went straight to work, but the French equipment was not as good as ours had been. They were expecting new advanced equipment any day.

Arriving on the French mainland, Jurek was enrolled in the Polish Highland Brigade (La Brigade Polonaise des Chasseurs du Nord) 1st Division, soon after April 1940, under the command of General Boghusz-Szyszko. It was integrated into the French 1st Division, intended for the Expeditionary Force to Norway following the German invasion on 9 April 1940. By May 1940 Jurek had an identity card issued for Harstad, Norway. The Polish and French troops were taken by ship from the northern French coast to Norwegian waters. They were heading for the battle of Narwik.

Battle of Narwik, April 1940

The first major battle of the Allies during the Second World War occurred in the mountains and off the coast of the city of Narwik, Norway. The naval battles were fought on 10 and 14 April between the British Royal Navy and Nazi Germany's *Kreigsmarine* navy. The land battles lasted two months and were fought by Norwegian, French (including Foreign Legionnaires), British and Polish troops against German mountain troops and paratroopers. This was the biggest battle of the war since the Polish invasion eight months earlier.

There were difficulties for the Allies. There was no unified command, and cooperation between the forces involved was not always smooth. Even within the British forces, the Army and Navy commanders had difficulty cooperating. In the second week of May, the Norwegians (using ski troops) and French (using alpine troops) advanced successfully on the Germans. By mid-May the Allies took the initiative and achieved significant victories, then the French Foreign Legionnaires took Bjerkvik and advanced north east to where the Germans were withdrawing. Polish troops were to advance there, from land on the west side of the fjord, but heavy terrain delayed them. The Germans then escaped through a gap in the Allied advance. The Allied attack was stalled while waiting for air support. On 28 May, a naval bombardment commenced from the north and Norwegian, French and Polish advances led to the first major Allied victory of the war on land. It seemed only a matter of time before the Germans would surrender. They were pushed from the north by the Norwegians, from the west by the French and from the south west by the Poles. However, orders from London required retreat under cover and evacuation. The attack on Narwik would disguise the retreat and the destruction of the iron-ore harbour. A possible Allied victory, one of the first in the war, which might have changed the course of the war, was turned into defeat, ultimately leading to the evacuation at Dunkirk.

The Norwegian government and commanders met this change of plan with disbelief and bitterness. The Norwegians still hoped to defeat the Germans alone and, as late as 5 June, the Norwegian brigades attacked. On 7 June the King and government were evacuated from Norway to Britain. All Allied troops were evacuated from Narwik in early June. Three Polish passenger ships, including the MS *Stefan Batory*, took part in the evacuation operation. One Polish ship, the *Chrobry*, was sunk by German bombers. Narwik was retaken by the Germans and on 10 June the last Norwegian forces surrendered.

The cold and snow was a common enemy for all troops at Narwik, and most of the Allies were poorly prepared. Only the Norwegians were fully equipped with skis and able to use them. The Germans achieved the successful invasion and occupation of Norway, and the Allies evacuated Norway in June 1940. The 1st Brigade of the North, where Jurek was assigned, fled to France; other troops fled to Britain or Morocco. The British government decided to evacuate the British Expeditionary Force, as well as several French divisions, at Dunkirk.

The fall of France

During the year of '*drôle de guerre*' (or joke war, phoney war), the inactivity by the Allies had settled into a waiting game which in France had sapped morale. The blunders of Narwik lost the French leadership their prestige. The Germans meanwhile were busy re-equipping and honing their plan of campaign. It has been argued that France could have won the war by an offensive in September/October

1939, but missed the opportunity to its great cost (Nord, 2015). It could have taken advantage while Germany was engaged in invading Poland, with a full quarter of Germany's armoured units in action in the east – the Reich was vulnerable at that moment. However, the French were determined to fight a defensive war – the Maginot line was the culmination of the First World War experience which still encapsulated their view of war, so they never seized the opportunity to attack. Yet the French had sufficient weapons and aircraft, and it was by no means inevitable they would lose in the summer of 1940. Nord describes a 'national awakening' in favour of fighting the Germans which occurred too late, only once France was under invasion. Faulty decision making following the Germans' unexpected invasion through the Ardennes forest set France up for defeat (Nord, 2015). Rigidity of thinking at the top of the military was at fault, as well as the reflexive defence mode.

The German forces launched a second operation, and with air superiority and their armoured mobility (using hundreds of tanks) overwhelmed the remaining French forces. They pushed deep into France, arriving in Paris unopposed on 14 June 1940. This caused a chaotic period of flight for the French government and effectively ended French military resistance. German commanders met with French officials on 18 June with the goal of forcing the new French government to accept all of the agreements in an armistice offered by Germany. Chief among the French government leaders was Marshal Pétain, the newly appointed prime minister and one of the supporters of the armistice. The Second Armistice, at Compiègne, was signed by France and Germany on 22 June 1940, which resulted in a division of France. Germany would occupy the north and west, Italy would control a small occupation zone in the south east and an unoccupied zone, the *zone libre*, would be governed by the Vichy government led by Marshal Pétain in the south.

France had fallen, and with it any hope of support to Poland. Two million Belgians fled before the German onslaught, to be joined by millions more French. No one had envisioned such a mass exodus. There was a breakdown of public services and the authorities abdicated control. The sight of so many soldiers in flight added to civilian demoralisation. The German military bombed refugee columns. The population turned against the government and General Pétain took the opportunity of seizing power and moved away from the principles of the French Republic. In the armistice negotiations the three-fifths of France subject to occupation was to be paid for by the French; Alsace and Moselle were occupied and annexed to Germany. Captured French soldiers (1.5 million) were required to stay in prisoner-of-war camps and France had to surrender asylum-seekers and German refugees to the Nazis. A ceasefire was effected and Marshall Pétain's government relocated to Vichy in the south of France. France's war was over.

However, General de Gaulle did not give in. He made a radio appeal on 18 June 1940 calling on the French to continue the fight. It became a rallying point for the Resistance in its anti-German campaign. When Vichy (French-held France) started to enact anti-Semitic legislation in autumn 1940 there were protests, including from the church and clerics. The Vichy regime became increasingly unpopular. It was right wing and collaborationist. Civil unrest gradually became organised and the French Resistance was born.

Polish troop movements in France

In June of 1940 following Armistice, many escaping Polish soldiers travelled to Vichy. Their aim was to reach the UK, the only ally still fighting, by St Jean de Luz or via Spain and Gibraltar. Most of the Poles headed for Toulouse, as did Jurek, where they were assisted by the Polish consulate operating until September 1940. This was soon closed, and secret evacuations of fleeing soldiers were organised. These were opposed by the Vichy police, and by the German Gestapo (secret police) who established themselves along the French/Spanish border. There were 27,000 Polish troops who escaped to the UK immediately, whilst a further 6,000 Polish men chose to stay in France in the occupied area and to demobilise on site. Jurek was one of those who stayed in France to continue the struggle.

Janina Struk writes about how her Polish father escaped from France to England by ship in this period. She was able to piece together his story after he died, from postcards he had left on his journey (Struk, 2013):

> By the time my father reached the harbour on 23 June, two Polish ships, the Sobieski and Batory, packed to capacity, had already sailed. Two British ships, the Ettrick and the cruise ship Arandora Star, were anchored outside the breakwater, unable to enter the harbour because of heavy seas. But it was the drama of their departure that is most vivid in the memory of the townsfolk – events in which the local fishermen played the crucial role. For three days and three nights, they braved the notorious swell of the Bay of Biscay to row the refugees in their fishing boats to the ships.
>
> The Ettrick sailed that afternoon. The Arandora Star started to load passengers, but the swell made the operation treacherous. By seven the next morning in calmer seas, the ship was ordered inside the breakwater so embarkation could continue. There is no official list, but according to reports, there were perhaps 5,000 crammed on board. In mid-afternoon it set sail for Liverpool. A few hours later, at 12.30am, the armistice came into effect. It stated that no more ships were to leave.
>
> My father was aboard the Arandora Star. . . . the last ship destined for Britain from the last free port in France, berthed at Liverpool docks at 7.35am on 27 June – my father's 24th birthday. That afternoon, the German army rolled into St-Jean-de-Luz along the route that the Polish trucks had driven just a few days before. He had had a lucky escape. Operation Ariel rescued 200,000 people – 25,000 Poles among them – in one of the biggest evacuations of the war, but it never captured the public's imagination in the way that Operation Dynamo at Dunkirk had done a month earlier. For the rest of the war, my father and thousands of other Poles stayed in Britain and

fought alongside the allies. He served in Polish air force squadron 307 as an aircraft mechanic.[3]

Jurek, like many other displaced Poles who remained, undertook clandestine work with the French Resistance. His official demobilisation was in June 1940 in Fégréac, in the Loire Interior. He changed his surname to Krause, took on the identity of a French Canadian and was put in charge as 'chief' of 26 other Polish fighters. The list of these men still survives and includes Jan (Jonny) Krasinski, a Count by birth, but also a displaced soldier. He kept his own name in France and became a close friend to Jurek throughout the war and after. We don't know whether Przemek and Erwin were on the list under assumed names, but they were to meet Jurek later and remain friends post-war. The aim of the group of Poles was to travel to Vichy (unoccupied) France to continue the fight against the Germans. The Poles all stayed in Toulouse in July 1940 with the Polish Consulate, who issued Jurek with papers for a 'mission to accompany seven people' (presumably the group was split into smaller ones). The Poles travelled south east, heading for Grenoble near the Alps.

There were various escapades on the way to Grenoble. One foraging exercise led to the discovery of a large stone jar of wine, from the plentiful Loire vineyards. Aware they could not carry it, and concerned about drunkenness, Jurek smashed it, to the others' dismay. Cigarettes proved the most useful form of currency. In fact wine proved so cheap and plentiful they later used it to clean their shoes. The group walked through the French countryside at night and slept during the day. On one occasion they were offered hospitality at a chateau. Jurek was invited to join in a game of tennis by the French *Comte*, his host, which he was pleased to accept. Later he was given fresh clothes to wear when he left. He found money in the pockets. He went back to return the money, thinking it had been left accidentally, and knowing the family would face reprisals for helping refugee Poles. However, the French aristocrat had intended the money for Jurek, in sympathy for the Allied and Polish cause. He hadn't wanted his wife, *la Comtesse*, to know.

The Red Cross worked with the consulates and in a network across Europe to aid combatants and civilians in need. They helped with communications through their couriers, and with lists of foreign nationals and combatants taken into prison or forced labour, and also sent parcels of provisions. By Christmas Eve, 1940, the Red Cross had obtained a room for Jurek in the Hotel Terminus in Grenoble, a stucco regency building near the station, still standing today. For this he used his real name, enrolling as an undergraduate studying Business and Economics. We have his id card (student number 571, 1941–2) and a receipt for 300 francs, for some expenses. He then started his clandestine work with the French Resistance. His role would be to travel around Vichy France as a courier delivering messages and other secret documents and materials. He had no official documentation, since he was not a French citizen, but would always give a cover story about his journey and was usually allowed on his way.

The beautiful city of Grenoble is located at the base of the Alps in a corner of France not far from Switzerland and Italy. The university, a hive of resistance, involved the Red Cross, who were able to get escapee soldiers enrolled as students. There are photographs of Jurek and his friends at the university at a Polish students' society. In one, Jurek is making a speech in a room full of smartly dressed students, the room bedecked with a large Polish eagle banner. He also seems to have had leisure time – in one photo Jurek is playing cards with a group of fellow students outdoors in the mountains. He was always fanatical about playing bridge.

The city of Grenoble, after the armistice of June 1940, was a place where the Resistance movement began, as more and more of its citizens joined the effort. The University of Grenoble and its professors provided constant support to the Resistance movement and, towards the end of 1942, several of its departments began producing false documentation for young people – giving them the identity of students – to prevent them from being assigned to forced labor. Towards the end of 1942, a group of *Maquis* (resistance fighters) was formed in the nearby Vercors region by the arrival of people who refused to be sent as forced German labor. This group became an important symbol of the Resistance.

Forced labour camps in France had started before the war, when thousands of Spanish refugees, two-thirds of them Republican soldiers, had poured over the southern border in February 1939 following the defeat of their forces by Franco's troops in the Spanish Civil War (Farmer, 2004). In winter and early spring 1939, these refugees were evacuated inland and dispersed among a variety of internment camps operated by the Ministry of Defence. In April 1939, the French government decreed that all able-bodied foreigners receiving asylum in France should be put to work. The formation of these foreign labour companies served as a way to acquire much-needed labour, restrict foreigners' access to the regular labour market in competition with French workers, and was a way of policing foreigners.

The newly founded Vichy regime took control of the numerous internment camps that dotted the southern zone and their associated companies of foreign workers. These were labour battalions, or GTE (*Groupements de Travailleurs Etrangers*), with six groups of approximately 41,000 workers in the south east. As of March 1941, around half worked in agriculture and almost a quarter on building hydroelectric dams, mining coal, or in the chemical and metallurgical industries. The remaining quarter laboured in the Forestry Service, the Department of Mines and Bridges or for regional or local governments. The ways in which workers were grouped and housed reflected the nature of their contracts: either living in makeshift barracks or with the person for whom they worked. Workers did not receive a salary, but were granted a bonus depending on their productivity and an allocation for their families.

Moving around Vichy France was becoming more difficult by the summer of 1942. In November the city of Grenoble was occupied by the Italians, and a year later by the Germans, and life under true occupation began. The Resistance was at this time training and providing weapons for forced labour evaders. Little by little, they joined the *Maquis*, organised in the woods and mountains surrounding

Grenoble. Gradually, the irregular groups took action, destroying power lines and transformers, stealing the local forced labour files, destroying the *Fort des Quatre Seigneurs* and stealing large amounts of stockpiled explosives. The British had made contact and were infiltrating into France from May 1941 to aid the Resistance group. De Gaulle formed his own agency in London to independently aid French Resistance efforts, although he failed to coordinate with British efforts. At first the resistance groups were scattered and lacked cooperation, then in June 1941 all groups in France merged into a larger group, proving the effectiveness of more coordinated resistance action.

Jurek's cover story on his various travels as courier for the Resistance was that he was travelling to join the French Foreign Legion in North Africa. This permitted travel and was usually believed; French police would let him on his way, saying '*Oh, chagrin d'amour!*' (reasons for joining the Foreign legion were meant to be failed love affairs). But Jurek's luck was to run out; on board a train, the French gendarme noted there was a deserter from the Foreign Legion at the back of the train under escort, and told Jurek to travel with him. Jurek was obliged to do so, and ended up joining the French Foreign Legion. In the first few weeks he had a medical examination, but told them a mastoid operation in his ear at age 18 had led to chronic loss of balance (this was untrue), which meant he failed the Foreign Legion medical. Rejects were handed over to the Vichy police, and imprisoned as displaced persons without papers. Jurek then had a spell in a French prison, which he noted was like a medieval dungeon with damp running down the walls, the worst in Europe; nevertheless, it was preferable to German deportation and concentration camp.

The authorities in Vichy France were also sending consignments of Jews to German concentration camps. One such consignment was short of the required number, so the police took random prisoners to make up the numbers. Jurek was selected but managed to bribe a guard with a valuable watch and evaded deportation. He then remained in Vichy France, assigned to forced labour. This included coal-mining (particularly difficult for Jurek, who was over six feet in height, working in cramped conditions) but on request for a change was given forestry work, which he preferred. Eventually he managed to escape – whether through Red Cross assistance or through his Resistance comrades, is unclear. The time was coming to leave France.

Flight to Spain, 1943

Spain in 1943 was ruled by a fascist government under Franco, and although neutral in the Second World War was trying to recover from the effects of its vicious civil war of 1936, thought to have cost more than half a million lives. It was, however, one of the few routes from France through to the British territory of Gibraltar, and hence sea passage to Britain. Jurek escaped from Vichy France prior to the German invasion in 1943 and managed to cross the border into Spain. We don't have specific details of his route, but Jan Karski describes his own passage from occupied France to Spain in the same year. Making contact through the French

Underground with a young Spanish couple, Karski secured a travel permit to Perpignan and was given a guide to get him to Barcelona. They travelled for miles by bicycle over difficult roads, at night-time; then onward by fishing boat, in which Karski and the guide hid for two days. A new guide was consigned to take him hiking through the Pyrenees (Karski, 1944, 2012). Each section was fraught with danger and the possibility of being caught by French or German soldiers or police on one side of the border, Spanish on the other.

Karski met up with other secret Polish travellers and all were told to say they were Canadian. This had also been Jurek's cover nationality. It was explained that if Canadians were caught in Spain the British authorities could extradite them. Karski and his group travelled by train to the outskirts of Barcelona, and spent several hours walking to the city. Any stops at cafés required ordering without speaking as none of them spoke Spanish. A rendezvous point was reached and an interview with the Consul General who helped Karski get to Gibraltar where, on meeting a British general, he left in an American bomber to get with some urgency to the British authorities in London. Karski met General Sikorski in London, who listened to his critical eye-witness report and awarded him a medal (Virtuti Militari) and gifted him his own silver cigarette case.

The exact route Jurek took from France to Spain would be similarly arduous. Once in Spain, poor and on the run, he recalls the cold of winter and having nowhere to go, looking through windows to see the Spanish celebrating Christmas. He was rounded up as a displaced person by the Spanish police and put into a prison in Figueres, Catalonia. He seems to have remained there until April, when he gained his freedom, again through the action of the Red Cross and permission to go to Madrid. He was using the pseudonym Jerzy (Yerzy) Krause. In Madrid he is documented as staying in a small family hotel on the Calle de las Conchas on 2 June 1943. His living conditions there were much better. He later described visiting the Prada museum and art gallery, and is pictured with a female friend, Juanita, smartly dressed and walking along the promenade.

Jurek reached Gibraltar in July 1943, to rendezvous with General Sikorski and other Polish troops. He wanted to fly to England and nearly managed to get a seat on the plane with Sikorski and his aides, but at the last minute he was told there was no room for him. He stood by the airfield, frustrated, and watched the plane take off then nose-dive into the sea. Sikorski, his daughter, and other personnel were drowned but the pilot survived. Jurek was part of the army cortege watching over the lying in state of General Sikorski's coffin for the next night and following day. The event was reported in the newspapers – Jurek retained a cutting from the *Gibraltar Daily*. Sabotage was of course suspected, as much from Soviet Russia as Germany, but exhaustive investigation in recent years has not been able to confirm this. The loss of Sikorski was a tremendous blow to the Poles – he was highly effective both politically as prime minister of the government in exile, but also militarily as commander-in-chief. He had the ear of Churchill and the British military establishment, and was a seasoned officer having fought in the Polish–Soviet war. On his final trip, he had been escorting Polish troops back to London after visiting General Ander's Polish troops in Italy, at a critical time in the war. Sikorski died but Jurek, by luck, survived. He later managed to get a place aboard a ship sailing from Tripoli, this vessel having berthed in Gibraltar on its way to Liverpool. Jurek reached England.

Enigma

There were many other Poles who followed the same route as Jurek through France on their way to England. Perhaps the most notable were three young Polish mathematicians who had worked on the stolen Enigma machine and had cracked the first German Enigma codes in Poland before the war: Jerzy Rozycki, Henryk Zygalski and Marian Rejewski. The sophisticated German code system Enigma used in the war had a code finally cracked by Alan Turing at Bletchley Park, England. However, this was only the final part of a long story of how the Enigma encoding machine was discovered and brought to England. The key Polish code breakers, already experienced in working on Enigma, left Poland and followed the same route as Jurek through Romania, to France, then to Spain, Gibraltar and eventually to the UK.

The Poles discovered a version of Enigma as early as 1928 when monitoring German radio traffic. A commercial Enigma machine was accidentally misdirected as a package to Poland and was taken by the Polish authorities for analysis (Budiansky, 2000). British codebreakers had also enjoyed a few successes against early Enigma machines in the mid-1930s, but the Poles made more progress because of their use of mathematicians rather than linguists as codebreakers. By 1938, Polish cryptographers had been reading 75 per cent of intercepted German radio transmissions enciphered using the Enigma machine. They kept their success a very closely guarded secret (Calvocoressi, 2011). In September 1938 the Germans changed the Enigma procedures for enciphering messages and further developed the complexity of the machine. This meant that Rejewski's previously successful scheme no longer worked. In July 1939 and with the invasion of Poland imminent, the Polish cryptographers decided to share their Enigma results with the French and British code-breakers. At a meeting in woods just outside Warsaw they shared their knowledge, giving the allies copies of the German Enigma machine and revealing their methods. The three Polish code-breakers then escaped through Romania to attempt to link up with a French code-breaking team at Château Vignolles, just outside Paris, to continue their work.

In October 1939 they joined a joint French–Polish–Spanish decoding unit at the château, and by the end of the year they were again managing to decode messages sent by the German Enigma machines. Following the German invasion of France and entry into Paris, the three cryptographers were evacuated to Algeria but then returned to Vichy France from September 1940. Rejewski posed as a professor of mathematics from a school in Nantes and worked at the Château des Fouzes in a secret French intelligence unit. Unfortunately, on 9 January 1942 his colleague Rozycki died when his ship sunk on its return from Algeria. Then, once the German troops had occupied Vichy France, the secret intelligence unit in the Château was in severe danger and was evacuated on 9 November 1942, three days before German soldiers discovered it.

Rejewski and his remaining colleague, Zygalski, moved around many of the cities of southern France avoiding capture. They eventually decided to cross the Pyrenees to reach Spain. Despite being robbed by their guide at gunpoint, they reached Spain, only to be put in prison. Their experience mirrored Jurek's. The Red Cross personnel included them on a list of Polish Prisoners who were to receive packages, and were later able to secure their release in May 1943 when they were sent to Madrid. From there they made their way to Portugal and, after transfer by Royal Navy ship to Gibraltar, they were flown to Britain where they arrived on 3 August 1943. Rejewski then joined the Polish Army in Britain. He was never sent to Bletchley Park to assist in the decoding operations being carried out there – it seems the authorities were unaware of his extraordinary talent. Neither he nor the other Polish encryptors received any acclaim at the time; their role was only revealed in 1973. At that time Rejewski was living in Poland, working in an undistinguished job and harassed by communist authorities, who suspected his wartime role. Zygalski remained in England, holding a professorship in Mathematics at Surrey University.

Katyn uncovered

The year 1943 was a terrible one for the Poles. In April the massacre at Katyn came to light, just when Jurek was released in Spain and one month before General Sikorski was killed in the plane crash. The Katyn site was found by German soldiers advancing against Russia, who on reaching the border district came across the mass graves. On 11 April 1943, the German radio service started to broadcast on the German Home Service the discovery of Polish mass graves in the Katyn woods near Smolensk, Russia. This coincided with the point at which the British foreign secretary, Anthony Eden, was meeting with the US President Roosevelt, who advocated keeping on good terms with Russia to avoid the spread of communism. As soon as the Katyn graves came to light, General Sikorski insisted on an international enquiry, to be led by the Red Cross. The Germans allowed a deputation of key international observers and experts under the Red Cross to go to Katyn to examine the graves. Dr Wodzinski, a medical doctor and expert in forensic medicine at Jegellon University, Krakow, and also a member of the AK Home Army, was one of these experts.

There was great shock at both the scale of the suspected massacre – over 20,000 men – but also at the selection of those killed: military officers, officials, administrators, teachers, political leaders, doctors, lawyers, academics, writers and priests – a class-based 'politicide' – a different focus from the other genocides taking place (Harff and Gurr, 1988). In countries covered by the Geneva Convention, officers in particular would be expected to be protected if taken as prisoners of war. Wodzinski flew from Warsaw to Smolensk with a delegation of senior Warsaw figures, and was joined there by international experts in forensic medicine including professors from Budapest, Prague, Slovakia, Bulgaria, Italy, Finland and Switzerland. My grandfather, Hugh O'Neill, in England recalls that a scientific colleague of his was also called to go (O'Neill, 1995). They remained for five weeks to oversee the exhumation and examination of the evidence of the bodies and the grave, with careful documentation made. There was silent German observation but no interference. It was as though the war had stopped, by common agreement, at this particular place of horror, while war continued across the rest of the continent. Statements were taken from locals who witnessed or knew of the massacre. The work of the international team involved lifting the corpses, examining them and determining the cause of death; searching the bodies for personal documentation for identification, and labelling them with unique numbers; then re-burying the corpses in new communal graves. In the following month, May 1943, a delegation of British and Colonial prisoners of war from German *Oflag* (prisoner of war) camps were sent to examine the site. A report was later filed by a British captain, Stanley Gilder, on 22 November 1944, corroborating the general information provided in the final commission report.

After extensive international investigation, the report proved unconclusive about the perpetrators. More members of the German Army units came to see the mass graves. Russian soldiers refused to help, and were found to be filling the site with water to hamper the exhumation. A secure radio signal from the head of the Underground organisation in Warsaw, labelled 'Despatch No. 52 Most Secret', was sent on 24 May 1943. An unauthorised copy was obtained by O'Malley (British Ambassador to the Polish government in exile in London 1941–5), with directions for it to be treated as 'particularly secret'. In a concise ten-point report it gave precise descriptions: the location and sizes of the mass graves; the arrangement of the corpses; and their uniforms and possessions – as many as 76 per cent were readily identifiable. It was noted that nothing but watches had been removed from the men. All the corpses had a bullet wound to the back of the head. The revolver shells and ammunition were still evident in the graves. The clearing in the forest at Katyn covered several square kilometres and was the site of prior NKVD (Russian secret police) rest houses. The local civilian population stated that in March and April 1940 one transport of 200 to 300 Polish officers used to arrive each day. This report was sent days after the end of the Warsaw ghetto uprising in May 1943.

The British services became involved in April 1943 when they interpreted a message about Katyn on their radio transmissions, concerning the unearthing of mass graves. A memorandum was written entitled 'Katyn and Afterwards' for the Foreign Office. Poles in London already knew of the missing officers, the location and the likely instigators. Jan Karski had been witness to much of this, as well as to the fate of the Jews. They were shocked at being compelled to remain silent by the British about the Russian perpetrators of the massacre. Their response was described cynically in a memo from a senior British official as having 'almost childlike faith in the honesty of purpose'. The Poles were unable to believe that Britain and the US would abandon their interests in favour of Soviet Russia after all their sacrifice.

Such cynicism was foreign to their culture and traditions. The worry at the time in London was that the timing was close to the planned (second) uprising in Warsaw and the planned western invasion was close. They could not afford to affront the Russians. The legacy of this cowardly act was to remain for decades to come.

Discussion

The theme is identity, and the chapter focuses on Jurek and his use of subterfuge in continuing Polish resistance to the Nazis in France. This began with a long journey across Europe, an open battle at Narwik and then clandestine work for the French Resistance. This took personal purpose and competence. It also took substantial organisation and networking from the military, the consulate, the Red Cross, the University of Grenoble and other authorities. For example, on the journey through Romania and Yugoslavia thousands of passports were created for fleeing Poles, clothing distributed and funds provided. After Narwik, overseeing demobilisation of troops including the Poles, and use of Polish consulates to issue papers and safe passage either to England or to remain in France, was a big undertaking. Finally, being able to accommodate a number of potential combatants in university enrolment, with the aid of the Red Cross, required careful planning. Such clandestine movement of populations requires great resources and shared purpose under dangerous circumstances. In psychological terms it also requires the trust of each individual in the linked networks, as well as sufficient camaraderie and goodwill of those on the same side to enable effective joint working, regardless of language or culture, but with a common purpose of resistance. Jurek was fortunate in already being fluent in French, and having sufficient resources of trust, social skills and competence at subterfuge to undertake this successfully. No doubt he was also lucky. The main themes of this chapter are shown in Figure 6.1.

A friend told me that Jurek's story reminded her of Geoffrey Household's *Rogue Male*, a book written in 1939 about a man on the run after having tried to kill a foreign leader (thought to be Hitler) in Germany (Household, 1939, 2014). He is caught, tortured, but then escapes, reaching England where he is still on the run from his pursuers who want to kill him. A solitary, action narrative, told by the main agent himself who is never named, he uses his skills as a game hunter to evade capture. He also uses his high social class to convey authority and this allows him to pass in various situations, a different sort of camouflage (Household, 1939, 2014). Whilst in *Rogue Male* the narrator mainly uses his skills on the land to survive, I suspect Jurek rather used his skills with people to the same effect. He must have been able to use social camouflage. He seems to have been able to keep a cool head and to remain purposeful. Reading the book by Household reminded me of the danger and anxiety of being hunted and hounded across a continent: never belonging, always having to move on. This would cause substantial strain. Many would not have survived it.

Resilience seems abundant in this narrative – not only for Jurek and his colleagues, but for the large numbers of Polish fighting men who all made their

134 Poland and England: the second generation

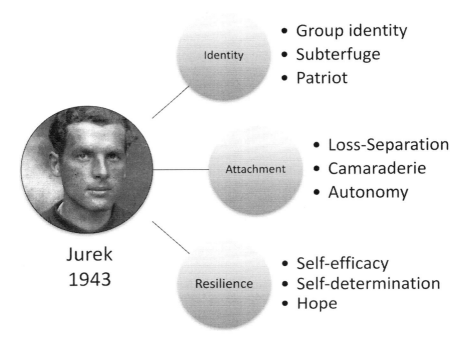

FIGURE 6.1 Summary of the themes in Chapter 6

way west, finding various resourceful ways of crossing the continent. Jurek had the background and education to help his survival. For someone in clandestine work it probably helped that he was a personable young man, intelligent, socially skilled, charming, cultured and good-looking. The French aristocrat who helped him apparently saw no social distinction between them. I rather like the insouciant manner in which they played tennis, oblivious to the conflict around them.

The Polish community too was resilient in the way it organised itself. There are several examples of Poles setting up not only camps but also schools on these travels. Polish schools were set up wherever there were Poles en route. Ander's army – Poles on their long trek from Siberia – saw schools established in the Middle East, Africa and places where they settled. These were paid from Polish funds – deducted from the soldiers' pay. There is a saying, 'If two Poles meet together in the desert, they will start a newspaper'; it seems that if a few more Poles get together then a school will emerge.

This chapter is about identity – the cultural and personal identity retained by displaced men – intent on fighting for their country but many thousands of miles from home. For Jurek and others like him, it entailed a change of name and a masking of his true nationality. He was to continue his clandestine work when he came to England with further name changes. He must have had a talent for secret work. Although throughout he had some knowledge of his wife and mother in

Poland through letters received, he was not to know for some years of Myszka's fate or that of his cousin Stas.

The secrecy of massacres also serves as a deletion of identity of those killed. The Katyn massacre was kept secret. The full Red Cross report was smuggled out of Poland after the war in 1946 to the British Foreign Office, where it was filed away unseen until 1972. The Russians under Stalin never admitted responsibility. They denied the timing (dating it a year later, from 1941 when the Germans were invading that area) and reported that the dead men were construction workers killed by the Germans, accusing the Red Cross of complying with a fascist pact between Sikorski and Hitler in concocting the account. This denial was re-enacted at the Nuremburg trials of Nazi war crimes, the full evidence never presented. It was judged a German atrocity and no individual was held responsible. The aftermath of Katyn was to live on for several decades because of cover-up and deceit. Poles were not allowed to publicly honour the dead of Katyn. Disputes over the siting of a war memorial in London were not resolved until 1970, where all public areas were refused, until eventually it was sited in Gunnersbury cemetery, Ealing. The British authorities insisted on discretion in regard to its label. The Poles had inscribed just two words: 'Katyn, 1940'; the Russians raised a storm of objections (the date points to the culpability). It remains a hidden memorial to the 22,000 individuals killed in the first months of the war. I visited it for the first time last year. It is imposing, tall and made of black granite. There were flowers and candles still being left by Poles in memoriam. Responsibility was eventually admitted by Gorbachev when Premier of Soviet Russia, but the perpetrators, then still alive, were never indicted. When questioned, they were unable to see why the killing of officers, academics, judges and other upper-class men constituted a crime (Maresch, 2010).

The themes in this chapter are subterfuge, secrecy and hidden identity. In attachment terms there is separation and isolation from family, but camaraderie with fellow travellers. Resilience comes through a strong sense of purpose, determination and hope.

Notes

1 www.bbc.co.uk/history/ww2peopleswar/stories/31/a2331631.shtml
2 www.bbc.co.uk/history/ww2peopleswar/stories/31/a2331631.shtml
3 *The Guardian*, Saturday 21 December 2013, www.theguardian.com/lifeandstyle/2013/dec/21/polish-fathers-miraculous-wartime-escape

7

ISOLATION

England fights, Warsaw rises (1943–45)

> Life doesn't make any sense without interdependence. We need each other, and the sooner we learn that, the better for us all.
>
> Erik Erikson

Introduction

In terms of Erikson's stages, this chapter and the next concern aspects of intimacy. 'Isolation' is a negative characteristic associated with this stage and 'Fidelity' the positive characteristic. The developmental task in emerging adulthood concerns the selection of a partner as main attachment figure, to create a new family with offspring and to be a source of support, trust and safety. This 'other' is a person with whom one is willing to share the proceeds of work, procreation and recreation, and to value as much as the self. Intimacy with a close other does not always occur, or does not always last. This may be due to internal (psychological) or external (social) barriers and the resulting state can at times be one of isolation and self-absorption. This chapter focuses on isolation to describe Jurek's solitary time in England, continuing the war effort alone, leaving his family behind on the war-torn continent. It also refers to Maria living alone in Warsaw and trying to survive. The city of Warsaw is also isolated as it rises up alone against the Germans, ultimately unaided by its allies. This latter isolation involved abandonment and betrayal. The people of Warsaw, including Maria, all lost their homes. Jurek became stranded abroad without a home. Through all of these trials there is, however, *fidelity* to the cause by Jurek, his mother and the Warsaw population.

In terms of family documentation used in this chapter, there are some shipping records, documents from Jurek's engagement in the British forces and letters from Maria after the war explaining some of her experience and a reminiscence from Jurek's cousin Marysia on returning to Warsaw. But there is little personal family information from the Warsaw Uprising itself. The account is therfore supplemented by published eye-witness accounts. I have chosen to focus these events specifically on the area where Maria was living in Zoliborz.

England and SOE

Records show Jurek boarded the Cunard ship *White Star Sumaria* on 24 July 1943 in Gibraltar, (passenger number, 892), travelling 3rd class, the ship having started its journey in Algiers. His address is given in the shipping documents as 'Polish HQ'. The ship had hundreds of passengers: there were many Poles, including the Polish Legation, military forces and navy personnel. However, there were also a number of other military personnel – Belgian, French, Dutch, Czechoslovak – as well as the French Fleet Air army. There were also a number of 'distressed British seamen' presumably rescued from a damaged ship. In the upper-class accommodation were British civilians and government officials, with others listed as Belgians, Latvians and Spanish.

Jurek arrived in Liverpool, England, to grey skies and rain. Whilst glad to be away from German-occupied mainland Europe, the first sight of this new country was somewhat sad and depressing. A fellow Pole, Jozef Hartley (original name Zachwieja) gives his account in the BBC archive of wartime experience. He came to England in similar circumstances, the month before Jurek arrived:

> On 26th June we arrived in Liverpool and on my first night in Britain I slept on a bench in Liverpool football stadium. Next morning we were put on the train to Scotland. Mostly Crawford, Biggar, Moffat on the A74 main road to Glasgow. The area became a tent city over the next three months, as we reorganised, demobbed the French army and uniforms, joined the British Army (Polish section). With the risk of the Germans invading a soft part of Scotland, the Poles were tasked with defending the seashore from Montrose to Dunbar. Headquarters were in Lord Moncrief House at Bridge of Earn near Perth. My company of signals was stationed here. After a few days, my troop from General Sikorski in France, was sent to Dundee as a reserve HQ. This was cover, as our main duties were taking down German messages to see if they could be cracked. Two months later, six Polish professors joined us to study the messages. Some high ranking officers thought we were wasting our time, but after a year the professors were recalled to General Sikorski's HQ at Rubens Hotel, Buckingham Palace Rd, London. We heard a rumour that the professors had cracked one code, but that the British had taken the project over.[1]

It was not long after Jurek came to England that he applied, and was recruited by the Special Operations Executive (SOE) service, Polish section. This was a secret organisation of combatants trained to fight behind enemy lines. His clandestine work with the French Resistance, his military schooling, his physical fitness, good social skills and his calm, unflappable manner must have made him seem suitable for this demanding wartime role. Jurek himself never described the process of selection to his family (the official secrets act remained in place for many years after the war). However, Jozef Hartley describes the process at the Rubens Hotel in London:[1]

> With more new boys from Eastern Poland arriving, a second Polish army corps was forming. I became an instructor and went on parachute training. After this, five of us were sent to London to the Rubens Hotel. From here they kept contact with the Polish Underground. We were interviewed by Polish and British officers. I had to show where I was born on a map. I was out. They kept three, but two of us had to return to Scotland. After the war, I learned that the three had been dropped near my home village, but on the wrong side of the border and the Germans killed them.
>
> I had to stand by for the next drop. I was injected and vaccinated, but the Russians got there first and the drop was abandoned. News arrived that General Sikorski had died in a plane crash in Gibraltar. I was chosen, with a few others, to be part of the funeral procession [in London]. We stayed in a big house on the Bayswater Rd facing Hyde Park. Six others were from my town in Poland.

SOE was a new form of warfare, initiated by Churchill to aid resistance movements in Europe. It had no precedent formats or procedures. It was led by Hugh Dalton, academic and barrister, and leading senior labour politician, who was later Minister of Economic Warfare. He was instructed by Churchill to 'set Europe ablaze'.[2] SOE's remit was to determine where resistance movements in Europe existed and, once targeted, to create and maintain contact and finally to aid sabotage efforts against the Germans. Its role was to undertake subversive operations in enemy-occupied territories. These agents were not spies, but trained combatants working in secret (Crowdy, 2016). In order for SOE to place agents on the ground in occupied Europe, it first had to find suitable candidates, individuals who could pass for locals. These agents (both men and women) received extensive training and were usually parachuted by plane at night to specific locations behind enemy lines. SOE used small Lysander aeroplanes, difficult for German observers to locate but tough enough to land on crude, makeshift runways. The agents had an extraordinarily difficult task, requiring high levels of competence and bravery, and the mortality rate was high (Crowdy, 2016).

By mid-1941, SOE agents were beginning to land on mainland Europe. They had a number of difficulties. A pre-arrangement was always agreed with the local resistance 'reception committee', informing them that a drop was going to take place. Flights were often stopped at the last minute, due to poor weather. These secret 'reception' committees were very much at risk from breaking curfew regulations imposed by the Germans – more importantly, though, because the risk of informants having told the Germans about these drops was a constant danger.

Isolation: England fights, Warsaw rises **139**

The work of the SOE became more sophisticated and more successful as the operatives and their managers gained more experience. Training was carried out in great secrecy. Various aids were devised (NationalArchives, 2014). SOE required clandestine radio communications, so a special wireless set was developed weighing less than 18 kg and carried in an ordinary suitcase. Every SOE group sent to occupied Europe included a qualified radio operator. All operatives were trained in parachuting, unarmed combat and self-defence, and some were trained in the use of explosives (Jurek took this role). All needed fluent language skills for the target country. Finally, all SOE operatives had to perfect their 'cover story' to confirm they were not from Britain. Any slip would have been fatal. Attention to detail was minute. For example, no British made shoes could be worn, or British-made cigarettes smoked, and all clothing and possessions had to be local in origin.

SOE's Polish section was one of the first sections, dating from the first experimental flight in 1939 to France (Tucholski, 1984). The agents in this section were almost exclusively Poles, but it was directed by British senior administrators and the officers and instructors were often British. It worked closely with the government-in-exile under General Sikorski. The Polish section was able to aid the overall SOE organisation. This was achieved through its swift intelligence networks on the continent, but also via its experience of the design and construction of clandestine wireless sets, and a flare for forgery. The agents in this section were known in Polish as *Cichociemni* (pronounced 'cheeko-chemny'), or 'dark and silent ones', because of the nature of the clandestine work. It worked closely with the AK home army in Poland (Tucholski, 1984).

The Polish SOE was run by Lieutenant-Colonel Jozef Hartman, 'the father of the *Cichociemni*'. He was in his forties by the time he arrived in SOE and was too well known to become an operative as military figure and prior aide-de-camp to Marshal Piłsudski. He was tasked to run the training and running of this section. It was based at 'Station 43', Audley End House, near Saffron Walden in Essex (Valentine, 2006). It was common for large country manor houses in Britain to be requisitioned in secret by the army during the war. This elegant house, once used by Charles II, had its historical interior features boarded over to make it a plain billet for soldiers. The heating and plumbing were poor and agents often had to be driven to the public baths in nearby Cambridge. The entrance was through an impressive oak door forming the north porch. A photograph of a Polish celebratory meal in the great hall shows the tall, protective screens in front of the staircase. Only on visits after the war did any of the men realise the original splendour of the mansion (Valentine, 2006).

The rambling house and gardens became home to 70 Polish trainees between March and August 1944. The stay was usually of six months. These were all combatants with army uniforms and army pay. Earlier training had been undertaken elsewhere in the UK. The first phase was usually held in the West Highlands of Scotland, for paramilitary courses and commando training. Candidates were also taught to live off the land, by snaring rabbits and eating wild food. There were also sessions where agents were dropped in isolated locations and expected to arrive at an agreed point, miles away. Whilst the details of Jurek's experience are not known, later he was to casually comment that he found the Scots accent difficult to follow, and was completely bemused when alone and boarding a tram in Glasgow during the war to be charged 'ha'pence three farthings', which made little sense to him in terms of the currency of pounds, shillings and pence. Some foreign trainee soldiers were actually turned in to the police by a vigilant populace as possible German spies. Later training sessions were at Largo House in Fife to practise trapeze skills, a preliminary to parachute training undertaken at Ringway, Manchester. Jumps started from suspended air balloons and then from aeroplanes, both in daylight and at night. Informative films showing parachute-jumping techniques were used to overcome language barriers and aid instructors. The SOE operatives were not allowed to learn English during their stay, or to fraternise with the locals, in order to retain their cover.

The selection was intense and the training rigorous. In Jurek's division they were all men, although women also played an important part in SOE. Any individual who did not complete the full course was sent back to his army company. The trainees were not necessarily very young – the average age was 30, extending to 40s and 50s. Jurek would have been 30 when he joined (although admitting to 27, he lied about his age when applying as a student to Grenoble University). The decision to join was entirely voluntary – candidates were not told at selection which force had accepted them. By 1943 the call for volunteers had brought nearly 2,500 applications, both men and women. Character, competence and commitment were essential:

> . . . only people of very high moral calibre and demonstrating high skill in acquired specialisations were sent into the country (Poland) . . . The principal of initial voluntary recruitment was maintained, but with the addition of applying stringent criteria as far as candidates moral standing, as well as looking at their psychological predisposition and physical condition. This further selection was applied during the training of agents, which was very strict and rigorous.
>
> Tucholski, 1984, p. 75

Whilst we don't have Jurek's records from his time in SOE, his later assessments in the RAF give him a score of 100 per cent for character and leadership, including: 'impressive appearance and bearing; quick thinker; adjusts easily; effective, forceful speaker, considerate of others; usually the leader; absolutely reliable; sterling character; self-controlled under difficulties; vigorous and enthusiastic; acts promptly on own initiative'. The assessing officers clearly thought highly of his potential.

Agents chose their own code names. These were necessary first for anonymity, but also to simplify Polish surnames for British military use. Jurek chose *Bronisz* (meaning defender) and used this as his given name, becoming known as Andrzej (Andrew) Bronisz. He was issued with an army uniform and provided with a distinctive special forces shoulder flash – wings with a red circle and the letters 'SF' – which he kept all his life. He was part of a division of Poles sent to train in various UK locations, but ending up at Audley House. The only document referring to this period gives all his details and shows him as a member of the Polish army. A requirement was that he did not learn English or mix with English people; this would help their cover when dropped behind enemy lines.

Jurek learned to parachute at a training site at Ringway and was awarded his Polish parachute wings. The training was intensive and the men had to be extremely fit. He recalled that his group of fellow fighters were also taught unarmed combat, knife fighting and judo. The men were organised into small groups, each man being a specialist, with Jurek becoming the specialist in explosives. He kept his notes about different chemical compounds needed for the explosives, carefully handwritten in Polish with diagrams, which we still have. The groups were to remain working together when they were dropped behind enemy lines. They were provided with light, collapsible motor cycles they could carry on their backs. Jurek recalled some of his training as perilous. One training exercise was in a derelict factory, with no floors but with a round metal pipe extending from one exterior wall to the other near the roof, a sheer drop below. The training exercise involved the men having to cross from one side of the ruin to the other, using this pipe. Jurek did it with his feet and hands crossed over the pipe (which was wet and slippery with rain) and travelled suspended. One of his fellow trainees who tried to walk across it fell and was killed. Jurek was reunited at SOE with Jonny Krasinski, a friend from France, which pleased them both. A photograph shows the two of them marching in uniform cheerfully down the front drive of the elegant manor house where they were billeted and trained.

Meanwhile, as Jurek was training in England and out of contact with his mother or Myszka, the situation in Warsaw was becoming more dire. He had had no word from them since Christmas 1942 and did not know whether they were still alive. He did, however, know that an uprising was to be planned.

Warsaw uprising

The hardship suffered in Warsaw in the first years of the war continued. There was, however, now frequent contact with London. Over three hundred Polish agents had been flown in by SOE. They landed with weapons and kits for making weapons. They brought plans, orders, couriers and large amounts of money for financing the resistance movement. They were also able to tell the isolated Polish Underground movement that they did indeed have an ally in the British. There were barriers to the communication, nevertheless. The flight from Britain was difficult and arduous due to the distance and location east of Germany. A two-engine Whitney plane had to be equipped with long-range fuel tanks to cover the eleven-hour flight over occupied territory, with constant danger of being shot down. However, from December 1943 a dedicated Polish air force flight was operated from Brindisi in Italy. These flights were extremely hazardous and many were shot

142 Poland and England: the second generation

down. Not only Poles but also South Africans, New Zealanders and others took on these 'mercy' missions, flying supplies to Warsaw while being fully aware of the dangers (Davies, 2004).

In the late spring of 1944, the Soviets had been winning battles against the Germans and were moving rapidly westward. On July 23 an attack by the Soviet Red Army annihilated the German defences on the River Bug. Soon the rumble of artillery could be heard in Warsaw, and the Kosciuszko Radio Station, transmitting in Polish from Moscow, repeatedly broadcast appeals 'to arms'. On 31 July 1944, at a 6:00 pm staff conference at the Head Quarters of the AK, General Bor-Komorowski, its Commander-in-Chief, decided the time for the uprising had come, with the Russian allies having advanced near to Warsaw and the Germans having no time to bring in reinforcements (Davies, 2004). The order to start the uprising was issued. The SOE had flown in the British civilian and military leadership essential to its operation. In August 1944 the Polish Underground in Warsaw, with knowledge of the Western Allies, began its uprising against their occupying German forces. As with the Jewish ghetto uprising two years earlier, the Poles had reached a point of no return. Despite their consistent armed resistance, after five years of starvation rations, random shootings and round-ups to the Pawiak prison before deportations to Auschwitz, a denouement was imminent. There was every sign of the war being won by the Allies following American entry into the war effort and Soviet successes in defeating the Germans in the East. The liberation of Paris was imminent. The Polish command in Warsaw decided to launch an attack on the Germans occupying their city on 1 August 1944. It was led by General Bor-Komorowski.

First day of the uprising in Zoliborz

Maria was still living in Zoliborz, at 21 Krasinski Street, and the fighting became focused on her neighbourhood. The first day of August saw skirmishes starting much earlier than the planned 5pm start, beginning in Zoliborz at 1:50 pm, following others in the city centre and Wola district. Julian Kulski Jnr, a young soldier in the AK in the Zoliborz district, describes his role on the first day of the uprising:

> It was a parched summer morning. At dawn we got orders to move into a house at Tucholska Street, off Krasinski Street, where our whole platoon had gathered. Here, additional arms were distributed among us. Along with a few others, I was chosen to go on patrol to Suzina Street, our pistols and Sten guns hidden under our jackets. We were to protect another detachment of our company, which was engaged in moving arms from one of our hideouts. Our orders were not to shoot unless first fired upon. When we got to the corner of Krasinski and Suzina Streets, we divided into pairs at the intersection and waited, more alert than ever before to everything that was happening around us. We did not have to wait long.

> ... At that moment, a German patrol truck drove quite slowly down Krasinski Street. Seeing the column, the Germans brought the vehicle to a screeching halt and opened fire on the men in the middle of the boulevard. ... The firing was still fierce, and bullets whined over our heads as we lay flat in the green centre strip dividing the boulevard. I kept firing back. ... Having a few minutes' respite, we unpacked the arms and distributed the guns, hand grenades, and ammunition among us. I drew an old Polish army rifle- the Warszawiak 1937-with ammunition. Then we took up positions in the buildings along Krasinski Street.
>
> Kulski, 2014, p. 222

This first fighting, then, was on the street where Maria lived. Kulski goes on to describe how on this first afternoon two huge German trucks, loaded with special SS anti-insurgency commandos, stopped on the avenue and began firing with machine guns and rifles. The resistance fighters returned fire. Two of their men were hit. Then the Germans sent a 'sharpshooter' to gauge their position:

> With the support of a heavy Tiger tank, the Germans attacked the building at the corner of Krasinski and Suzina Streets, so we decided to move to Zeromski Park. However, when we got to the lower part of Krasinski Street, we realised that we would have to attempt to cross it while it was being swept with tank fire. The German machine guns were placed so low, that the bullets were cutting the leaves off the potato plants growing in the centre strip of the boulevard.
>
> In spite of this we had to cross the boulevard. Crouching, with my rifle in my hands, I ran at a terrific speed, but I got pinned down in the middle of the road and was unable to proceed. Then, the tank trained the muzzle of its big gun on my position and the first shell exploded about twenty-five meters from where I was lying. The next was even nearer, so there was no time to think. We all jumped up and with one rush covered the distance to the other side of the boulevard. ... When we entered the building on the other side of the street, we left our wounded with the medics, and a nurse dressed my wound and gave me some water. As we sat in the courtyard, an old lady blessed us with the sign of the cross. She was crying with joy and excitement because the longed-for hour of the uprising had really come at last.
>
> Kulski, 2014, p. 223

As night fell the shooting stopped, and Zoliborz became quiet again apart from the sound of burning houses. The survivors of the dispersed units began to gather on the streets, some of them coming from further away in the city. They all regrouped on Krasinski Street where the company was stationed. They learned of their heavy losses. After a short break the order came to fight again, but the insurgents then lost Zoliborz. The premature start alerted the Germans, who had sent in several truckloads of SS-Polizei together with three tanks supported by Luftwaffe bombing. The insurgent leader told his men to disengage and regroup. This meant an overnight march north to the Kampinos forest to join the partisans and attract more volunteers back to Warsaw.

The first day took a terrible toll. At the start of the uprising the AK had 41,000 soldiers in Warsaw. There were 2,000 dead at the end of the first day. The Germans reported 500 of their soldiers as either dead or wounded but with several hundred taken prisoner by the AK. The uprising was to last for 63 days at a similar pace – makeshift soldiers and civilians fighting the fully equipped and militarised German troops under airfire from Luftwaffe bombers. The insurgents did well in the cobbled Old Town and the working-class Wola district bordering Zoliborz and the town centre, where there were fewer Germans. By 8pm they had taken the eighteen-storey art deco Prudential building and cornered the German high command. The German Governor, Fischer, and senior officer Stahel, who had just arrived from Austria, were ordered to prepare Warsaw for a siege but found themselves unable to leave the building on the first day of the uprising (Borowiec, 2015). Another success for the AK was a find of ammunition hidden behind sacks of flour and sugar guarded by only a single German gunman. On the negative side, the insurgents were driven out of the east bank of Praga nearest the Soviet advance, and had abandoned Zoliborz. They also failed to take the aiport, and the two main bridges across the Wisła. Whilst there was hope of the British sending their SOE agents to help with the fighting, there was a shortage of weapons, which put the insurgents at a grave disadvantage.

By the morning, civilians wanted their part in the uprising. In the city centre they asked the Polish guards where they should build the barricades. Trenches were dug, pavements torn up, abandoned tram cars upended and enough barricade provided to stop a tank (Borowiec, 2015). A platoon was ordered to help them. Polish music played while they worked – the German loudspeaker system previously used to issue reprisal threats was now in the hands of Poles who played the Polish National Anthem and other rousing music. Later, General Bor-Komarowski used the loudspeaker to address his soldiers. There was a holiday atmosphere – Polish flags were unfurled, girls kissed soldiers, housewives brought out tea, bakers bread, and there was enthusiasm about the wins on the first day. The electricity plant was captured, which enabled the hospitals and arms factories to continue. The Poles made a pledge to uphold the Geneva Convention with German Wehrmacht soldiers taken prisoner. They did not, however extend, this to the SS. The insurgents succeeded in capturing most of the Old Town.

Meanwhile in Zoliborz, Home Army soldiers were sent in, reinforced with volunteers from the countryside. Hospital and food distribution points were set up. Home Army canteens were set up with one meal a day guaranteed for their soldiers. The evenings were warm, windows were open with the occasional sound of a piano being played, or even the BBC playing over the loudspeakers. Maria would have witnessed this in Zoliborz where there was so much action. We later hear that Maria lived in the cellar of her building during the uprising, with the

Lubomierska family and their daughter Barbara, whom Jurek was later to meet in England. The women in the family all helped in the soup kitchens feeding the insurgent soldiers. Maria's nieces, Danuta and Marysia, who had bravely worked for the AK in the 'grey' guide division as couriers taking messages in secret across parts of the city, did what they could. We don't know what role Maria's brother-in-law, Olgierd played, given his officer status and extensive military training, but it was likely to have been substantial.

The Germans retaliated with reinforcements. On 3 August, Hitler's directive was to liquidate the population of Warsaw without regard to gender or age and to destroy the buildings without compromise. Advancing through the Wola district, the Nazis burned the houses and murdered en masse the civilian population. The Armoured Division advanced into the centre of the city, driving civilians in front of its tanks as a protective shield for the purpose of disassembling the barricades.

By 4 August 1944, there was no change with the centre of the city completely controlled by the insurgents (Davies, 2004). On the same day, at 8 am, General Bor signalled London to demand ammunition and anti-tank weapons. However, there were no communications from the Russians, no Soviet bombers had been seen over the city and no sound of gunfire from the advancing Russian army. London communicated Warsaw's need for immediate military help to Stalin, whose troops were approaching Warsaw on the Praga bank. On 2 August, a secret order from the Kremlin had reached Marshall Rokossovsky, the Commander-in-Chief of the Soviet 1st Byelorussian Front, to cease the advance on Warsaw. On 5 August, Stalin replied to the British:

> I think that the information which has been communicated to you by the Poles is greatly exaggerated and does not inspire confidence. The Home Army of the Poles consists of a few detachments, which they incorrectly call divisions. They have neither artillery nor aircraft nor tanks. I cannot imagine how such detachments can capture Warsaw, for the defence of which the Germans have produced four tank divisions, among them the Hermann Goering Division.
>
> Davies, 2004, p. 265

At 1 am on the night of 5 August, British Halifax planes flying from Italy made the first Allied air drops of weapons, awaited since the first hours of the uprising. They parachuted arms into Warsaw and, hitting the target, the Protestant cemetery in Wola. The same day, after midday, the Germans launched a counterattack in the Wola district. Artillery, heavy machine guns, battle tanks and air raids were used. At 2 pm SS troops stormed into the Wola Hospital, shot the staff of 60 and the 300 sick and wounded patients, a number of whom were wounded German soldiers. The next day over 30,000 Warsaw civilians were murdered and burned in the Wola suburb by the Germans. Women and children had been used as human shields by the Germans throughout the fighting, but the massacre at Wola involved the wholescale shooting of civilians. Early reports were immediately broadcast by the insurgent radios. Hospitals were then attacked by the German troops and nurses raped. The Marie Curie-Skłodowska institute of oncology in Ochota was attacked and the hospital of St Lazarus was set alight. This in itself has the status of a massacre. More Poles were killed at Wola and Ochota in one week in August 1944 than the 33,000 Ukrainian Jews at the infamous Babi Yar massacre (Davies, 2004).

On 12 August, Churchill telegraphed Stalin imploring his help. The following day Stalin stated he was dissociating himself totally from the Warsaw 'reckless adventure'. Stalin realised that the outbreak of the uprising and the continued fighting in Warsaw would compromise his plans for the future Soviet takeover of Poland. Entering Warsaw in August to aid the Poles would have been an easy move, but it would have meant tacitly agreeing to Poland's AK Home Army, and the London-based Government-in-Exile. Stalin washed his hands of both. On 20 August, President Roosevelt and Winston Churchill sent a joint appeal to Stalin urgently requesting supplies and munitions to be sent to the Poles in Warsaw. They pointed to world opinion focused on Warsaw, which would see the lack of action as abandonment. Stalin refused access by Allied planes to the airfields he controlled. Then on 24 August, the insurgent press reported the liberation of Paris. A rather sobering comparison. In France, when US General Patton reached the River Seine, the Parisians rose without communicating their plans to the Western Front's Commander-in-Chief, General Eisenhower. On de Gaulle's insistence, Eisenhower changed his original plan and allowed Leclerc's Free French division to liberate Paris after only one week of fighting. This was good news for Paris, but Warsaw was not given the same consideration. These two ancient capital cities had very different treatment. The Poles were magnanimous, applauding the Parisian liberation, broadcasting in French from their Radio Lightning: 'In the midst of our own struggle we greet the news of the liberation of Paris with profound and sincere joy' (Davies, 2004, p. 306). Warsaw's Old Town was in agony. General Bor-Komorowski recorded in his memoirs:

> Late in the evening I climbed for the last time to the observation point in the upper floor of the few remaining buildings. I wanted to have a last look at the Stare Miasto (Old Town). Everything was covered with clouds of smoke and dust of the bombardment. The fire was now less intense. At my feet lay the whole of Stare Miasto – or rather the ruins of what had been the city – enveloped in a pall of dust and smoke.
>
> Nothing but ruins remained of Warsaw's oldest buildings: the Church of Our Lady, the charred cupola of the Blessed Sacrament convent, the shell-furrowed roof of St. James's Church in Freta Street, and the remnants of the Cathedral tower. The market place was a confusion of craters and rubble. The destruction of Stare Miasto was the heavy price which Warsaw had paid to be able to hold on. The work of six centuries now lay in ruins.
>
> Bor-Komorowski, 2010, pp. 304–5

During the uprising, the only liaison between city sections and pockets of resistance was through the sewers. Around 3,000 insurgents were evacuated through the sewers from the Old Town, the city centre and Zoliborz, in such secrecy that on 2 September the Germans, unaware, continued heavy bombardment of what was now a completely deserted section. On 4 September, the British War Cabinet sent Stalin an urgent message complaining of his lack of cooperation, with the whole world watching the Warsaw Uprising and its outcome. Stalin delayed answering. Day by day, food supplies dwindled in Warsaw city centre. Zoliborz, where the hostilities started and were to end, had a quieter time in the middle of the uprising. Poles in the other districts joked: 'They play volleyball in Zoliborz!'

On 9 September, General Bor-Komorowski reported to London that Warsaw's endurance was almost at an end, with only a few days left of supplies and munitions. On 13 September, the Soviet troops reached the outskirts of Praga on the East bank of the Wisła. For the first time since the start of the uprising, the Warsaw population began to consider a German withdrawal from the city as a possibility. In the afternoon, the Germans blew up all four Warsaw bridges over the river. Soviet planes dropped fliers into the centre, to Zoliborz and Mokotow, with greetings and promises of airdrops of weapons, ammunition and food. On 15 September, fog on the British airfields prevented supply planes taking off. It was only at dawn on 18 September that the effort got under way; 110 Flying Fortress aircraft were sent with 73 Mustang fighters for escort. Of the dropped supplies, less than 20 per cent fell into the AK insurgent bands, the rest falling into German hands (Davies, 2004).

The battle to capture Praga over the river lasted four days. The Germans had reinforcements and improved defences. The Russians realised that fording the Wisła and taking the left bank would be costly in terms of lives lost, so they assigned the task to General Berling's Polish First Army, which had been formed in Russia and was fighting under Russian command. A total of three attempts were made, the last in the early afternoon of 19 September. Unsupported by planes or artillery, over two and a half thousand Polish soldiers of two battalions made it across to the west bank. Nearly all were killed by the German gunners. There was no Russian loss of life in the assault.

Meanwhile in England, the Ist Polish Independent Parachute Brigade stationed at Stamford, Lincolnshire, was to aid in the liberation of Warsaw. One or more of their number had already been dropped into the city to aid with the fighting. The training had been completed by spring of 1944, and expectations rose that the Brigade would be sent to Warsaw. When Britain told General Bor-Komorowski and the Polish troops that facilities for transferring the Brigade to Poland did not exist, troops in the Brigade went on hunger strike, supported by their commanding officers. But there was no mutiny, the troops stayed loyal. These troops were instead sent to Arnhem – a position circled by German Panzers where only one-fifth of the 20,000 survived (Davies, 2004).

Jurek, meanwhile, had gone through gruelling training in England, with his band of fellow Poles, to be dropped over Warsaw for the uprising. He recalled boarding the plane ready for take-off, but the operation was cancelled at the last minute. The Allies were not going to rescue Warsaw. Churchill countermanded the order to send the specially trained SOE Polish troops to their capital city. The response was despair and desolation as the men realised that Warsaw would be lost. For Jurek it was his home city, and he believed his wife, mother, aunts, uncles and cousins were there fighting as civilians, now with no hope of victory.

The last days of the uprising in Zoliborz

The district of Mokotow, just south of the centre, surrendered on 27 September. Insurgents continued to defend themselves in the city centre and Zoliborz, further north. The Germans launched the *Sternschnuppe* (Falling Star) operation aimed at the liquidation of the Kampinos Group in the forest. The next day a general offensive on Zoliborz began. The district, defended by about 1,500 insurgents, was attacked by over 8,000 soldiers, supported by armoured vehicles. On the 29th, a massive attack was carried out on Zoliborz. The following day General Bor-Komorowski radioed London to say[3] 'Our fight is breathing its last. All we need now is food. Only an immediate Soviet attack could save us. . . . We stand no chance'. He thanked all his AK soldiers for their efforts in the common cause. The same day at German headquarters, talks started in the morning with AK envoys over surrender in Zoliborz. The insurgents were ordered by their commanders to lay down their weapons. The Polish delegation obtained consent for a ceasefire from dawn to dusk so that the civilian population could leave the city. General Bor-Komorowski signed a treaty on the suspension of arms and capitulation of the AK Warsaw Corps. After 63 days of unremitting fighting, AK units prepared to leave the ruined capital.

The surrender took place at the Technical University of Warsaw where Jurek and Myszka had studied. The building was fire damaged but still standing. The six surrendering officers, among them General Bor-Komorowski, with three dressed in pre-war officer uniforms, all sang the Polish national anthem. The soldiers and civilians who lined the streets joined in the singing. Finally, Colonel Munter in full dress Polish uniform and wearing his medals from the 1920 Polish–Soviet war saluted them at the barricade. A Wiermacht German major saluted back and asked for the 'honour of taking them into captivity'. The Polish officers saluted in return. Then all senior officers were driven off to the railway station in a fleet of cars and put in a closely guarded first-class carriage. They were sent with hundreds of other Polish officers to a Bavarian Oflag prisoner of war camp (Davies, 2004).

Half a million civilians, women and children were marched after surrender to Pruszkow, outside Warsaw, to a transit camp. This included Jurek's family members Maria, Grazyna and Waclaw and their daughter Marysia, and others. The great Warsaw Uprising had ended in defeat. The capital of Poland, a city of over a million inhabitants, was completely destroyed – much of it during those 63 days, the rest following surrender. Hitler's orders were to liquidate the city and to create a lake in its place. Over 200,000 Poles, including 10,000 AK soldiers, perished in the two-month uprising. Another 20,000 soldiers were sent to German prisoner-of-war camps. The Germans had sustained casualties of 15,000 dead and 9,000 wounded.

According to the terms of the capitulation, Home Army soldiers who laid down arms were to be treated as prisoners of war following the Geneva Convention of July 1929. The same was to apply to soldiers in the Home Army taken prisoner during the fighting. Non-combatant personnel were also to be treated according to the Geneva Convention. No collective penalties were to be applied to the civilian population who remained in Warsaw during the fighting. These terms were never kept.

Wira, who was a teenage member of the AK, describes what happened to her:

> Around 5 October a few days after capitulation, I marched out of Warsaw with our army. We had been ordered to gather on the edge of Mokotow fields, a massive common area, and we made our way up there in small groups. At the gathering point, under the watchful eyes of the Germans who stood at the front, we organised ourselves into lines. Groups of civilians had come to watch and look for family members. . . .
>
> We lined up six abreast – boys of my Company with weapons in hand at the front and women soldiers, including me, behind them. There were about a hundred of us in my group and we were leaving within the newly formed 72nd Infantry regiment. We held our heads high, all wearing red-and-white armbands. I was still wearing my Wellington boots. I watched as the boys at the front started marching first; they laid down their arms in large containers before moving through Mokotow fields and we followed behind them. As we marched past the standing Germans, some of them saluted us. Later I heard that Heinrich Himmler had described the fighting during the Warsaw Uprising as the fiercest since the beginning of the war, comparable to the fighting in Stalingrad, which had been between two well-armed professional armies. We had lasted much longer than anyone could have expected. We had also treated German prisoners humanely. All this had apparently gained us a degree of respect among their soldiers.
>
> Szhlachetko, 2015, p. 99

Wira describes how she learned later that just before the Germans raised Warsaw to the ground, they loaded 33,000 railway wagons with furniture, paintings, artefacts, personal belongings and factory equipment to take to Germany. Only 15 per cent of Warsaw's buildings were still standing. She and her young soldier companions were marched 15 kilometres east to a combatant transit camp at Ozarow. German guards marched alongside them the whole way. The combatants and civilians were not allowed to speak. They were told they were heading for captivity in Germany. They finally reached Sandbostel camp, a prisoner-of-war camp that already housed Polish prisoners. Wira stayed there for three months, and was then moved to Oberlangen in the remote marshlands of north west Germany. Others from the uprising also arrived, with 1,700 female soldiers living in thirteen barracks. Food was scarce and all were hungry. Finally Red Cross parcels started arriving. Education was continued, with the prisoners who had been teachers setting up classes. The severely cold winter was brutal. Wira describes the setting as like a concentration camp. They were finally released in April 1945 at the end of the war, by the Polish 1st Armoured division.

What remained of Warsaw was seen at the end of October 1944 by Swedish journalist Ivar Versturlund. He reported that some fires were still burning. Smoke still lay over the ruins and here and there fires would flare up again. There were signs of fighting everywhere and at least five barricades still blocked each street. He confirmed that all civilians capable of work had been deported to labour camps, the remainder distributed throughout towns and villages in Poland. The deported people wore white armlets with red crosses. Their plight was indescribable. There were thousands of orphans and lost children. Only German personnel remained in Warsaw. The German officers accompanying Versterlund told him that German patrols shot at sight any civilian with no special permit to stay in the city. There were eight to ten such executions every day. The victims were called 'marauders'. On 17 January 1945 Soviet troops captured Warsaw, or the ruins of Warsaw. Correspondents from the British and American press stated they had never before seen such destruction:[4] 'Warsaw is a vanished city', they said. 'It looks as though the city has been buried for years and only just dug up. . . Warsaw, once one of the great capitals of Europe, was now just a historical expression.

Maria after the uprising

In a later letter, Maria gives the only clue to her experience during the uprising: she talks of Barbara (*Basia*) Lubienska, who Jurek met in England after the war and became a close family friend:

> I spent the whole of the uprising with the Lubienski family in a cellar. I remember Basia very well, I also know that her mother is no longer alive. She was a good woman, the best of mothers and a paragon of a Polish patriot. I've also seen the wedding photo of Basia.

In a later letter she says:

> I won't dwell on the years of German occupation because there aren't enough words of terror and despair, but all that was as nothing compared to the two months of August and September in 1944. On 1st October after capitulation, those who were left alive had to wander away looking for somewhere to live. I spent half a year in a village 25km from Krakow. On 23rd March 1945 I returned to Warsaw which was in ruins. By some miracle our house

survived although it was very badly damaged, without a roof, but it could be used. Of course I left with only the clothes I was wearing and returned to completely nothing . . .

After the uprising, Maria was evacuated alongside other citizens but separated from her family. Approaching her 60th year, she found herself alone in the south of Poland near Krakow. She made her way back home after the war ended, to her street in Zoliborz, to find her house still standing. She managed to enter her apartment and laid claim to one room while another family forcibly claimed the rest of the space. She did not know at this point what had happened to the rest of her family, who had been evacuated separately. The story is taken up by Marysia, her niece:

> Then I remember . . . our forced exit to a camp (Durchgangslager -Dulag) in Pruszkow also our removal from there, and our arrival in Kielce where we stayed with good people – without any possibility of contact with Aunt Maria. . . . The first one to come back to the ruins of Warsaw was my father at the beginning of 1945 – because he got a job in an institution, where he used to work a long time ago, the Treasury. Then it was situated in the huge buildings of the Railway headquarters in Praga (Praga suffered little damage compared to the terrible destruction of left bank Warsaw). The ministry also had accommodation at its disposal and gave rooms for the use of its workers, father as well . . .
>
> Father sent us a letter every week. In one he wrote that nearly all the buildings in Warsaw had been burnt or completely destroyed, but some buildings were saved by some miracle. So every Sunday he went round Warsaw to the places where family or friends had lived – in the hope that some building had survived and he would find someone close to him who had survived. And indeed – a miracle! In Zoliborz many houses still stood – with bullet holes and broken windows – but still standing. And in some the windows had even survived. He saw that one of the buildings that had survived was the one in which Aunt Maria had lived.
>
> Father wrote that he entered the courtyard and then went up the staircase. He saw a closed door. He knocked loudly with his fist. And a real miracle! He heard a woman's voice asking: 'Who's there?', 'It's me Wacław Ostrowski. I'm looking for Maria Czechowska'. The door opened. Aunt Maria stood on the threshold. Delighted – but at the same time fearful. She asked in a trembling voice: 'What about Grazyna? What about little Marysia?' She cheered up when she heard: 'They are in Kielce. They are living with respectable people.'
>
> She invited my father to come in: 'Come in, come in! We must talk! I'll make some tea and something to eat'. As she was reaching for matches and the spirit stove, with a kettle filled with water, my father said: 'There's no need, no need! Let's talk . . .'.

Writing in 2016, Marysia continues her remembered narrative:

> And it was during that talk that Aunt Maria said that in one of the rooms of her two room apartment, some strange people were living who were trying to obtain from the city authorities, 'the allocation of one of the rooms of a large bourgeois apartment to them'. Consequently she no longer had the same freedom of movement as before. However she had a lot of space in her room and would try to get a spare wide bed, so she invited Grazyna and little Marysia to spend the Easter holidays with her, on 1st April. My father thanked her and said that we would definitely visit her, but would stay with him at the Ministry's allocated accommodation. From my visit with my mother, to Warsaw, I clearly remember that we had to get off the train at the Dworzec Zachodni (station) because all the other stations in left bank Warsaw had been destroyed by the invaders.
>
> I also remember that passengers were taken from the station to the pontoon bridge across the Wisła, not by bus, but on lorries which had chairs and benches in them and you had to get on by movable wooden stairs. The roads had been cleared of rubble, so that you could drive along them quite easily, but on all sides we were surrounded by a nightmare: from piles of rubble to scorched and blackened walls with black holes for windows, then more and more of the same. . . . I remember my mother's and my journey by bicycle rickshaw (a vehicle that is having a renaissance in Warsaw after a long period of being forgotten, then it was commonly used, as it was during the occupation) to Aunt Maria in Zoliborz. Luckily she was at home and we talked warmly with her . . .

Aftermath

Hitler's reaction to the fall of Warsaw was one of elation and merciless revenge. The demolition of Warsaw proceeded methodically for more than three months while the Soviets watched impassively from over the river, making no move (Davies, 2004). The beautiful historic houses in Warsaw were destroyed, street by street, by German soldiers even at a time when their main army in the west was in the process of being defeated by the Allied invasion. If successful, the uprising and the resulting liberation of Warsaw would have allowed the Poles to establish political and military independence from Stalin, leading to the establishment of a non-communist Poland. Stalin understood this and sabotaged it.

The Yalta conference in February 1945 as the war ended was between the Big Three leaders – Roosevelt (USA), Churchill (Britain) and Stalin (USSR). They met to discuss war strategy and the post-war world. Shortly after the meeting opened, Stalin took a firm stance on the issue of Poland, citing that twice in the previous thirty years it had been used as an invasion corridor by the Germans. Furthermore, he stated that the Soviet Union would not return the land annexed from Poland in 1939, and that the nation could be compensated with land taken from Germany.

While these terms were non-negotiable, he was willing to agree to free elections in Poland. While the latter pleased Churchill, it soon became clear that Stalin had no intention of honouring this promise. As Stalin subsequently reneged on promises concerning Eastern Europe, Yalta was blamed for American and British ceding of Eastern Europe to the Soviets. Many came to view the meeting as a sell-out that greatly encouraged later Soviet expansion in eastern Europe and north east Asia. There were many recriminations after the fall of the Warsaw Uprising. Shockingly these were not regarding the lack of effective British or US support, or to the betraying Russians, but rather to the AK command in Warsaw. General Bor-Komorowski was hounded with such recriminations; and after the war, the Soviets held trials for sixteen underground leaders held in Moscow's Lubyanka prison (Davies, 2004).

There was further humiliation for the exiled Poles in Britain. In June 1946 London hosted the British Commonwealth, Empire and Allied victory parade. Fifty-one countries that had been at war with Germany before its surrender were invited to participate. An invitation was sent to the communist Polish government, who refused. No invitation was given to the 200,000 members of the Polish armed forces in the west who had fought under British command and were still in Britain. Protest was made by Churchill, senior figures in the RAF and a number of MPs, but the organisers were intent not to offend the Russians by inviting representatives of the Poles who had fought with the allies. Poland therefore had no representation at the victory parade despite its steadfast, sacrificial and crucial support of the Allied cause.

Discussion

I have chosen to focus in this chapter on Warsaw during the 63 days of the uprising, to reflect the experience of my grandmother Maria and the area where she lived. The events of those two months seem sufficiently significant to me to merit a chapter, even though this narrative as a whole covers over a hundred years. My grandmother, Maria survived the onslaught in her flat in Zoliborz. This was by no means an area free of fighting – the beginning and the end of the uprising took place there, but neither was it the worst location and didn't suffer, for example, the type of massacre that befell the Wola district. She lived alone, although she had close family and friends nearby. Finally she was evacuated from the city, not knowing whether any of her family were still alive. She admits to feeling terror. She had no knowledge of whether her son, Jurek was living. Later she says she had a Mass celebrated for Jurek every day. Her religious belief was very strong and was no doubt an element of her resilience. She had no way of knowing that Jurek had been training to come and help Warsaw in its uprising, but that he had never been sent. The themes of this chapter are summarised in Figure 7.1.

Jurek was able to adapt to subterfuge. In this period he was learning how to be a highly skilled agent behind enemy lines, going through very rigorous training. In the final event he did not use this training. This was very frustrating for him

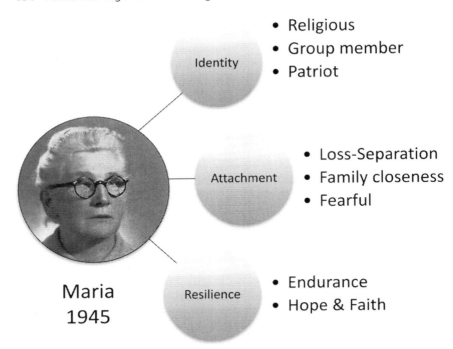

FIGURE 7.1 Summary of the themes in Chapter 7

and afterwards he felt disappointment that he could not be the hero his father had been. However, if he had been dropped on Warsaw as planned he would almost certainly have been killed and then this story would not have been written. So resilience also includes chance happenings and is dependent sometimes on random decisions made by governments.

Resilience also includes perseverance and optimism. The Warsaw citizens had both. Despite extreme privation, they managed to maintain hope and to direct their actions towards the survival of their identity, community and culture. During the 66-day uprising, the ritual activities of life were continued including weddings, christenings, masses and funerals. These were all self-affirming. It is unlikely that they would have had more chance of survival if they had acquiesced to the German army. For many, religion was key. It gave them hope of a future, whether in this life or the next. Religious ritual was ongoing and a comfort.

By implication, attachment behaviour was also high in the city. There are numerous stories made public of families protecting each other, being separated but then reuniting and being mourned when lost. Family members kept their clandestine behaviour with the AK secret from each other, to protect them, but then resistance eventually became so widespread that everyone was involved. Attachment was one of the most important aspects of life, often more so than food and shelter. For Maria she had her siblings, in-laws and nieces near at hand, as well as friends. For Jurek the attachments were close friends and fellow combatants, some of whom had come with him from Poland to France, and at least one who was with him in SOE. He was however, separated from his two closest attachments, his mother and his wife, and had no recent news of them. His volunteering for active duty in SOE for the campaign to help Warsaw was also a measure of his attachment not only to them but to his city.

On the world stage, if there was shame attached to the Allied command for their treatment of Poland, and despite Churchill's personal regret, it was not publicly voiced. There was still both fear and admiration for Soviet Russia. Russian propaganda deflected shame onto the Warsaw population themselves. This deflection of blame onto a victim is familiar in psychological literature. It occurs when the public and institutions accept perpetrator justification for hostile or criminal actions, and where there is failure to recognise and empathise with victim/survivor experience. Effectively the public and authorities side with the perpetrator and believe the biased account. This occurs particularly in the arena of sexual offences and domestic violence (Fugate, Landis, Riordan, Naureckas and Engel, 2005). Victims can become re-traumatised by their loss of reputation and diminished identity. So in the aftermath of the Allied victory, the Polish action in starting the Warsaw Uprising was questioned, with Bor-Komorowski made to justify his actions and implications of blame attached to the Warsaw population for their resistance. In fact they had little choice – the Germans would have destroyed them and their city regardless. It was a grand gesture, the gains being moral standing, cohesive community and psychological resilience, even in defeat.

Curiously, the greatest admiration for the Polish resistance in Warsaw was expressed by the Nazi oppressors. When the civilians, women, teenagers and children capitulated, and were made to march out of the city, German soldiers and officers saluted them. There was recognition that this was the largest and best organised civilian defence action on record. One can't help but wonder what the regular Wiermaht soldier felt about this merciless attack on civilians. The German soldiers would have had to obey their command, and were even terrorised by the SS on their own side into acting cruelly. They could hardly have seen such actions as honourable. Trauma can be experienced both by victim and perpetrator. The German soldiers were forced into inhumane actions by the SS police who were placed in each unit, using terror to force the soldiers to fight. Many of them committed suicide. Diary entries found on a German soldier taken prisoner (Kurt Heller) by the Home Army during the fighting included the following, reported by General Bor-Komorowski, as published in one of the information bulletins sent to London. The German soldier with his comrades was cut off from his main division:

> 16.8 Terrible hunger. At night we are terrified. When first stars appear, think of home, wife and my boy who is buried somewhere near Stettin. Can't take it all in. Now am in same position.

> 17.8 Poles tried to smoke us out by fire and bottles of petrol. More men lost their nerve and committed suicide. Frightful smell from corpses in the street.

> 18.8 Completely cut-off from the outside world.
>
> 19.8 No hope of relief. Surrounded by Poles. Who will be next for the mass grave down the courtyard?
>
> Bor-Komorowski, 2010, p. 278

Davis quotes another young German officer writing home to his parents on 5 October 1944, and risking severe punishment in stating his views:

> The capitulation was undoubtedly one of the most extraordinary things you can imagine. The reality of it puts all drama, all tragedy into shade. They came out with fully deserved honours after true heroism in battle. In truth they fought better than we did. What we can learn from it is the following; 1) that nothing sensible can come from this sort of subjugation of an entire nation. Sad but true? 2) we don't have a monopoly on fortitude, spirit, patriotism, and sacrifice (we can't take the Poles' credit away from them). 3) that a city can defend itself for months on end, with much heavier losses on the attacker's side ... and much can be learned from this by a neutral observer. 4) That although a fighting spirit and a pure and courageous approach can achieve a great deal, in the end this spirit will always succumb to material advantage. Can history ever be just? Not here. However strong the idea of nationhood, the fact of power will always overwhelm it.
>
> Davies, 2004, p. 481

The British press were seeking to come to terms with the capitulation in Warsaw. Many were shocked into making bold statements of support after the restraint they had been under during the uprising. They were offended by the denunciation of General Bor-Komorowski, led by the Soviet Committee who had labelled him a criminal. They reiterated that the British and American governments recognised him and the uprising army as a combatant force protected by the Allies (Davies, 2004). George Orwell upheld this view, supporting the Poles against the Russian propaganda in *The Tribune*, 1 September 1944:

> It is not my primary job to discuss the details of contemporary politics, but this week there is something that cries out to be said. Since, it seems, nobody else will do so, I want to protest against the mean and cowardly attitude adopted by the British press towards the recent rising in Warsaw. As soon as the news of the rising broke, the *News Chronicle* and kindred papers adopted a markedly disapproving attitude. One was left with the general impression that the Poles deserved to have their bottoms smacked for doing what all the Allied wirelesses had been urging them to do for years past, and that they would not be given and did not deserve to be given any help from outside. A few papers tentatively suggested that arms and supplies might be dropped by the Anglo-Americans, a thousand miles away: no one, so far as I know, suggested that this might be done by the Russians, perhaps twenty

miles away. The *New Statesman*, in its issue of 18 August, even went so far as to doubt whether appreciable help could be given from the air in such circumstances. All or nearly all the papers of the Left were full of blame for the *émigré* London Government which had 'prematurely' ordered its followers to rise when the Red army was at the gates. . . . Now, I know nothing of Polish affairs, and even if I had the power to do so I would not intervene in the struggle between the London Polish Government and the Moscow National Committee of Liberation. What I am concerned with is the attitude of the British intelligentsia, who cannot raise between them one single voice to question what they believe to be Russian policy, no matter what turn it takes, and in this case have had the unheard-of meanness to hint that our bombers ought not to be sent to the aid of our comrades fighting in Warsaw. . . . The Russians are powerful in Eastern Europe, we are not: therefore we must not oppose them. This involves the principle, of its nature alien to Socialism, that you must not protest against an evil which you cannot prevent.[5]

The Uprising Museum in Warsaw provides an excellent detailed and personal exposition of the uprising. This has only been in existence since 2014, the 60th anniversary.[6] Under communism, any historical account of this momentous event was forbidden. The official account was that those involved were 'capitalist enemies of the state'. The Poles had to hold on to their memories in secret until the Berlin wall tumbled, and they were able to express them again. There is black-and-white footage of the uprising, the film sent by the Allies to record events. The people shown – under-nourished, living amongst the rubble and ill-equipped – nevertheless face the camera with bright eyes and smiles. Despite ragged clothing, they have taken the trouble to dress, tidy their hair and clean their faces, and clearly take pride in their resistance with immense community spirit. Their optimism is boundless. They held marriages and funerals and regular Catholic masses during the uprising. They understood the lessons of psychological resilience. This does not necessarily save lives, but it gives lives meaning and purpose. They have dignity and this reinforces their identity. Like the Polish Jews, two years earlier, they made a collective decision not to go as 'lambs to the slaughter' but to end in a final leonine roar. They had no illusions about their fate with the Germans. Whether they resisted or not it was death and denigration, but the Warsaw population kept buoyant under duress. The films are compulsive but hard viewing. The museum deals with individuals and their heroic actions. The many diaries and photographs kept to record events are highlighted with individual vignettes and case studies. This makes it very real for the young Poles and children three generations and nearly 70 years after these events, who visit in large numbers. The story survives.

Notes

1 www.bbc.co.uk/history/ww2peopleswar/stories/31/a2331631.shtml
2 www.bbc.co.uk/history/worldwars/wwtwo/soe_01.shtml
3 http://info-poland.buffalo.edu/classroom/uprising.html

4 https://search.warwick.ac.uk/website?source=http%3A%2F%2Fwww2.warwick.ac.uk%2Fservices%2Flibrary%2Fmrc%2Fstudying%2Fdocs%2F&q=292–943.8–1-b
5 http://alexpeak.com/twr/trriw/
6 www.1944.pl/en

SECTION III
England
The third generation

This, the third section, represents Erikson's final stages of development (Figure 8.1) and introduces the third generation of the family. This takes place largely in England. It describes Jurek and Christine meeting, marrying and bringing up their family of four daughters in the UK. It also describes Maria coming to England to live and being reunited with her son and meeting her young grandchildren

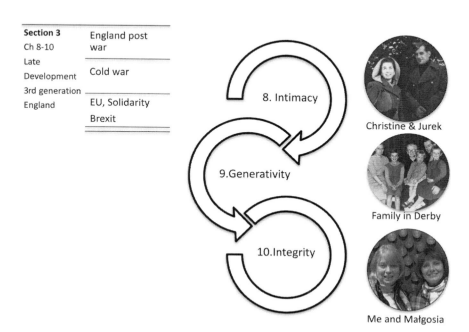

FIGURE 8.1 Erikson's final stages of development

160 England: the third generation

(Figures 8.2 to 8.6). It takes the narrative up to date, discovering new links with Polish cousins, aunt and nephews, and with Poland itself, now a full member of the EU. It covers the more positive aspects of intimacy through happy marriage, generativity in terms of a new family growing and integration in terms of coming to terms with the full impact of tracing family history on later members. There is none of the war experience of the prior sections, apart from that of the Cold War with the Soviet Union – otherwise a period of peace.

Photographs section 2

FIGURE 8.2
Stas Leinweber, 1939

FIGURE 8.3
Myszka, 1942

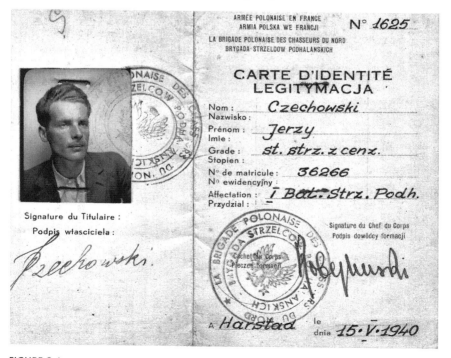

FIGURE 8.4
Jurek mobilised to the French army, May 1940

FIGURE 8.5
Jurek (left) in the French army, 1940

FIGURE 8.6 Jurek's student card, Grenoble, 1941

K.V.2 7H7ILiusa

POLISH ARMY

SOLDIER'S NAME AND DESCRIPTION

708617

Name (in Capitals) BRONISZ

Christian Names (in full) ANDRZEJ

Date of Birth 16.10.1916

Place of Birth: Parish Płock; In or near the town of Płock; In the county of Poland

Trade on Enlistment urzędnik państw. civil servant

Nationality of Father at birth / Nationality of Mother at birth: Polish

Religious denomination R.C.

Photographed Number 31939/AP/108-I

Signature of Soldier Bronisz Andrzej

Date

DESCRIPTION ON ENLISTMENT

Height 1,75 ft. ins. Weight 82 Lbs.

Maximum Chest ins. Complexion fair

Eyes c. brown Hair d. blond

Distinctive Marks and Minor Defects

31939/AP

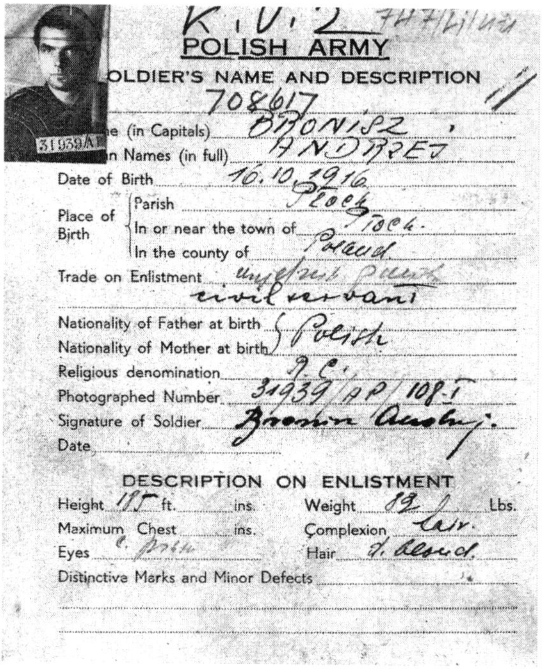

FIGURE 8.7
Jurek in SOE as A. Bronisz, 1944

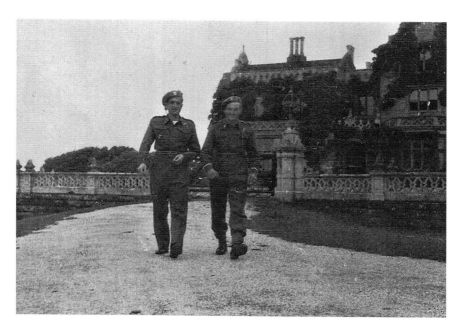

FIGURE 8.8
Jurek and Jonny, SOE training, 1944

8

INTIMACY

Marriage and migration (1945–50)

> The richest and fullest lives attempt to achieve an inner balance between three realms: work, love and play.
>
> Erik Erikson

Introduction

This chapter addresses the positive aspects of Erikson's adult life stage of 'Intimacy'. The associated virtue is 'love'. This section gives the more positive parallel to the isolation described in the last chapter. Jurek finds a safe haven in England, having joined the Royal Air Force in England after the fall of Warsaw, leaving SOE which then disbanded. He remained in the RAF until two years after the war, having met and fell in love with Christine. He regains contact with his mother, Maria in Warsaw, each learning the other is safe. It is a period of consolidation and rejuvenation after the trauma and loss of the earlier phase. However, the earlier period casts its shadow: it is in this period that the loss of Myszka is confirmed and mourned. Whilst it is known that Stas is missing, the Polish community learn of the massacre at Katyn even though the details of his death are not known publicly for decades. In terms of identity, the issues are around migration, conflicts about returning home and barriers to integration. There is no longer subterfuge needed given times of peace, but some level of cultural camouflage is required for the Polish community in Britain given the Soviet threat and reach.

In terms of the Polish nation, it also represents a period of consolidation and rebuilding, the country finds itself in a bleak period of isolation. There is no international recognition of the Polish contribution in defeating fascism. There is no apology or compensation for its massive losses from the German or Soviet authorities, nor aid to rebuild its economy from the USA. Poland finds itself in submission to the Soviet regime, losing freedom of expression, freedom of travel and trust in authority or government institutions. It has no safe haven, it finds itself rather a 'hazardous' haven. And yet, as before, the nation proves capable of biding its time, building itself up and looking for a future opportunity for rejuvenation, which it eventually finds with its Western European partners.

Post-war Europe

After the jubilation of the Victory in Europe (VE) Day celebrations, Europe was left in poverty with major destruction of buildings and infrastructure. Cities and factories had been bombed, transport links had been severed and agricultural production disrupted. Populations had been moved, or destroyed, and a tremendous amount of capital had been spent on weapons and related products. The continent was wrecked. The Lend-Lease Act of March 1941, the principal means for providing US military aid to foreign nations in the war, was suddenly stopped in September 1945. The British government pleaded for help and secured a low-interest $3.75 billion loan from the USA. However, the cost of rebuilding the country necessitated austerity at home. The Marshall Plan, a massive programme of aid from the USA to sixteen western and southern European countries, was aimed at helping economic renewal. Britain was required to modernise its business practices and remove trade barriers from 1948 (Kynaston, 2008). The following year saw the NATO military alliance formed between the UK and USA, along with Canada and nine western European states, to form a counterweight to Soviet armies in central and eastern Europe. Its premise was solidarity – an armed attack against any one member was an attack against them all and would provoke reprisals.

There was also the issue of German debt. The repayable amount was reduced to about 15 billion marks, and stretched out over 30 years. Repayments were only due while West Germany ran a trade surplus, and limited to 3 per cent of export earnings. This gave Germany's creditors a powerful incentive to import German goods, and assist reconstruction. The agreement significantly contributed to the growth of the post-war German economy. The question of German reparations after World War II, raised at the Yalta Conference in February 1945, had delegates agreeing on compensation in goods to the Allies. German reparations were obtained from the four occupation zones held by the British, French, American and Russians. The Western zones were merged in 1949 to form the Federal Republic of Germany (West Germany), and the Soviet zone became a separate country (DDR or East Germany). No country was to draw from other than its own area. However, the Soviet Union was to receive, in addition to reparations from the eastern zone, 10 per cent of the industrial equipment removed from the western zones plus an additional 15 per cent that the Soviets would pay for with food, coal and other products (Seathoff, 2009).

To facilitate the economy after the war, certain categories of victims of Nazism were excluded from the compensation otherwise given by the German Government. These included forced or slave labourers from the war period, most of whom were Polish. Where Poles were due compensation, for example, as victims of concentration camps, these were only allocated directly to the Soviet Union. Most were subsumed under the communist Comecon framework, with little benefit directly to Poland. Under Soviet pressure in 1953, the new People's Republic of Poland renounced its right to further claims of reparations. So again, Poland was recognised neither as a victor (for its significant role in aiding the Allies) nor a victim (for its substantial numbers lost in concentration camps or in slave labour). This was another blow to national identity. The issue has been raised again in recent years, post-communism, but Poles gave up any claim for reparations in 2004.[1] In terms of land mass, Poland was given the western territories and East Prussia from Germany, but lost the eastern Polesie region to Soviet Russia including the sites of the family estates of the Czechowski and Rodziewicz families.

By 1948 a fully Stalinist regime was established in Poland. All freedom of speech was denied, no discussion was allowed of the wartime alliance with the Western powers, and no one was allowed to speak well of the Warsaw Uprising, nor ill of the communist regime (Davies, 2004). The view of history proscribed that Soviet Russia had defeated the German Nazis single-handedly, democracy was to be replaced by 'dictatorship of the proletariat' and that the ruling party was beyond criticism. Anyone of a different view was considered dangerous and at the mercy of the state. Even in private, people learned to speak with caution – police informers were widespread. Children were taught in Soviet-style schools where denouncing friends and parents was formally considered admirable, ironically mimicking the fascist Hitler Youth (Figes, 2007). Yet the communist reputation as a repressive system was never the target for as much criticism and moral repugnance as fascism had been, and Stalin never reviled like Hitler (Davies, 2004).

Britain and Poles post-war

In Britain the end of the war saw a landslide victory for Clement Attlee and the Labour Party, elected on a manifesto of greater social justice with policies including a new National Health Service, an expansion of low-cost council housing and nationalisation of the major industries. But these policies were expensive, creating the Age of Austerity with pre-war levels of prosperity not returning until the 1950s (Kynaston, 2008). Rationing and conscription continued into the post-war years, with one of the worst winters on record in 1946–7. Morale was boosted by a royal wedding, the marriage of Princess Elizabeth in 1947, and by the Summer Olympics in London 1948, followed by the Festival of Britain in 1951. Reconstruction in London had begun but with little funding for it. London was a city in desperate need of large-scale rebuilding due to the Blitz bombing, with architects and planners seeing the opportunity for remodelling the city, reorganising the population and rejuvenation.[2]

At the end of the war, many of the Poles who had come to England as political exiles to fight for the Allies, stayed in the UK. In order to ease the transition from a Polish military environment to British civilian life, a corps of the British Army named the Polish Resettlement Corps (PRC) was created, with those Poles wishing to stay in the UK allowed to enlist for the period of their demobilisation. The PRC was formed in 1946 and was disbanded after fulfilling its purpose in 1949. Most Poles wanted to go home to their families, and their life before the war, but there were a number of barriers. The main one was the Stalinist communist government in Poland. It was widely known in the community that the Soviets had killed many Polish citizens during the war. For example, most knew about the Katyn massacre, but also about Russian betrayal in the Warsaw Uprising. Also, there were trials and executions of pro-democracy Poles after the war, and leaders of the Home Army were persecuted, imprisoned, sent to Siberia or brutally murdered (Davies, 2004). There were real risks to going back to Poland. The result was the 'Polish Resettlement Act 1947', the UK's first mass immigration law. Large numbers of Poles stayed, but many also emigrated to the Commonwealth, forming large Polish Canadian, American and Australian communities.

In the 1951 UK Census, some 162,339 UK residents had Poland listed as their place of birth. The communities were set up by former members of the PRC in the late 1940s and early 1950s. In 1946 the Ex-combatants Association was formed to work for the welfare of those who had stayed in Britain. Jurek was closely involved in setting up a Polish community organisation in Derby, where he eventually settled with his family. This was an ex-airmen's club, part of a large network over the UK, centralised in London. In different cities in Britain, around the hub of a Polish church Polish social clubs, cultural centres and a variety of adult and youth organisations grew up. The aim of these organisations was to ensure a continuation of Polish language, culture and heritage, as well as offering services for the families and children of the ex-PRC members.

The Polish community in Britain did not formally recognise the communist Polish government, so a Polish Government in Exile was formed, a continuation of the wartime organisation. It took up residence in Eaton Square, London. General Bor-Komorowski, who had reached London in May 1945, was made Commander-in-Chief for a year. He is remembered as a quiet, polite and extremely modest man whose main concerns post-war were for his young family and the Home Army Association, of which he was president. Bor-Komorowski had managed to survive German captivity to be handed over to the Americans at Innsbruck in May 1945. He had been protected by an SS cavalry officer, Hermann Fegelein, with whom he had been friends before the war on the international horse-riding circuits. Bor-Komorowski spent the rest of his life in London, where he played an active role in Polish *émigré* circles. He met Jurek and agreed to speak to the community at the Polish club in Derby. He died in London aged 71 from a heart attack on 24 August 1966. He was buried in Gunnersbury cemetery, Ealing, and nearly thirty years later, in 1994, his ashes were re-buried in Powązki Military Cemetery in Warsaw with full military honours, including the award of the Virtuti Militari medal.

General Anders took over as Commander-in-Chief, based in London. He has appeared little in this narrative, because he was not directly connected to Warsaw. However, he was key to Polish armed forces fighting for the British in Italy, and for the rescue of hundreds of thousands of Polish families forced into Siberian exile by the Russians when they invaded Poland (Davies, 2015). As the commander of the largest field formation in the Polish Army in the West, Anders readily accepted his political role after the war. He was considered a hero by the Allies for his overseeing of the victory at Monte Casino in Italy. He had a dramatic history. A cavalry officer in a Russian Tsarist regiment during the First World War, he commanded a force during the Second World War which, over three years, made an epic 9,000-mile journey through Siberia, central Asia, the Middle East and Africa, eventually to confront the Germans in Italy for one of the most crucial battles of the war (Davies, 2015). Anders was accused by the provisional communist government in Warsaw in 1946 of crimes against Poland, and his citizenship revoked. He then played an important role in the Government in Exile, and died in London in 1970. He was buried alongside his soldiers in the Polish cemetery at Monte Casino, Italy.

The Polish Embassy in Portland Place, London, was used by communist diplomats from the new Polish state in 1945. During the period of the Cold War they served to obfuscate what was happening in Poland, to mount surveillance on the exiled community and persuade as many as possible to go home. As the Cold War intensified, espionage became a central feature. The Soviets had successfully infiltrated the top of British Intelligence through the 'Cambridge Five' – Philby, Burgess, Maclean, Blunt and Cairncross – who were sending British secrets directly to Moscow. Another character, Tabor, a Pole who had been active in the wartime Government in Exile, also turned spy on the Polish community.

Wira, active as a teenage soldier in the Warsaw Uprising, settled in London after the war. Her view was that the British media post-war was very much in favour of Stalin and the press branded the Poles remaining in Britain as 'fascist', an offensive term they coined for anti-communists. She describes her experience in the Polish community:

> For many years, every correspondence with Poland was read by the communist authorities and letters were vetted and censured. Families in Poland were even coerced into pressing relatives abroad for information that could be used to undermine the Capitalist West. People tried to send informative books and news from England but little got through. High ranking officials and officers, like General Anders and General Maczek, particularly, were closely observed, branded fascists and publicly undermined. General Anders' Polish citizenship was withdrawn along with that of many of his senior officers.
> Szhlachetko, 2015, p. 132

Life for the Poles who settled in Britain was difficult, in competition for jobs and accommodation. In subsequent years many were to buy their own properties at low, post-war prices and rent rooms out to their fellow Poles. Despite labour shortages, the trades unions put up barriers to Poles getting certain jobs and there were reports of strikes because firms had hired Polish workers. The unions were very vociferous, insisting Poles should return to Poland. Wira describes difficulties getting accommodation, with signs saying 'rooms to rent, no Poles'. The British population was indifferent or hostile. The Poles came to believe their whole wartime contribution had been forgotten. However, Wira also notes that respect for the Poles who settled in England grew with the subsequent decades. Their reputation for hard work and honesty, being law abiding and contributing to society, eventually had impact. They were self-sufficient as a community, organised their own support systems and did not claim any welfare payments.

Warsaw, 1945

If life in London was difficult post-war, it was as nothing compared to the Warsaw experience. In January 1945, Warsaw was a sea of ruins. There was complete devastation of the city, home to over one million people before the war. The devastation of Warsaw had occurred throughout the war. Whatever was left was methodically looted and then razed to the ground by German action. The population was evacuated away from the city and district. During 1945 the citizens started to return and began to live amongst the rubble. The city needed rebuilding.

Post-war, the new communist authorities considered moving the capital to another Polish city, the preferred choice being Łódź, which had most of its buildings still standing. One idea was to leave Warsaw as a landscape of ruins, a war memorial for future generations.[3] The losses in urban architecture of Warsaw at the beginning of 1945 were estimated at around 84 per cent, with industrial infrastructure and historic monuments destroyed at 90 per cent and residential buildings at 72 per cent. All this made the rebuilding of Warsaw seem highly unlikely. However, demand came from its citizens. Starting in January 1945, there was a steady influx of people to the city, former residents as well as displaced persons, who flocked into the frozen ruins. They virtually started the reconstruction process on their own. On 3 February 1945, the National Council passed a resolution that called for the rebuilding of the capital. A week later the Office for the Reconstruction of the Capital (BOS) was formed.

With BOS, one of the most ambitious projects in history was initiated. No society had ever attempted to reconstruct the monuments and houses of a war-torn city, not least a capital city, on such a scale. The decision to do so was in stark contrast with the prevailing anti-conservation doctrine of the times elsewhere in Europe. The reconstruction of Warsaw followed its own opposite tactic and a full reconstruction of whole buildings and monuments was undertaken, based only on existing documentation (hidden during the war), memory and cultural resources like the detailed drawings of Warsaw by Caneletto. It also meant that a large part of the rebuilt city would be a replica. Whilst the initial range of the reconstruction proposed was eventually drastically reduced, huge parts of the Old Town and the Royal Route were meticulously reconstructed. This pioneering and unique effort of reconstruction was given international recognition in 1980, when Warsaw's Old Town was selected as part of UNESCO's World Cultural Heritage list (Szypowska and Szypowski, 2005). In 2011, the Archives of BOS were recognised as one of the most valuable examples of human documental heritage, appearing on the 'Memory of the World' list.[4]

The rebuilding of Warsaw happened despite the economic devastation of the country by war. Poland was not part of the American Marshall Plan aid, which funded German rehabilitation. This stopped at the frontier with East Germany. The communist Soviet empire refused such funds on Poland's behalf. In fact, the sole source of financing the rebuilding was through donations made by the people. Established in 1945, a social rebuilding fund (SFOS) was the only legitimate state institution to deal with financing the reconstruction effort. It was not dissolved until 1965. Thus Warsaw was truly rebuilt by the whole nation, with donations and workers coming from all around Poland, much of it volunteer work. The widespread enthusiasm, caught on newsreels from the period, cannot be dismissed as communist propaganda. To facilitate the reconstruction effort the communist regime introduced Bierut's Law in November 1945, nationalising all land and buildings within the pre-war borders of Warsaw. Without it, the rebuilding of the capital on this scale would have been impossible.

Maria in post-war Warsaw

We next hear of Maria from letters dated 1946. She returned to Warsaw early in 1945 after being evacuated to south Poland. At this point she still knew nothing of Jurek's situation, having last heard from him by letter in August 1942 from France, although she managed to get some information of him in 1943. During the Warsaw Uprising and its aftermath she had had no contact. In January 1946 she writes to someone she knows who might have information, and the letter survives:

> Dear Sir,
>
> On the recommendation of Mrs. J. Leonowicz, your Mother, I would earnestly like to ask you if could let me know whether you have any news about the fate of my son, Jerzy Tadeusz Czechowski, born 16.10.1913. The last communication I had from him was on 10.8.1942. In Spring 1943, thanks to your information, I knew that he was alive and well, since then there has been no news. Please forgive me if I am causing you any inconvenience, even more so that you yourself are suffering, but the torments of uncertainty, which I am undergoing because of the lack of information about my only son, may explain my boldness. I will be everlastingly grateful for any, even the most trivial, information. I thank you in anticipation.
>
> I enclose my most sincere wishes for your return to health.
>
> With respect, Maria Czechowska

At the end of February 1946 she finally hears he is alive and has his address in England – on receiving a letter from him on 14 February, she replies:

My Dear Son, Dearest Jurek!

I'm beginning my letter with your words: today I lived through the most beautiful day of my life. For nearly four years I haven't had a single word from you. I won't dwell on the years of German occupation because there aren't enough words of terror and despair. . . .[5]

Uncle (Olgierd) Czechowski's family were even worse off because their villa had been burnt. Myszka, your wife, was sent to Auschwitz in October 1943 and from that time there has been no news of her. From our closer family, Leszek, Mirek's brother, died in action in 1939 and Uncle Janek's (Jan's) two sons Włodek and Jurek were shot in the forest. Also, no signs of life from Stas, the son of Aunt Julia and Walek. The rest of the family are alive and managing somehow. I have already been working in an office for three months, I earn enough for a very modest living. What else can I expect in these very difficult post-war times, especially in this city of ruins? I am having some trouble with my hearing which I lost during the war; partly while living in an unheated apartment when I developed chronic catarrh in my ears and finally in September 1944 from a blow. This disability gives me a lot of trouble with my office work, but somehow they still tolerate me.

You write that there are great problems with returning home. I think you should wait patiently until travel becomes easier. I live in just one room; the one facing the street. The rest of the dwelling has been taken over by the family of a minor railway official. It consists of five people who even before my return, took over the whole part of the house that hadn't been devastated. I had to repair the room facing the street, that had been ruined during the Uprising, before I could move in on 8th July 1945. For three months I had to take advantage of the hospitality of neighbours.

Uncle Ostrowski's (Grazyna's) family have been allocated an apartment (68 Filtrowa Street). They are living with me and in a couple of weeks they want to leave me. Marysia is being educated at Fielcach with the Nazareth Sisters, she is the best pupil in the school. I must end my first letter to you in yet again changed conditions. I would so like to write and write about many things at length. I ask but one thing of you, my dear son: be of good cheer, believe in Providence, throw yourself completely on God's mercy and it will lead you to a happy ending. For the whole year, every day, a Mass is celebrated for your intentions and not a day passes without my praying for you. I hope that by the end of this year we can be together. If you have a lot of time, learn languages because this will give you a living in the future. There is a lack of educated bookkeepers. I bless you my dear child and commend you to the care of Mother Mary and hug you to my heart like I used to when you were tiny and it was good for you to be with me. The Ostrowski family send best wishes and hugs.

Kisses for your darling head, your Mother.

PS Skilled workers in all spheres are very much needed but as usual you have to have contacts It would be best to return, not individually but in a larger group of repatriates.

Maria seems not to have heard back from Jurek. She writes again on 5 April 1946:

My dearest Son,

Have you received the letter I wrote in reply to your letter of 14.2? Has nothing changed and are the possibilities for returning to this country still so difficult to find? I can understand your nostalgia, it is better to be in your own home even if it is poor rather than being the poor relation staying with someone rich. This year your name day (Saint's Day) occurs at the same time as the Easter holidays, so for both these reasons I am sending you, my dearest son, wishes for God's mercies, for only in their light will you find happiness and peace. Will I ever attain the happiness of wishing you this in person and being together? Do you think you might be able to find out something about the fate of Walus, Stas, or their mother? Nothing has been known about them for seven years. Also let me know what is happening with our relative T. Okszyc? What he has been doing since leaving France and now?

On 6th April the Ostrowki's are moving to a tied flat they have been allocated, so I will be left on my own. I have become strangely defenceless in facing life and I am more frightened of people than of disasters. At home I have a hostile environment, since they (other tenants) would like to get rid of me so they can take over the whole premises. Now I am old I don't know how to fight or defend myself. Work at the office tires me and I return home every day with a headache. I am so afraid that you didn't receive my first letter and the news that I communicated hasn't reached you. If communication with this country has not been made difficult, then write without waiting for my replies since some letters may be lost on the way. You probably know that your flat was plundered in 1939 and the furniture was sold. Not even the smallest keepsake was left. Whereas my flat was robbed of everything after the Warsaw Uprising. So we are both very poor. Write about your health, what you look like, and your frame of mind. I think that if you came back to the country you would be able to find a job. I send you hugs and kisses and commend you to God's protection.

Your Loving Mother, Maria

Maria receives a return letter from Jurek, but he has not received her latest letter. She writes again on 3 May 1946:

My Dear Only Son,

Yesterday I received a second letter from you dated 15/4 it took 17 days to arrive. I wrote to you for the third time on 5th April. It should reach you during holiday time, on your name day. I spent the holiday alone like so many previously – the sort of Easter we used to have during my childhood at my parents' house – we will never see again. The packages which you mentioned, I haven't yet received, so wait before you send any more. If they reach me I will let you know. I'd like to know beforehand what they contain, so that I can complain if there is anything missing. This happens quite often. At the moment I have such modest requirements and need so little that I don't want you to bankrupt yourself, my dear son. While I still have this job, I am managing somehow. As for my hearing, there is probably no hope of a cure. Firstly because of the cold in unheated apartments (seven winters already) I had chronic catarrh in my ears and finally I lost my hearing during the Uprising when I was hit by a so called '*szafa*'. The worst thing under the sun. It is a missile of compressed air. This was the only thing I was afraid of during the war and of getting into the hands of the Germans. Maybe there are hearing aids to help the hard of hearing, but there are no such luxuries here. I am earning about 3,000 złoty a month. To keep oneself in the most modest manner costs a minimum of 150 złoty daily. This is not enough for clothes or shoes. We are partly helped by UNRRA. I received one parcel for Christmas, one for Easter and some material for a coat. From 1 December I have been working in the head office, in accounts. Before, for eight months, I worked in a workers' canteen, peeling potatoes from 7am until 3pm, also washing and scrubbing floors and windows. This was rather hard work for someone my age, but I survived. I would have been there to this day if I hadn't been dismissed.

Jurek my dear, I didn't want to add to your troubles so I didn't tell you the whole truth straight away. Myszka is no longer alive. I received her death certificate from Auschwitz. She died on 10 January 1944. She stopped coming to see me about one and a half years before this and cut off any contact with our whole family for no good reason from my, or the family's side. I know that she, together with her mother and sister were doing well. They also never visit me. They live in Wolomin and didn't suffer during the uprising at all. One can't explain everything in a letter, so I'll give you all the details face-to-face. I am sure you are free. I keep praying that God will inspire you with good advice, because I don't know anything and am frightened of everything. My heart tells me one thing and my reason something else. The Under Secretary of our embassy in London is your colleague Marian Szuch who married Zosia Grunwald. If you could go and see him it would be pleasant for you both.

My hair is now completely grey and I wear horn-rimmed spectacles. You probably wouldn't recognise me, in addition I've become a cry baby, like a child. Kissing you an infinite amount of times, I commend you to Our Lady's care.

Your Mother, Maria

PS Greetings from the Michalski family. I would be very happy if you could send me your photograph. Are you well? How do you spend your time? Have you got job? And have you learnt English, which you always so admired?

Christine in England

Back in England, the O'Neill family remained in their house in Highfield Road, Derby, which Hugh had built for his family. Despite a short wartime evacuation, the family had remained in Derby because, after some initial bombing in 1941, it escaped further attack. It was later believed to have been protected by a new anti-radar device. For a time the family stayed with friends in the Old Rectory, Dalbury, just outside the town in the Derbyshire countryside. Christine attended grammar school, getting her school certificate and leaving aged 16 in 1942. Then she helped her mother care for her youngest brother, Daniel, who had a heart condition, and attended Derby Art College part-time to take a diploma in Art and Design. Hugh made a number of trips to London and witnessed the bombing there. He writes (O'Neill, 1995):

> I arrived at my hotel one night to find excavators working in floodlights at the end of the street to recover the bodies of twenty-eight people killed in a pub demolished by a rocket.

Hugh remained in Derby during the war, with responsibilities on the railway:

> Normal and abnormal problems continued to arise in my railway work, one scare being the discovery of leakages in poison gas 'containers' at some aerodromes. This proved to be due to fatigue cracks caused by long distance rail transport and the job required me visiting a poison gas filling factory in the wilds adjacent to caves used for storage purposes. Observations from on high also led to the discovery in my section of a rather amateur young communist spy.

He talks about social activities:

> In June 1940 some 20,000 Polish troops were brought from France and commenced training as airmen and soldiers, under their exiled government in London. A national federation of Anglo-Polish Societies grew up and I was Vice President of an enthusiastic branch in Derby, which 'adopted' one of the new Polish regiments. Arrangements were made for the soldiers to spend their leave periods in the homes of our members, and this proved remarkably successful and great friendships developed.

Intimacy: marriage and migration   175

The railways were to be nationalised on 1 January 1948, so Hugh decided to leave his job and return to academic life. With his family, he left Derby to take up a Professorship in Metallurgy at Swansea University in August 1947. He and Barbara, and all five nearly grown children, made the move to a detached, elegant Edwardian house in the city.

Jurek met Christine on 9 May 1945, on Victory in Europe (VE) day. She recalls the date in her diary. He was stationed with the RAF at Hucknall, near Nottingham, where he was training as a pilot; Christine was then still living with her family in Derby. Christine belonged to the Anglo-Polish association, which her father had helped form, and which helped the Polish soldiers and airmen stationed in England far from home. They organised social gatherings and dances and invited the soldiers and airmen back to meet their families and have meals together. When she met Jurek at the celebration dance, they had no language in common – Jurek spoke French fluently but was only just learning English; Christine had learned only German at school. Christine's younger sister, Pauline, did however speak French, and after they were introduced, Christine decided since she wanted to speak to Jurek they would have to manage without a common language. Christine writes later in a journal about their meeting on VE day:

> I remember him looking out of the Central Hall window onto the crowds of revellers in the street below and managing to have a conversation with him, the gist of which was the sadness of the Poles as the victory was not theirs. I remember saying to my friend Joy, 'I could fall for him in a big way'. She said to me 'it's easy enough, *"Parlez vous Francais?"*' I said, 'that's the trouble, I don't!

Pauline describes the Welcome club:

> I was 16 and Chris was 18 when we first went (with our parents) to what became known as the Welcome Club. In those days (1944) it was held in a large room above the Kardomah café which I understand my father to have hired/booked/rented for the purpose. It was open to servicemen from abroad and I remember Yanks, Canadian and Dutch as well as Poles. (The Americans didn't stay long, but the Poles had a language problem). We girls used to try and chat and dance with them and make them feel welcome, and mother and various adults used to make tea and sandwiches (those were the days!). That's all there was to it at that time – a weekly hop on a Saturday evening. Chris and I were completely overawed by the glamour, the lipsticks and the sexiness of the Wilcox girls who lived down Vernon St.
>
> Chris fell for Jurek in a big way though I don't know how they communicated as his English was vestigial and he only spoke Polish and French. Chris had taken German in school whereas I took French so I had to try to interpret for them. He often visited us in our house in Highfield Rd. I was too young to take anyone seriously and much too involved in

sports and swotting for A levels at school. So Jurek and I used to play tennis – we enjoyed that as Chris didn't play, but it sort of kept him in the family.

I was quite surprised when my father agreed to the marriage as he had no job, no vocabulary and I believe he had to obtain a death certificate for his first wife who died in Poland in the war. However they seemed very much in love and he was a Catholic, which was important to my parents, and father arranged with Alan Turner to employ him somehow. . . As far as I'm aware that as the end of our involvement with the Welcome Club and we all moved to Swansea in 1947 when I was 18 and father became a Professor and I became a student.

Jurek and Christine got to know each other, and corresponded while he was still stationed near Nottingham and she was relatively close by in Derby. His letters from that time have survived – Christine kept them all her life, carefully tied together with ribbon. There are a few from 1945, and a couple from 1946, including translated letters to and from his mother Maria. Jurek's first letter was 6 December 1945. It is written very neatly and probably translated for him:

Dear Krysia [Chris],

I'm most obliged to you for such a lovely invitation. Of course I will come to Derby. As you probably know, I am not anymore in Croughton. When we finished our JTW training I went to France where I had a nice leave. After this time period I came back to Croughton and there we were told by our authority that is no more flying training at all. You can imagine my feelings. I walked about like a blind monkey and at last came a glorious day with the great news: training has only been transferred to peacetime training, and I came to Newton. Few weeks ago I started to fly. I suppose to make my first solo in a short time.

Well dear, that's all about me. If anything more will happen during these next days I will tell you it personally. I will bring with me to Derby two or three boys. They will be Andrew, Danny and my friend Jonny. I have no idea where are the others. We shall be there about 8 o'clock. Well, dear, hoping to see you soon, I'll close now as it's getting rather late and I should turn the light off. Goodnight then, and lots of love, from Jurek.

Jurek's first letters are formal and polite, and written in alternating English and French – he is yet to become fluent in English. He is transferred to RAF Newton near Nottingham in the Midlands and clearly very relieved to hear he will still be flying with the RAF. His next letter, just before Christmas, is in French (Christine's mother Barbara translates) and he describes being ill with a stomach bug and unable to travel to Derby. This seems to be after he hears from his mother about the fate of Myszka, although this is not described overtly. He refers to 'documents' sent – this is likely her death certificate from Auschwitz. Jurek sends Christine Christmas greetings. By April he is visiting Derby more often, travelling by coach. He worries whether he is too old for her (an acknowledged 10-year gap, but in reality 13 years). He identifies her by her Irish background and says that, because of her, he has a very high opinion of Irish girls.

The relationship progresses with frequent visits. There were initial problems – he told her immediately that he had been married in Poland but had no idea what had happened to his wife. He also told her about his concern for his mother in Warsaw since she was alone and he had no siblings there to look after her. Jurek imagined he would go back to Poland. The most emotional letter is in November 1946, when Jurek has to make a decision about whether to stay in England or return to his mother in Warsaw. He writes:

Dearest Krysia,

This letter will be very difficult to write. It is difficult to write in Polish but it is impossible to write in English, as I want. At the beginning I want to send you my best wishes for your birthday. In Polish there is a [proverb] 'it is better to do late than never'. I didn't forget, I wrote a letter, after another letter, but I did not send it. Try to understand me. I was undecided. I had to choose between my country and emigration. If I say my country, I see my mother, Warsaw and everything I loved. I had a Polish Daily [*newspaper*] from Warsaw that was for us: 'You thought during the war to desert is the worst thing of all – today you desert and that is worse'. Don't laugh at me. The love of our country makes us the romantics, and we are romantics in this point. Put any Pole in the worst conditions he can sort things out (*se debrouiller*) very well, but he will be still romantic. If you can understand Polish I can give you the poem of Jan Balinski 'The Country of Chopin'. If you can understand the [ambience] of this poem, if you can hear the music of Chopin as a Pole, you will know all of us. I'm sorry Christine, I was thinking about my unborn [future] child. I thought he would never speak Polish, never understand Polish – he will be British, and that made me suffer. I'm very sorry Christine to write you that, but it is necessary. You are (British people I mean) proud of your British Empire – we love our poor country and [because] it is more poor, it is more loved.

And I love you Christine, that's true. In my decision you played a big *role*. I am in Resettlement Corps. The first condition of our contract is very *irritant* for my colleagues. 'You will engage to serve His Majesty as an airman for a period of two years Regular Airforce Service provided His Majesty should so long require your services'. Not for me. I'm still a monarchist. I prefer to serve for the *seigneur* than a *noveau riche* like Stalin. And I know I serve until that my service is not against my country. I'm born Pole for my life and death. Can you follow me in this poor writing? Can you accept me as I am and be a little Polish girl as I try to be British?

I'm so sorry for the weekend. I dreamed about it. Plenty of obstacles (*empecher*). One of my colleagues is ill and I had to replace (*remplacer*) him on duty on Saturday afternoon. I was going to send you telegram that I'm coming on Sunday morning when I received your telegram about Oxford. I couldn't go there and I didn't like to prevent (*empecher*) you to see your friends. I got your last letter on Sunday near 12.00. I'm on duty now from 24.00 (Sunday-Monday). I'm short a little of money because I bought the wireless for my mother, I want to send it with one Pole who is going to Warsaw. Also I had pain of my tooth and I'm fat (swollen) on one side. As you see I was (*discouragê*). I hope to see you next Sunday at Nottingham or Derby. I don't like to take now money for a day off, I want to have plenty of time on Christmas.

PS What a wrong idea you have 'finished with me'. I dream to be still with you and never leave you. All my love Jurek. 24/11/46

There are also a couple of letters from Maria in Warsaw addressed to Christine. In one, neatly printed and translated, she sends best wishes and blessings for Christmas and thanks for intervening with Jurek in writing more often.

The bulk of the letters from Jurek are from 1947, when the couple overcome the various barriers and decide to get engaged. The letters are written weekly, with only Jurek's surviving. Christine had received Christmas greetings from Maria in Warsaw, which Jurek translated for her. Christine also offers to send a food parcel to Maria in Warsaw through an American friend.

By March 1947 Jurek writes:

Dear Krysia

Thank you very much for your letter. I'm sorry you have had the trouble with this parcel. Send it to me, or wait until my coming. I'll not be able to come to Derby until next weekend. We are five at the guardroom, so everybody has a duty every day. Others, policemen, are on leave until 1st April. I'm so thankful to your parents for all their trouble about my job. I'm sending you two replies for my letter. It was too late written.

Thanks a lot for sending me the letter from my mother. I was waiting for it. My mother writes she can't demand my coming, but I know she wants it. I write that I want to marry you, and have a home here, that if she comes to England that will not be bad for me, that I want my son can speak Polish as good as English and she can help me for it. I never wrote her about my intentions. I hope she will comply. I can't make my mother unhappy. I'm sorry Krysia to write you about my troubles, but you must know all about me.

I invited Włodek [Myszka's cousin] to come to me for Easter. He is still too young to be (*solitaire*) during this holiday. Do you mind if we shall come to Derby for a few days? He got bad news from Poland that his brother was murdered in Germany by Germans. I'm sorry Krysia to send you a letter so sad like this. I'm still waiting for my posting but it will not be before the holiday. I'm sending you a few stamps for your father. I'm longing to see you again, to make to disappear my troubles. I'm ready to take any job, I'm not afraid of physical work.

Thank you once more for all Krysia, I hope to see you during holiday,

With love, Jurek. 23.3.47

Jurek left the RAF in 1947 when he was demobilised. He moved to London where he had three close friends from SOE and his flying days – Jonny Krasinski, who had been with him in France and in SOE, Andrew Nowina-Sapinski and Danny Rotert, who were both in the RAF. He also saw Erwin and Przemek, who had travelled through France with him. He shared digs with both Jonny and Danny at different times, but accommodation was hard to get in London, and harder for foreigners. His address is shown as Earls Court (Kempsford Gardens, SW5) and later as Sydenham (Kirkdale, SE26). His first task was to get a job, difficult for foreigners with poor English and at a time of great competition for jobs following general demobilisation.

A friend of Hugh's came to the rescue. Before the war Hugh had become friends with Alan Turner, an industrialist and Catholic convert who owned two textile mills in Derby manufacturing narrow fabrics. His wanted to run his business on Christian principles, concerned with staff wellbeing. Alan Turner had read that Leon Harmel 'one of the great pioneers of personnel management' had established textile works in France along similar idealistic lines, and so he became friendly with the Harmel family. The Ernest Turner Textile Group (Alan inherited it from his father) had a head office at Kings Cross, London, as well as textile mills in Derby. After Hugh made enquiries, Alan Turner offered Jurek a job as assistant accountant at the London office. This was based in Northdown Street, between Caledonia and Pentonville Roads a few streets from Kings Cross station. It still stands, a 1930s brick block, four storeys high, the width of three or four terraced houses, with many large, blue-painted windows suggestive of well-lit offices. Now the buildings in the street are cleaned and refurbished. In 1947 it was probably darkened by soot like many London buildings, and the area would have been rather poor and down at heel. But it was very central and convenient for the main London stations; also, not far from Sadler's Wells ballet and a bus ride from the West End.

Whilst perennially short of money Jurek managed to have a social life, as described in his letters. He was in a circle of close Polish friends and they would meet and eat together, attend football matches at Chelsea and Tottenham, and even Charlton on one occasion. He walked around London, to the parks and the markets. He went often to the cinema, and at least once to the opera. He and Christine also visited each other often, which meant train or coach trips between Derby and London, and later to Swansea when she and her family moved there. Jurek enjoyed visiting both cities, and became attached to her family, particularly her mother, who was very welcoming and a fluent French speaker. In Swansea, the family's Edwardian detached house was set in large garden, near a park and not far from the sea. Christine would often come to London with a friend and stay at digs nearby to Jurek. She also had a close friend, Marguerite Allmande, who lived with her family in London. Both Christine and Jurek spent time with Marguerite. She was from a French family, her father being a professor who had come as French Ambassador to England during the war and had been stationed at a large manor house near Derby, Kedleston House, where he had met the O'Neills. They welcomed Jurek as well as Christine. The couple's courtship progressed, Jurek proposed, Christine accepted and they planned their wedding.

Marriage and work in Derby

Jurek and Christine were married in Derby in May 1948. There is a short piece of film of the bride, groom, bridesmaids and family outside St Mary's Catholic Church on that sunny day in May, filmed by Alan Turner, family friend and employer. Jurek is in his airforce uniform, his best man Jonny Krasinski in army uniform. Christine is in a traditional long, white dress and veil and her sisters (Pauline and Helen) are bridesmaids, together with Alan Turner's daughter, Felicity. Hugh and Barbara are present, as well as both of Christine's grandmothers and numerous friends. Jurek has no family present, although his mother has sent her blessings.

They honeymoon on the Isle of Wight, where Christine had a friend whose family owned a hotel. She moves in with Jurek on their return to London, initially renting a flat in Highbury, north London, and then later sharing a flat with Johnny and his wife, Wanda Lubormirska, and their sons, Christopher and Dominic. Christine writes in her journal:

> We lived at first in a furnished flat, £3 per week at 97, Highbury Hill near Arsenal football ground, in May 1948. It was bomb damaged. Then when we were expecting Yolanda, we shared a flat in Forest Hill, South London with Count Jonny Krasinski and Princess Wanda Lubormirska and their sons Krzystof and Dominik. Then we had a flat in Highgate, 4 Holmesdale Road.

Christine was both impressed and amused at living with a count and a princess – not always the best qualification for undertaking household chores. Within a few months of marrying, Christine was pregnant and for the last few weeks of her pregnancy she went back to her parents in Swansea, in April 1948. She and Jurek exchange letters during this time – he from their flat in Sydenham:

4/4/1949

Krysia Darling!

Thank you very much for the letter, which I received this morning. It was a very sweet letter, darling. I miss you very much and I'm looking forward to seeing you in Swansea. Already it seems to me a long time since you departed.

Friday evening I've been with Włodek [Myszka's cousin] to the pictures as planned and enjoyed this film in which Greer Garson isn't so bad a woman as you told me. On Saturday I went to watch a match at Tottenham. Then I felt so tired I came back home and made some rearrangements in our room (not because I was tired but because I wanted to try some changes). Result worse than expected, but I enjoy the new look of the room.

On Sunday afternoon I met Erwin and went to visit Przemek. He spent all the time talking. I bought from Przemek a tennis racket for £1. It is a good one, but I have to change all the strings. No money at the moment. The bill for £21 came this morning for flat rent. Next Friday I will pay for February. I sent you the letter from LCL which came today. Send it back with remarks (*remarques*). I am afraid that Prof Allmande can get more for the flat in Golders Green than we can offer for it.

Whose wedding at Cardiff? I know nothing about feeding mothers. I believe only in pleasant dreams. How do you know I don't want a daughter? Maybe I am insuring myself calling for boy? Daughter is getting after (*closer to*) her father.

All my love darling, Jurek. (Remember me to all the family).

Finally the baby, a daughter, is born on 9th May, Jurek writes:

My dearest, darling Krysia,

What a big surprise, you are punctual like Princess Elizabeth! I was dead sure nothing would happen before Thursday or Friday and I hoped to be with you at this time. I guess you have had a comparatively gentle time, thank God. How does this little one look? How are you both going on? I know so little about it all.

As I wrote you, I spent Sunday afternoon and evening at Earl's court and stayed for the night. This morning Jonny phoned me about it. He couldn't tell me much, he was so sleepy. At first I could not understand what he was talking about. I can't forgive myself not coming home last night. I can't believe that something could happen yesterday. I think you didn't write me all about your feelings so I imagined everything would be four days later.

Anyway, all now is over and I hope you both are very well. There is a little conversation in the office and a little celebration. I brought cakes, which I paid for. I've hardly done any work.

I'm dying for news. I hope tomorrow there will be a letter with details. I just realised that I did not reply yesterday about your suggestion about Godparents. I think your idea is a good one and go ahead. Let me know when you think will be the best time for the ceremony?

I am sorry for this chaotic letter, but because of the excitement – I think I will be better next time. All my love to you both, Jurek.

182 England: the third generation

On the 10th he writes again:

> My darling Krysia,
>
> I'm so happy to know that you are very well and only need a good rest. I learned how brave you were refusing the gas. When Jonny phoned me, one of the thoughts that crossed my mind was – I bet she didn't use any anaesthetic. I'm very proud of you and feel very lucky to have such a girl. It's a long time since I've known you are an ideal wife and will be a perfect mother. I had a lot of opportunity to observe you dealing with Christopher [Jonny's son]. Of course I have no doubt that our daughter will be beautiful. Even two dimples doesn't surprise me at all – my Godmother (*Grazyna*) had them when young.
>
> Everybody here sends you congratulations. Wanda came back with Christopher, who has got very brown and with his blonde hair looks very well. Today I asked Mr Pennington to let me go on Friday. I should work next Saturday, so I will be back on Friday evening.
>
> Just now Mrs Allemande gave me a ring, she got a letter from Mother [O'Neill]. She congratulated me and promised to write to you. She asked about the name, I said we had not yet decided but it maybe Yolanda. Now I have an enormous job to write to all my family. I already wrote to my mother.
>
> I hope you are much better now and you will be quite comfortable when I come. I am so grateful to Mother [-in-law] for giving me all the news.
>
> All my love darling – give a kiss from me to our daughter, Jurek.

Christine talks about leaving London for Derby in her journal and the help received from two school friends who became lifelong friends – Margaret Hadfield and Eileen Drury. She writes in her journal:

> Jurek was transferred to Derby, my parents had managed to get him an office job with Alan Turner of Derby and London who made narrow fabrics. We had nowhere to live there as my family had gone to Swansea. My friend Margaret Hadfield loaned me her house as she was on holiday and I went to Derby with Yolanda who couldn't yet walk, to try and find somewhere to live. Anyone with a foreign husband and a baby was not very popular. Eventually my friends the Drury's at Dalbury rented us part of the Old Rectory. We were at Dalbury all winter, Yolanda going in a little baby seat at the back of my bike. I was very intrepid in those days! Then we had part of a furnished house at 208 Kedleston Road, in a house belonging to the Oleszkiewicz's and the Wesołowski's [Poles who become family friends].

The Old Rectory at Dalbury was six miles outside Derby. The Drury family were known to Christine since school days, and Eileen Drury was subsequently a lifelong friend. The village was tiny, with a Saxon church from the late 11th century, on the edge of the Peak District not far from Kedleston Hall. It has beautiful views of the countryside all around. Christine and Jurek rented one wing of the old house, and Jurek travelled into work each day at the Turner offices in Belper Road, Derby. Christine was at home with Yolanda, not yet a year old, and travelled around by bicycle.

This seems to be a happy time, although no doubt the house was cold and draughty in winter and they were somewhat isolated. Being situated in such a rural location, completely undamaged by war, must have been a time of respite from the many post-war difficulties. The young family subsequently moved into Derby, close to where Christine used to live with her family, and rented part of a house from a Polish couple. When a second child, Marie, was born (1952), they bought their first house in Chaddesden, a suburb of Derby. It was a 1930s brick semi-detached house with a garden on a quiet road with a nearby Catholic church and school, St Albans. I was the third daughter, born in 1955, and my youngest sister Joanna was born in 1959. Both of us were born at home in Albert Road, Chaddesden. The final element required to make the family complete was for Jurek's mother, Maria, to come to live with us in England. This eventually happened at Easter 1958.

Discussion

This chapter covers the rebuilding of cities after the war, and the building of intimacy and new relationships. There is also separation – from country and family – which becomes formalised in the Iron Curtain effectively cutting off travel across Europe. Yet family members adapt and find daily routines, which help them to rebuild their lives. Intermittent communication is finally in place across the continent.

This chapter sees a positive period of settling, requiring adaptation and creating new attachments. Mourning, adjusting to traumatic bereavement and life disappointment following the outcome of the war seem to be managed by Jurek without much emotional expression. Jurek did, however, talk to Christine about Myszka and her fate, but this was never discussed with us children in later years. This generation compartmentalised such painful memories and probably dug them deep.

To summarise the themes developed: identity revolved around adjusting to immigrant status. It also included social membership with both the community of Poles and the Anglo-Polish 'Welcome club'. Despite the dislocation and immediate loss of social status, this was a time when Jurek could express his real personal identity. He did not have to use a pseudonym or act in secret, with the proviso that he could not talk about his time in SOE because of the Official Secrets Act. However, the Polish community in Britain did have to adopt some camouflage – Jurek never made very public his upper-class origins, nor his father's status as a war hero, since these would have been potential targets for communist surveillance. The themes of this chapter are shown in Figure 8.9.

184 England: the third generation

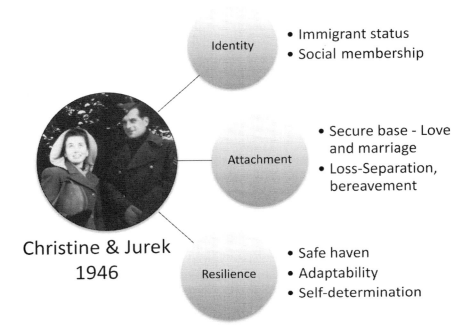

FIGURE 8.9 Summary of the themes in Chapter 8

In terms of attachment, Jurek and Christine together provided a secure base for themselves and later their children. There was loss – Jurek had to cope with the traumatic bereavement of learning how Myszka died. It occurred to me recently, at a funeral, that people like her who died in the Holocaust never had a funeral, no eulogy. Similarly for Stas – buried in a communal grave, now in a foreign country. Such losses in wartime perhaps inhibit the mourning process. I have no knowledge of how Myszka's parents or Stas's mother coped. There would have been many thousands of such losses in Poland. For Stas' family the details were not known for a long period of time, which must have intensified the grief. Jurek retained contact with Myszka's family; letters show that he saved money to send gifts to her younger sister, Didzia, who wrote to him in return; and he also befriended her cousin Włodek in London.

There was also continued separation between Jurek and his mother. He knew she was in straitened circumstances, ageing and experiencing health difficulties, but at least with Grazyna and other family members around her. He was unable to get to her, but sent parcels and maintained intermittent contact by letter. (He was never a frequent letter writer. When we were children, on receiving letters in Polish, when we asked what they said, he would reply 'just good wishes'.)

But again, there was resilience. Britain was a safe haven for the Poles; Jurek, like his compatriots, showed adaptability to the new setting and the self-determination to make a success of their new lives. Jurek had found himself without qualifications, a common language, family or connections in England and from an immigrant group reputationally damaged by Soviet political intrigue. But he adapted and made a good life for himself, and achieved high standing in the eyes of the community where he lived. In this he was helped a lot by Christine's family and friends. He attracted friendship and loyalty wherever he went. Women adored him. In terms of identity, Jurek voices his conflict of being a Pole in a foreign country with charges of desertion from the communist Polish press. There were, however, many kindnesses shown to him, and Jurek's resilience is aided by his attachments. He was able to take on work and was popular with his colleagues. He also managed with accommodation.

Jurek's wartime work was recognised by a French medal for fighting with the Resistance, and an RAF wartime medal. He was unable to talk about his role in SOE and tended to describe himself as having been in the RAF, even though this occurred just towards the end of the war. To continue the theme of heroism, it is notable that two major Polish heroes, Bor-Komorowski and Anders – now with a noted place in the history of the period were denigrated by the Soviet regime in Poland and labelled as 'fascist'. Both were hounded by that regime whilst living relatively quiet lives in the south of England. Both seem to have countered such reputational damage through the stoical support of their local communities, but it must have been bitterly disappointing to have such treatment despite great sacrifice and ultimately being on the winning side. Neither were properly recognised until after the fall of communism in 1989. Adam Komorowski quotes his father, Bor-Komorowski, writing in the 1950s:

> The darkest and most terrible moments in the Underground now seem beautiful and happy compared with the present day, because we had faith in victory and a happy end.
>
> Bor-Komorowski, 2010, p. xxiv

Notes

1   www.wsws.org/en/articles/2004/11/pola-n06.html
2   www.history.co.uk/topics/history-of-london/ww2-rebuilding-london
3   http://culture.pl/en/article/how-warsaw-came-close-to-never-being-rebuilt Mikołaj Gliński, February 3, 2015
4   http://whc.unesco.org/en/list/30
5   A section of this letter appears in the last chapter

9

GENERATIVITY

Family reunion and loss (1951–71)

> If there is any responsibility in the cycle of life it must be that one generation owes to the next that strength by which it can come to face ultimate concerns in its own way.
>
> Erik Erikson

Introduction

The penultimate Erikson stage of development is 'generativity', involving creating, establishing and guiding the next generation. The key role is of parenthood, but also of socially valued work to benefit society. The associated virtue is 'care'. Failure to develop this stage leads to stagnation. This chapter describes how Jurek and Christine settle down to married life, have children and how Maria comes to England to be reunited with her son and his family. It is the only section of which I have personal memory. My father uses his social, organisational and leadership skills to help the Polish community to become settled and thrive. He also makes two visits, along with the family, back to his home country, the first after a separation of 25 years. This chapter covers a period of 20 years and so only certain highlights are described in detail. These include Maria's journey to England and settling with the family in Derby, and her death in 1962; the first family trip back to Poland in 1965; the Polish community in Derby and the visit of Lee Radziwil in 1966; and the Rolls-Royce crisis in 1971 which led to major changes for the family.

The themes developed include the importance of community and roles within the family; the chapter describes a secure base for the family and a safe haven in the UK, with resilience attached to positive relationships, reunion and community resources. It also covers loss and bereavement and how the family responded.

Britain in the 1950s and 1960s

Britain still had economic difficulties in the 1950s. Some basic commodities like butter, meat, tea and coal were still rationed. There were also severe shortages of most consumer products, which prompted the continuance of the wartime 'make-do-and-mend' culture. The standard rate of income tax was high. Consequently most Britons had little surplus money and even less to spend it on. It was a time of austerity. There was a serious urban housing problem. The Labour government intended to pull down the slums and move their occupants either to new high-rise council flats or out of cities altogether, but local authorities lacked the resources to overcome the housing shortage. Nearly half the population lived in private rented accommodation – often in dingy rooms or bedsits with little privacy, comfort or warmth. Less than a third of all houses were owner occupied. The vast majority of buildings were still traditional in character and construction, and were built of brick or stone. All this changed rapidly in the late 1950s and 1960s.

The population of the UK was about 50 million in 1950 with only 3 per cent born overseas and the majority of immigrants white and European. At over half a million, the largest immigrant group was the Irish, and they made a major contribution to both the post-war rebuilding of Britain and the staffing of the National Health Service. Other immigrants had come to Britain as refugees from the Nazis, including over 160,000 Poles and Jews from central Europe. There was also an influx from Italy and Cyprus. The first post-war immigrants from Jamaica arrived on board the *Empire Windrush* in 1948, but by 1951 there were still fewer than 140,000 Black and Asian immigrants in Britain. Many suffered discrimination in employment and housing.

Poland in the 1950s

The first decade of communist rule was dominated by Stalinist repression, tensions with the Catholic Church and a strong-handed Soviet influence. Waves of purges and show trials shook the army and bureaucracy. Education became patterned after the Soviet model. Real power was exercised largely through the security services. Yet some concessions were made for Poland – the Stalinist leadership refrained from fully nationalising agriculture on the Soviet model, to appease Polish feelings and resentments. These resentments gained force and expression after Stalin's death in 1953. A 'thaw' in the Soviet Union by Kruschev became echoed in Poland. By the mid-1950s, 100,000 political prisoners had been freed. But discontent mounted, leading to worker protests in Poznan in 1956, followed by an echoing uprising in Budapest, Hungary. In Poland, the surge was met by the appointment of Gomulka as leader (First Secretary of the Party), and for a while there was wider tolerance for diverse opinion. In 1968, however, there were student demonstrations against the government countered with a political offensive in which many government officials and party members accused of anti-socialist or pro-Zionist sentiments were removed from office, and an estimated 12,000 Polish Jews left

Poland. Following a drought and harsh winter in 1969, another generation of workers took to the streets to protest against food prices. The next year the police fired and killed scores of striking workers, killing 44 civilians and Gomulka's rule collapsed. The new party leader, Edward Gierek, sought to appease and reassure an alienated nation, and rebuild a weakening party with consumerism. Vast amounts of money were borrowed from Russia in order to build factories that would produce exports and raise living standards. Nevertheless, after a few years many of the factories lay unfinished and Poland was burdened with a mountain of debt.

Maria comes to England, 1958

Housing in post-war Poland through the 1950s and 1960s was still problematic. Improvement in housing provision under the communist nationalised system was dependent upon the success of industrialisation. This was to pay for the housing development, but also dictated housing demand in large cities or industrial areas (Andrzejewski, 1965). Building was critical, but early restrictions were made on occupancy rates and allocation, and rent was frozen at a low level. The state and local authorities were the only investors. An increase in building occurred in 1957–9 after a change in policy and the potential for cooperative and private building. This led to a doubling of the number of flats and increase in the rate of housing construction and a tripling of housing investment. There was a large population growth in towns post-war and a corresponding growth in the number of rooms. The speed of change in towns was double that of the country as a whole.

In 1950 there were shortages of flats for people, and overcrowding, particularly in towns. In 1960 nearly four million people, 27 per cent of the urban population, were living in overcrowded dwellings.

Maria remained in her one room, part of the flat she had originally owned at the same address in Zoliborz. She had difficult neighbours, those sharing her own flat at number 21. A letter from a friend a few years later outlines the issues:

> And now a bit of gossip about our building. Of course the tenants from no. 21 keep jumping down each others' throats, only the other tenants are a bit frightened because he can also throw insults at them just like they do. One of the tenants gassed himself in December. Maybe you remember him, he lived on the ground floor with his wife and mother-in-law, Cziesniewski, a little man without moral values. The mother of Mrs. Kwiatkowska gets about but doesn't look at all well. She asked me to send you her regards. Mrs Kw. has signed over her flat to her dentist daughter. Her neighbour lives alone.

The problem neighbours made life difficult for Maria – she knew they wanted to take over her room to increase their flat size, which made her cautious about leaving her flat even briefly. She also had to suffer from overheard family rows and from the neighbours' aggression to other tenants. It made her life more insecure. Whilst she had relatives in Warsaw, they did not live in the immediate area – Grazyna and her family were in Filtrowa Street, between Mokotow and Okeica; Maria's youngest brother, Wacek and his wife were in Kielecka Street, in Mokotow just south of the city centre. The latter had a one-room apartment with a small separate bathroom and kitchen, up several flights of stairs in a bullet-strafed stone pre-war building (we visited it in 1965). Grazyna and her husband had an old apartment, with an original ceramic stove and a limited number of large rooms with tall windows. They shared the neighbouring flat with close friends, who became relatives when their children married. By the mid-1960s, Grazyna's daughter, Marysia and her husband Andrzej, she a successful author and he a photographer, owned their own small house for their family of three in Falenica.

Family and children in Derby

Jurek and Christine had another baby girl, Marie-Christine, in 1953, the year of the Queen's coronation. The family were living in Derby, in a three-bedroom 1930s semi-detached house with a garden in a quiet cul-de-sac in the outskirts of the town, backing on to fields and farmland. This was a settled family period. Jurek worked first at Turner's company whilst Christine stayed at home with the two young daughters. I was born in 1955, and this was the size of the family when Maria came over from Warsaw to join us when I was aged three. Joanna was born the following year, after our grandmother arrived.

In August 1956 Jurek left his job with Turner's, having worked there for nearly 10 years. His reference describes him as conscientious and hardworking, trustworthy in handling large amounts of money, and a good timekeeper with little time off for illness. Jurek himself chose to leave, and he is 'heartily recommended' for other positions requiring 'initiative and responsibility'. His next job was in the finance department of Pickford's Heavy Haulage, where he stayed until 1962. Following this he worked at Rolls-Royce Ltd and trained in the newly emerging computer programming department, working as a commercial programmer until 1971. In terms of leisure, Rolls-Royce had its own bridge club and competitions. Jurek was still an avid player, belonged to the bridge club and frequently won the champions cup – a statuette of the 'Silver Ecstacy' that graces the Rolls-Royce cars, and which stood on our mantelpiece for a number of years.

Letters from Maria in Warsaw

Five letters survive, sent from Maria to Jurek from late 1957 until just before she arrived in England in March 1958. The Polish borders started to open to individuals wanting to join their families in the West, a slight parting of the Iron Curtain, but the process was not easy. It took Maria almost a year to finalise her exit. This included selling her apartment lease, difficult because of her problematic neighbours. Initially only a 12-month visa was to be issued. Proof was needed of Jurek's income in the UK to support her. She weighs up whether to travel by ship or airplane, and the implications for taking her belongings. She receives help from her sister-in-law Grazyna and niece Marysia.

She writes again in February 1958:

> My dearest son,
>
> I received your letter of 28th January an hour ago, with the certificate from your place of work. All the affairs concerning my journey to you are progressing very slowly, as one says 'like a stone'.
>
> In the first days of January I received permission from the National Bank of Poland, Overseas Department for a departure paid for with Polish currency. But so what, since I am still waiting for an overseas passport, for which I gave all the necessary papers on 31st May 1957. Also in January we learnt that the cost of a passport rose from 350zl to 5000zl. I borrowed money in the hope that when I sell what I intend, I will be able to repay the debt. Meanwhile, although there are many applicants and nobody questions the price, the business of selling is not progressing because of the opposition to those living with me. They frighten everyone away. Everyone is frightened of the hard labour of living with them. So, I don't have a passport and without it I can't obtain a visa, and I don't have the money for this expedition. I had to cancel my place on Batory for 3rd March and move it to the next sailing on 31st March 1958. Maybe during this time I will be able to deal with the finances and obtain, at last, a passport and visa.
>
> Grazyna is taking care of all these things – like a sister, she worries about me and arranges everything. My brothers are very ill, and the elder, Stanisław, suffers seriously and nearly hopelessly with heart problems. I can't even visit him because the hospital is far away and the weather is dreadful. I don't have enough money for a taxi and I don't feel brave enough to take the tram because of the crowding and the cold. Everything hangs on the impossibility of selling supposedly my own property, but it is rather the property of others. As soon as anything happens I'll write at once to let you know what is going on.
>
> My dear son and best daughter-in-law – what have you decided about how I am going to travel from the port: by train or by car? That is your decision, not mine, and I agree to whatever you decide, because I know it will be considered and carried out with the best intentions to please me. At times, when nothing seems to go right, I think that my destiny is so cruel that it won't allow me to see you and then I lose hope. I am as if shackled to the end of my life, of which there is not much left.
>
> Grazyna is coming, maybe she will bring some good news. Then I'll complete this letter.
>
> Your loving mother and grandmother, Maria

Finally the date is set; Maria has sold her apartment and is to sail on the MS *Stefan Batory* at the end of March 1958:

> I am staying with Grazyna until the date of departure. I have got rid of my apartment, and I am leaving for Gdynia on 29 or 30 March and Batory sails on 31 March. It is supposed to arrive at the English port on 2 April, but I don't know at what time. I hope that someone will be waiting for me because I am like a small child and won't be able to manage on my own. I'll have two suitcases, one large and one small, a bag and a walking stick, which I use when I'm walking. I'm travelling in a grey coat with a brown collar. My friend and previous colleague from the office will take me to Gdynia and will help with embarking on the ship. I have a first class ticket, an overseas passport and a British visa.
>
> I am very tired from the difficult and hard experiences of the last three months – at times I thought that I would abandon the journey because of the many difficulties and my lack of strength. Of course if it wasn't for the endeavours, energy and intelligence of Marysia Szypowska and Grazyna – I would never have managed, because difficulties piled up from hour to hour and became greater with every step. Marysia is occupied at the moment with organising my belongings and worries about me as if I were her actual mother. She even neglects her little, beautiful daughter because of me. Independently of this letter, we will send you a telegram within the next few days. I would be very happy if you would send a cable after receiving the telegram, that you know about my departure on 1 April and that you will be waiting for me, then I will have a peaceful journey. This will be the first time I will see the Baltic Sea which I have never seen before.

Travel by ship

Maria came to England sailing first class on the MS *Stefan Batory* from Gdynia on the Baltic coast. She stayed a few nights with her nephew, Bogus (who was a student) and his parents, her brother Jan and sister-in-law Jadwiga. She also met Barbara (Basia) who was to marry Bogus, and become mother to Ania and Karolina. Ania relates:

> My mother Basia met your grandmother when she was still Bogus's girlfriend. She came to Gdansk first (where we lived) and then went to Gdynia accompanied by my father to board 'Batory' on her way to England. Your grandmother was very well dressed, her hair nicely done, very elegant. She was also very nice and open towards my mother – she accepted her as future family. She told her she had known Jadzia (Jadwiga) Cygler from Płock, probably from school, and it was she who introduced Jadzia to her brother Jan [Ania's grandparents]. She was very happy to go to England to join her son and his family. . . . Maria left some money for my father for lunches [he was still a student].

Maria's luggage was carefully itemised and sent separately by freight and arrived in London to be transported to Derby some weeks later. It must have been a sad, but rather glorious, journey on this still elegant ship.

Jurek and family drove by car to Southampton where the ship docked – a full car of two adults and three children – it must have been packed on returning with Maria. It was a black, second-hand Buick. Jurek inherited his father's love of large cars. As many will remember, in the 1950s cars were unreliable, and there was a minor breakdown, both on the way down to the coast and on the way back. However, a fortuitous meeting in a small village near Southampton with an AA man on foot led to its speedy repair. However, it did lead to a night sleeping in the car, the first of a few in my childhood holiday experience.

Maria settled well into a quiet family life in Chaddesden, Derby. She went to Polish mass weekly with the family and visited the Polish club. She did not make any close friends in the quiet street where the family lived, but spent her time with the children, receiving frequent letters from her family in Poland and helping with cooking and running the home. In 1960 my other grandmother, Barbara, died suddenly following a routine operation at the age of only 61. Hugh and the family all mourned the passing of this kind, warm, literary woman of whom I have only a very vague memory. Maria offered condolences to Christine. With a bequest in Barbara's will, Christine and Jurek were able to buy a Victorian house in Vernon Street, Friargate, in the centre of Derby. A fine detached house with a long garden, it was in need of repair but was large enough to house the family of seven as well as enabling rooms to be rented out to lodgers. The following year, Jurek changed jobs to go to Rolls-Royce. Christine also worked there briefly in administration, amongst other jobs, but then a few years later got a teaching job in Friargate House School. This was owned by Mrs Lorna Wibberley, who was a founding member of the Anglo-Polish association in former years and a philanthropist who aided many young Polish women and families who came to England alone. Christine was initially taken on as an Art teacher, being requested to help with the choir by playing the piano, but later was given her own reception class. She enjoyed teaching, always insisting that the small local children pronounce her Polish married name correctly.

There was good postal communication between Warsaw and Derby, so Maria received regular letters from Grazyna in Warsaw. The letters talk about health (a common concern of older women), and how hard their adult children work and delight in caring for their grandchildren. A common theme in the family has been grandmothers playing a large part in their grandchildren's upbringing – inter-generational transmission of culture by child care practice. Grazyna looked after her grand-daughter Małgosia whilst her daughter was pursuing a literary career; Jadwiga (Maria's sister-in-law) looked after her grand-daughter Ania while her parents were pursuing academic studies. My own grandmother, Maria, looked after me and my sisters whilst my mother was working.

Maria cooked the evening meal so we were familiar with Polish cooking, and spent time with us when we were not in school. She would read to us, sing, play cards, teach embroidery and otherwise stimulate us with conversation. We received

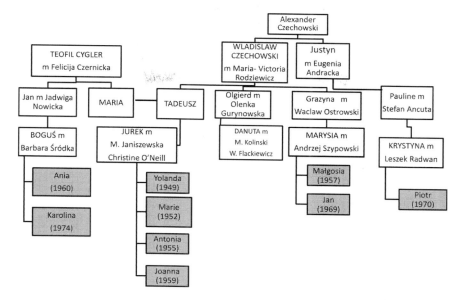

FIGURE 9.1 Third generation of the Czechowski family tree

Polish comics (*Miś*) sent from Warsaw: Grazyna sent them after her own grand-daughter, Małgosia, had finished reading them. I still have them. My grandmother particularly doted on my sister Joanna, the youngest grand-daughter, born after she had come to England.

The family tree shows the next generation of children with two sets of (second) cousins at this point. Małgosia is grand-daughter to Grazyna on the Czechowski line, and Ania is grand-daughter to Jan and Jadwiga on the Cygler line. They were born in the late 1950s and early 1960s. Their younger siblings, Jan (brother to Małgosia), Karolina (sister to Ania) and Piotr (son of Krystyna, grand-daughter of Paulina Czechowska), are of a slightly younger generation, born after 1969. In communist Poland there were social restrictions on having large families, as well as constraints on family size created by the housing situation. In two of the families, therefore, there were sibling gaps of twelve to fourteen years. This led to either child being brought up as though an only child. Figure 9.1 shows the third generation of the Czechowski family tree.

Cousins in Poland

Jurek's cousin, Marysia, married in 1954. She met her husband, Andrzej, who was a neighbour and family friend. Marysia was very bright, did well at school and university and took up a writing career. She sent Jurek pre-publication copies of her plays and poems, which we still have. When Marysia planned to marry Andrzej, she wrote to Jurek in June 1954:

My Dears,

I'm writing to you for the last time as Miss Ostrowska, because in two weeks' time on 27th at 9am, my wedding will take place in the Cathedral. I haven't let you know earlier since I haven't known the date until the last minute. The date was dependent on matters of accommodation, holidays and a thousand and one other matters. I expect you would like to know what sort of prince is snatching me away? Well he has about as much of a prince in him as I have of a geisha, but that really isn't important. He is a good and wise person, studied humanities and has many hobbies among others photography, opera and motorcycles. I will feel like the owner of a farm of thoroughbred 'horses'.

Of course our wedding will not remind you in any way of your somewhat fairy tale ceremony but we want to love each other at least as much as you. Of course I haven't mentioned to Andrzej – he is called Andrzej Szypowski – about your domestic habits, quite the opposite. I tell him edifying stories about wives who sleep 'til noon, who clean for their husbands, serve breakfast etc. I am afraid however that this is still too little. I must tell him about wives who bake cakes and those with yeast. I only know how to bake shortbread because that is always successful.

On the whole, I am pleased at the smallness of the room in which we will live, at least I will have an excuse to send my husband to work. The flat as I've already mentioned will be rather cramped (a cricket would have to move carefully so that with a bigger jump he wouldn't fall out of the window) but we have made great efforts to find a place in the suburbs. Maybe in 1956 we will be able to move there. In the meantime?

We probably won't go away anywhere for our honeymoon because it is difficult to arrange holidays and we will only have two free days – but this isn't important. That's all about me and my affairs. Write and tell me what is happening to you.

Many kisses for everyone, Marysia.

Their daughter, Małgosia, was born three years later, in 1957. Soon afterwards the family moved to the countryside just outside Warsaw, in Falenica, where her mother, Marysia, continued as a writer and her father, Andrzej, as a professional photographer. Both increasingly worked from home and travelled. They produced a number of historical travel books on Poland, which were popular and sold well. Małgosia spent a lot of time with her grandmother, Grazyna, and grandfather, Wacław, and with her father's parents living in the adjacent flat. When Małgosia visited she could see both sets of grandparents.

Grazyna writes of the family at Easter 1960, when her grand-daughter is three years old:

Holidays, holidays, and the holidays are over. Despite my announcements and promises I weakened and baked a cake. To my despair, the cake didn't rise. I baked two types of cake and I added dried fruit to one, which came out quite well. On the first day of the Easter holiday we went out to the country for lunch. The table was laid in the traditional manner with flowers, wild oats, cranberries, cakes and meats. There were only a few of us there.

I don't know why, but Andrzej was very depressed. A mother knows best what her son needs. So we sat at the table. Małgosia sat in her armchair. Everyone went up to her to share the egg and wished her well and she wished everyone all the best and a Happy Easter. It all looked quite funny but very solemn at the same time. We spent a very pleasant day. Małgosia was a dear, good and so clever. It was a bit cold so I told her that I would take a jumper and scarf to wear. She looked at me, a little worried, and said, 'But Granny you are only borrowing them?' When I said that this was so, she said 'Do it up well so it doesn't fall off.' Tell me, where does the child acquire such a feeling of possessiveness? No-one has mentioned such a thing to her! She is very obedient and won't touch anything without permission, just like Marysia once upon a time. Is this inherited? She makes the most of being outdoors but the weather has not been very good. There were a few warm days, then it turned cold and now it is raining. It's true that we need this because it has been very dry, things are slowly turning green but not as much as before. The trees are only just beginning to blossom.

We haven't been to Falenica for a long time. The children [Marysia and Andrzej] are going on a trip to prepare articles and photographs for two weeks in the middle of May. Can you believe, Marys, that we don't go anywhere! I who used to enjoy visiting people, sit at home with Wacek and this is fine. Even to go to Falenica seems an effort. Only occasionally we go to our neighbours for bridge. Thank God our health is good. We will go there then to look after Małgosia. From Monday Małgosia is going to nursery school. I am curious how she will react to this. I think she will get used to it quite quickly.

Grazyna goes onto describes her childcare role:

During those two weeks we delighted in the company of Małgosia. She is very lovable and no trouble at all, except she missed her parents. She would cuddle up to me and say, 'While my mummy is away you are my mummy'. Sometimes she would be thoughtful, even a little sad and when I asked her what was the matter, she would reply 'I don't know'. She was so happy when they returned but immediately checked – 'but you won't go away again?' While she was away Marysia had a few meetings with her readers. She was surprised how the students [at the horticultural school for farmers] were able to listen, to react to the spoken word and to discuss. On the whole Marysia, who often travels to the country, returns satisfied but very tired because of travelling and the preparation she has to carry out. On the 30 June they are going to submit their work and if it is accepted, that will be a great success. God willing, they should earn a reasonable amount of money.

> On 10 June it was Małgosia's name day. She received a lot of presents. She was dazed and at the same time tired by all the excitement. We bought her a bed for her dolls and I made a mattress, sheet, coverlet pillowcase and undersheet. On the next Sunday we went to Falenica again to look after her in order to give her parents time to get on with their work. We also went on this Sunday 26/6. First of all I waited until I could write about Małgosia's fourth birthday on 10 April. Then I waited for the photograph which I am sending you. I then started waiting for her name day on 10 June, but in the end I got round to writing.

Marysia and Andzrej enjoy their material success by buying presents for their parents. Grazyna later writes:

> Imagine what a surprise the children prepared for us. On Sunday 9th April they brought Małgosia to us and went out somewhere themselves. After an hour they appeared with three enormous packages. It turned out that they gave both sets of family a television each. I was so surprised by this that I burst into tears that they were spending their money on such things when they have so many needs themselves. But they were so pleased that they had given us pleasure that I didn't have the heart to reproach them – so today we are watching and listening. It really is a great pleasure because we never go anywhere, neither to the theatre or the cinema. My dear, good children.

She writes about Małgosia:

> What can I write about our treasure? As usual she is a good dear child, intelligent, obedient and determined. Thank God she is generally healthy but catches cold often. Maybe they dress her too warmly – but this isn't anything serious. She already has scarlet fever and measles behind her. The worst illnesses have passed! Thank God they passed lightly. She goes to nursery school very willingly. She is very fond of her father, he also idolises her – he is an ideal father. He knows how to approach a child. He is always sincere. Marysia doesn't have this ability. She is too matter of fact. She talks to her like an adult – but she lacks warmth and tenderness towards the child. Her relationship with her father is quite different.

There is also some correspondence from Jadwiga Cygler to her sister-in-law, Maria, in England. She is mother to Tadek (to whom Jurek was close growing up) and Bogus, who was much younger and didn't really know Jurek before the war. The family had by then moved to Gdansk, on the Baltic coast of North Poland. Jadwiga writes at Christmas 1959 to her sister-in-law, Maria. This is shortly after Jurek's youngest daughter, Joanna, is born and before her own grand-daughter, Ania, is born:

Dear Maria,

I hope that this letter reaches you along with our best Christmas and New Year wishes for you, Jurek and his family, sincere wishes for health and prosperity. What is your news? How is your health and the health of your nearest and dearest? I wrote to Wacek [Maria's youngest brother] and he replied. From that time we are in close contact with each other. Only one thing surprises me, that even though I mention Mira [Wacek's wife] in every letter I haven't received a single word from her. This embarrasses me a little, since I would like to write to Wacek more often but I feel ice from the other side, so I have decided not to write often even though I can see that Wacek is glad to receive my letters and replies warmly. Last time I asked for a photo of them both, since I know that if I were to meet Wacek on a street in Warsaw I wouldn't recognise him. I meant to go to Warsaw in November to visit them but after the changes that have occurred here I wasn't able to go. We have moved to a new apartment, in the same building, but with a separate entrance and a gas cooker, which pleases me very much. We are healthy but very busy from dark mornings to dark evenings. Winter is here with a vengeance, with ice and lots of snow. We are staying at home for Christmas since Bogus must get some rest in order to have the strength to deal with increasingly hard and difficult work. Has Jurek's child arrived? Maybe it's a son, then my congratulations.

I can't write anything interesting. I go shopping, then I cook, do the washing and in this way whole days pass, especially since they are so short at the moment. Apart from this I am still very tired after the move and I have very sore fingers which makes writing difficult. The writing is not very clear but I am sure you will forgive me. I would very much like to write more often and exchange thoughts with you. Let me know if this would be possible. Once again, my dear, receive my best wishes. Bogus and Basia also send their wishes. Hugs and kisses for you and for Jurek and his family, my best wishes. Jadwiga Cygler

Maria's illness

My grandmother Maria went through substantial negative changes in her life in terms of social conditions and social standing. She seems to have endured it with good grace. In later life she was thrifty and extraordinarily conservationist about simple household items. (This is also a Polish characteristic, but whether only of the Poles from that era, I don't know.) I have a handwritten book of her Polish recipes, about 80 pages worth, each written in meticulously neat printing, with no errors. She also retained her remarkable sense of style and was always elegant and well-dressed whatever the setting. She was also forgiving – when a family moved into our street with a German mother and Polish father, she immediately went to offer friendship. The Schwartz family became lifelong family friends. I believe the four years she spent with us in Derby were calm and restive ones.

Maria became ill with cancer and had surgery on 2 April 1962. She confided in her sister-in-law Grazyna by letter that she considered forgoing treatment. Grazyna was direct about the need to keep her health and it is clear Maria's poor health was more long-standing. The implication is that she knew of her illness before she came to England. Grazyna writes:

> I am so happy, sister, that you decided to undergo the treatment. You should have done this three years ago. But thank God that you have eased your suffering. My dear Marys – how could you!! Don't go against the will of God. God wants you to live this way and you for your part must do everything to be healthy, after all Jurek needs you. Your operation was such a distressing and painful experience for him, so you must reward him by living and being healthy. And Joasia [Joanna] so needs her beloved grandmother. I am so sorry that I am so far away from you or I would straight away knock these bad thoughts out of your head. So, my dear, for Easter we send you sincere wishes for good health and that you may overcome any resistance.

Maria succumbed to cancer and died on 23 April 1962, aged 77 years. This was 42 years after she lost her husband, Tadeusz. She had lived only four years in England, but these were happy years with her son, daughter-in-law and grandchildren around her. Whilst separated from her family in Poland, she had frequent postal contact. These last years were lived in relative ease. She had lived through three wars, with fighting close to home in Warsaw for most of them. She had seen huge technological and social change, lived through trauma and deprivation, only to see her country return to the Russian domination of her childhood. But she and her son, and many close family members, had survived and went on to rebuild their lives. Her religion remained a comfort to her throughout her life. She died knowing the family lived on. She was buried in Derby cemetery. Her name and dates were also carved on to Tadeusz's gravestone in Pawązki cemetery in Warsaw. The family in Warsaw were informed by telegram. None were able to come for the funeral, but all sent condolences and Jurek sent details and photographs. Grazyna continues to write to Jurek; in a letter from January 1963:

> Dear Jurek,
>
> I am so grateful for your letter and the photo. I was really worried about what was happening with you, dear son. I can believe how difficult it is for you. That telegram is always fresh in my mind – more than once I wanted to write to her about our joys and sorrows. Nobody understood me like she did. Your photo is very nice. You look so like your father. Do you really look as well as you appear in the photograph? Your mother always worried that you looked so poorly. How is your, and your family's health?
>
> Here, the New Year started unhappily. On 19 December Uncle tripped over while going out through the entrance and broke his leg. Thank God,

there weren't any complications but he is immobile for six weeks. He spent a week in hospital but he is at home from 27 December. Małgosia had mumps, so Christmas was quite sad. On New Year's Eve the children took me to Falenica. I feel quite well. Marysia and Andrzej, as usual, have huge amounts of work. Marysia has the last deadline for the work on Konopnicka. So they work in the outbuildings where the literary association has a place, since at home it is quite impossible. They have two rooms where it is difficult to isolate yourself from your surroundings. Andrzej is working on albums of Opole, Paczkow and Jelenia Gora. So he needs peace and quiet but they are happy and satisfied with their work. They are enormously helped in their work by having a car. They bought a Moskiewicz.

Do you have any work now? Do you have any lodgers? How is Krysia managing such a large enterprise? What a pleasant surprise today, when I received a letter from Yola I was very moved. Naturally I will keep sending the girls magazines and 'Stolica' for you. Are there any other publications you would like?

Dear son, once again thank you for the letter. Maybe you will write again soon? But I emphasise that I will not be offended if you don't. I will write from time to time. Dear Yola wanted to write to me so there will be a contact with you too.

My dears, sincere best wishes for the whole family

Grazyna, Wacek and family.

Jadwiga, living in Gdansk, writes further in 1962 and there is talk now of a visit:

I am living, as you probably already know, with my youngest son Bogus, who got married in 1958. They have a two-year old daughter, who I love very much. Bogus has achieved his doctorate. He is now preparing himself for the next step of assistant professor but this can occur only after about three years, since at the moment he doesn't have the conditions for writing his thesis. His wife, Basia, has a Master's degree. They both work from morning until night, sometimes very late, while I spend whole days with Ania (my grand-daughter) and I look after the house. We are looking forward to your promised visit to Poland. I hope that you will want to visit us in Gdansk while you are here. You are always welcome. If it's not too much trouble please write from time to time to your old aunt. Your girls are very delightful and pretty, as is your wife.

Jurek and family visit Poland, 1965

The first opportunity for Jurek to visit Poland was in 1965, when he returned for a summer holiday taking Christine and the four children. The visit was by car, with the family camping *en route*. There was a stay with Polish friends in Belgium. This was Barbara Merrimen, née Lubienska, with whom Maria had spent the Warsaw Uprising in a cellar. Her husband, Richard, had been a teenager in the Warsaw underground army. It was a very pleasant reunion. Christine sends a letter to her family, father and siblings, (a regular 'round robin') describing the trip. She describes entering behind the Iron Curtain:

> ... we got to the borders of East Germany in the early afternoon. We felt very excited at going through the curtain – to coin a phrase. We queued up to sign all our forms about currency and things. We found the people unsmiling, unhelpful and unfriendly – not a *word* of English among them. Luckily my German stood up to it. There were the towers with guns and searchlights. We got through all the officials and guards to the last one. He asked for the '*Grosses Papier*' which we hadn't got, to our alarm, so back we had to go to re-queue and get it, nobody told us anything about it. This time we got through. Jurek's a bit windy about E Germany as it is more under Russia's thumb than Poland, he didn't want to stop at all there. I drove in East Germany. We saw the cooperative farms, but the men weren't working, leaning on their tools watching the cars go by.
>
> Eventually the scenery changed to pine or fir trees, then we came to the Polish border. The German authorities were very anxious about what money we had with us. That seemed to be their main worry. The border there is a very dramatic bit of country, near Frankfurt-on-Oder, the river Oder is the boundary – a wide river with very dramatic banks. We crossed over it, it was early evening – and a very exciting moment for us. Then we had to queue up for signing more forms and queuing up to change some money for Polish money. We had to queue up for so long, it was now dark. Our first sight of Polish countryside was a dark quiet deserted country. With tree-lined roads as we went along, and cobbled roads through the villages and small towns – to Poznan. As it was late by then and we were all tired we stayed the night in a hotel in Poznan. Very luxurious, by the way.

Finally the family reach Warsaw:

> Next morning it rained – torrentially, and we made the trip to Warsaw. Our first impression of Warsaw wasn't that inspiring – that particular road doesn't give a good impression and it was pouring. We found Jurek's Uncle's flat in a nice tree lined street near the centre of Warsaw. We had a great welcome from Jurek's Uncle [Wacek] and Aunt [Mira]. His uncle is his mother's brother, a youthful looking man of about Daddy's age, with beautiful snow-white wavy hair. He is retired, but his wife [the daughter of a general] still has to work in an office to get a pension to keep them going. She was younger than him, a bit like mother, with grey hair in a bun and glasses.

Uncle Wacek had a sort of garden allotment with a little chalet in it. These allotments are very popular and expensive. All locked up and with a man and an unleashed dog to guard them at night, as there is supposed to be a lot of hooliganism. (They use that word, which is an Irish surname!) In Poland though, we didn't see any sign of it, except our camera, first-aid box and a box of chocs, a present, was pinched out of the car, which we were always very careful to keep locked up, but somebody managed to get in.

This garden was lovely with roses, peaches, strawberries, apples and all sorts. The chalet was very nice too, furnished as a little bedroom for them to spend weekends in. So Jurek and I slept there and we put the tent up just by it and the children slept there, but we ate at Uncle's. But the first evening it was pouring with rain so we all slept at the flat. They have one room, a little kitchen and a little bathroom. They have a sort of double bed used as a sofa, all the bedding goes in a draw underneath it, and then another double bed, which lifts up against the wall during the day. Three of the kids slept on that with their sleeping bags. Jurek and I on the other bed, Yolanda on a chair which made up into a bed, and noble Uncle and Aunty on the floor on two of our lilos. So eight people in one room!

We visited all his relatives, mostly old or ageing ladies, all the men have died or been killed off. Some of the places they live are the ultimate in dreary depressing rooms. But I expect they are used to them, and don't realise how they look to us. They all cried and embraced Jurek, and gave us marvellous meals, gifts and goodies.

There is only one little girl descended from this crowd, they are either unmarried or childless. Jurek's father's sister (Grazyna) has a daughter (Marysia) who is quite a star turn. She writes, has recently had a biography of a woman poet published. She gave us a copy – she is younger than me – and the mother of this one little girl [Małgosia]. She writes for the radio, magazines and a series of Tourist books about Polish towns, with photographs taken by her husband, a professional photographer [Andrzej], which we also have. They have a car [very unusual in Poland] and a little house only for themselves [also unusual]. We went on a big sight-seeing trip with them in two cars and back to their house for a meal. The husband took lots of photos. We shall send them to you when I get them.

Christine sums up how she saw Poland:

> ... poverty and very low wages. Living accommodation still very short, everybody only allowed so many square feet. Food still difficult – *no* meat visible, they have to queue for hours to buy it. Milk must be bought before 8am, otherwise none. Milk very scarce or non-existent in cafes etc. No imported fruit like oranges, bananas etc. Shops mouldy – Don [brother-in-law] would have a fit if he saw the standard. Small windows – artistically arranged, but nothing interesting or exciting to buy. Rather shabby and

> second-rate. We bought some spoons with our zloty, and the glass of the showcase was broken and repaired with Elastoplast – in Warsaw! Any pre-war buildings still standing, covered in bullet holes, still! And there are tragic little places on the street with plants and flowers and little plaques saying on such a date so many people were put against the wall and shot, in street roundups by the Germans.
>
> Now for good points. Fantastic hospitality of the Poles. Even with their hard life, they give you the most marvellous time, wonderful food, beautifully cooked, presents, and such a welcome. Beautiful countryside, a lot of graceful silver birch trees and pine woods. In the south the mountains are lovely – lots of unusual wild flowers we don't see here. Some lovely weather – boiling hot. Also some of that torrential rain as well. Complete freedom – except for leaving the country. Churches packed. Masses continuously every half hour, people standing and standing outside as well. Extraordinary!

The drive back to England was eventful with car breakdowns, near escapes on unmarked dead ends on East German autobahn bridges, being towed across the East German border by a furniture van, but eventually home to England:

> We drove straight to Ostende, of course we had missed our intended boat by a day. We caught the boat at midnight and got back about 1 o'clock midday. England looked marvellous, beautifully painted, marvellous shops. We stopped at the first eating place on the M1 and were thrilled with the food, the super spotless toilets, the hot air drying the hands, and all the plumbing working so well (which it doesn't in Poland). Jurek finds everything changed from before the war and the people too – only the hospitality unchanged. So now he feels he belongs here not there, which is gratifying.

Polish club in Derby

Much of my parents' social life in Derby had revolved around the Polish club, and this is something we as children had grown used to, along with other Polish children in our community.

Polish social clubs sprang up in the 1950s all over the UK. Over 1,500 Poles settled in Derby where the Polish Airforce Association was formed; its first meeting was held in 1948 and Jurek was to become a founding member and subsequent chairman. Premises were needed, and in 1950 this local club applied to the central organisation in London for a loan to buy property; this was granted the following year. A suitable property became available in Osmaston Road, not far from the railway station in Derby, in April 1952. It was named 'Dom Polski' (Polish House) and by June the first applications were made for a Polish Saturday school, scouts and guides and an ex-combatants' association with a benevolent fund. It started with a membership of 130, but this was soon to grow. By 1955 a fund was launched for extending the premises and by the following year a hall was built and made ready for use. It became a hub of the Polish community, holding weekly dances. It also held an initiative of volunteer Polish women, 'Stokrotka', in which Christine and some other English wives were active, to aid with social help in the community. The club was again extended in 1966, Jurek making trips to London to secure the loans, and it was to see its silver jubilee in 1977.

Jurek and Christine spent many happy years involved with Dom Polski and the Polish community. There are many pictures of dances, displays of Polish folk dancing, festivities, Christmas celebrations for children and other happy events. Jurek regularly played bridge and poker with his fellow Polish card players for relaxation. As children, we were frequently there running around, doted on by friendly adults, supplied with quantities of lemonade and peanuts. Our Saturday Polish school lessons were held in the convent at St Mary's church, until the new Catholic centre was opened. We felt it was a chore, but learned to write in Polish, learned Polish music and dancing and made Polish friends.

In 1966 there were special celebrations for the millennium of the foundation of Christianity in Poland. Celebrations were held in Polish clubs all over the UK. To coincide, there was an official opening of the newly extended Polish club in Derby in October 1966. The opening was undertaken by Princess Lee Radziwil (née Bouvier), sister to Jackie Kennedy and wife to a Polish prince, Stas Radziwil. He was cousin to Jurek's friend, Wanda Lubomirska (Jonny's wife). So Jurek was able to make the contact and offer an invitation, which was graciously accepted.

The millennium celebrations in Derby involved special Masses held at a Nottingham football ground, with a rally of Poles from all parts of the Midlands; the Bishop of Nottingham co-celebrated Mass with nine Polish priests. There was a combined Polish choir from Birmingham, Leicester and Nottingham. Princess Lee opened the new hall and attended the pageant – with *tableaux vivant* of scenes from Polish history and the dedication of a new Polish Catholic centre in Kedleston Road, Derby. There are pictures of General Bor-Komorowski being invited to speak, sitting alongside Jurek at the head table of a large gathering. It would have been interesting to know of their conversation. Bor-Komorowski died later the same year.

In 1970 Jurek received a commendation and medal from the association for all his work with the Polish community. Christine was later to receive the same honour. Polish communities were similar across England. Jola Malin, who is my contemporary but brought up in West London of Polish parents, describes her experience:

> The Polish community initially centred on the Sunday Catholic mass and Saturday morning Polish school, which also developed 'harcestwo' the scout movement for young boys and girls. As children we just accepted the routine of attending Polish school on Saturdays (after a full week of our normal school), and though it was seen as hard work sometimes, learning Polish

geography, history, language and literature, it also included the fun of learning to sing and dance. The Polish daily paper became essential reading for the adults, whilst also exchanging local news at their shop with imported Polish produce. The new generation were bilingual, learning to speak Polish at home and English outside. Though many of our Polish customs focused on religious festivals, others were light hearted and fun.

Malin, 2013, p. 88

At this time Jurek was also active in the first Race Relations Board set up in accordance with the Race Relations Act, 1965. Legislation had been passed following racial tensions surrounding the arrival of Commonwealth immigrants in the UK from the 1950s. The legislation aimed to ensure that their rights were protected.[1] The Race Relations Boards were there to assess and resolve individual cases of discrimination. The Board's duties continued and expanded in 1968. As new communities from South Asia and the West Indies settled in Derby, their politicisation resulted in a growing emphasis on their religious and cultural identity. The Poles were part of the new multi-culturalism that was emerging.

The Czechowski family flourished in Derby, having another memorable holiday in Poland in the summer of 1970, travelling over more of the country – for example, to Gdansk to see the Cygler family and to Płock to see the house where Jurek was born. We revisited the now ageing older generation of family members, who were delighted to see us. The family was growing up. My oldest sister, Yolanda, then left Art college and was working in fashion design in Nottingham; Marie went to live with grandfather Hugh in Swansea while she completed her A-levels; I was doing my O-levels at grammar school in Derby, and my younger sister had just joined the school. Christine was teaching at Friargate House School.

In 1971, Rolls-Royce was nationalised after losing money on its aero engine production. There were extensive redundancies in their plant in Derby. This included Jurek, who lost his job after nearly 10 years, in spring 1971. For the first time, aged 58, Jurek was out of work. He felt disillusioned with working for large companies and wanted to open his own business – he did, after all, take his undergraduate degree in Business Studies. At the same time, my older sister Yolanda had developed a successful career in the fashion industry working for large companies in Nottingham and Manchester, including Marks and Spencer. She too felt like a change, came back to Derby and decided to start her own fashion boutique with her father. With a bequest from great-uncle Leonard – Barbara's brother, who had come to live with our family after his mother's death in the late 1960s – a property was bought in Normanton Road, and refurbishment undertaken to start 'Yolanda's Boutique'. Jurek spent May and June at home while this was in planning, given some free time to spend in his beloved garden and walk around the town. It coincided with me being at home revising for O-levels so we spent some time together, just the two of us. He still met up with friends and played bridge on a regular basis, and still spent time at the Polish club.

Then one evening, 23 June 1971, Jurek had a major heart attack whilst playing cards with some friends. He was rushed to the Royal Infirmary; Christine and Yolanda both went to the hospital, major surgery was initiated but he did not survive. The family was in shock, as was the Polish community who he had served. Numbers of well-wishers called at the home in Vernon Street bringing food in the Polish custom, the death reported in the local newspaper, and telegrams sent to the Polish family in Warsaw. The funeral was attended by many hundreds – St Mary's church was full to overflowing. A Polish choir from Nottingham sang medieval Polish choral works. There was a long funeral procession at Nottingham Road cemetery with an abundance of flowers. Jurek was buried alongside his mother, Maria, and a black marble headstone marks their names and dates in Polish. It was the end of an era. Two years later I left Derby for university and never lived in the town again.

Discussion

Jurek's attachments in his family were loving and stable. His marriage to Christine was successful and his four daughters had a caring upbringing. The family attachments in Poland also seem to have flourished, with grandmothers' hands-on care of their grand-daughters, parents very busy working and building successful careers, but also family minded and committed. The families all stayed together. This provided security in day-to-day life and, in children, provided resilience going forward. The reunion between Jurek and his mother must have been a great high point in their lives, and her last four years with him and her grand-daughters would have been a source of pleasure to both. It also benefited us children having her care and links to our Polish roots. It was pleasing that we made a second trip to Poland, which proved to be the year before Jurek died.

The family in Derby were well assimilated culturally. The Polish influences remained strong. Jurek kept a very strong sense of his cultural identity, and was highly committed to the Polish community in Derby. He made visits to the Polish centre of the ex-combatants' association in London, visiting the Ognisko club in Kensington as well as the centre in Balham. As a young child I often accompanied him and my mother on these trips. It seemed an adventure to visit London at the weekends. However, Jurek no longer had close friends in London. Those with him during the war had all emigrated to America and he had only irregular postal contact. We don't know what happened to them.

The family needed resilience after Jurek's sudden death. There were difficulties around family finances that needed to be met. This was also during difficult economic times nationally – the three-day week under Ted Heath and electricity shortages. The family pulled through, with Yolanda providing for most of the family income. But somehow the heart had gone out of the family and soon after I went away to university in Exeter, followed not many years later by my younger sister who went to university in London. My sister, Marie, studied nearby in Nottingham

206 England: the third generation

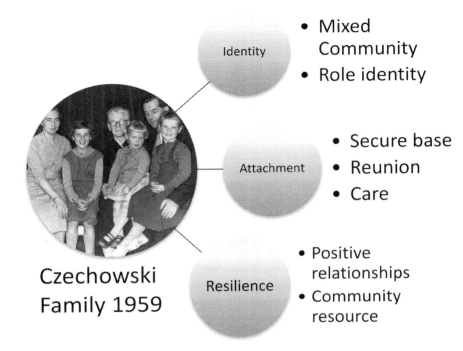

FIGURE 9.2 Summary of the themes in Chapter 9

but later, after her children were born, also left the area to go to Gloucester. Only Yolanda stayed in Derby and within close reach of our mother, Christine.

In terms of the three themes of the book, I have identified some above which seem to fit with this period of family life in Derby (Figure 9.2). In terms of identity, the Polish community was certainly of importance in imparting cultural identity and role identity, additionally for Jurek's work with the Race Relations board. It also covers the different wider family roles as parents and grandparents.

In terms of attachment, the family home provided a secure base for the members within, and a period of respite for Maria. Reunion refers to Maria coming to England to spend her final years with her only son and his children. Care refers to the caring between generations, particularly childcare. Resilience is shown in terms of positive relationships and community resources for keeping the family together and functioning.

Visiting Derby, 2016

In September 2016, and during the writing of this book, I made a visit to Derby on the occasion of my mother Christine's 90th birthday. I stayed in a new hotel next to St Mary's church, the church where my parents married and where my grandmother and my father's funerals were held, in the centre of this ancient town. In walking to my mother's nursing home near Friargate, where we had once lived, I traced the route I took daily to St Mary's Primary School, usually with my younger sister. It is entirely changed, with a new road layout and slum houses cleared, but the brook we walked along is there still, now thick with reeds and wild flowers, intentionally so according to the accompanying ecological plaque. It is certainly more picturesque than when it was a brook at the back of textile mills in the 1960s. These large, brick buildings are actually rather a magnificent reminder of Victorian industrialisation and, now refurbished, are part of the new Derby University. The distances walked are shorter than I remember. I realise that as well as time being experienced differently as a child, so are distances. My geographical understanding of the town is poor, a child's view in all. This is not helped by the new road system intent on taking the unsuspecting visiting driver away, and out of, the city.

At dinner in the hotel the music playing is that which played before I left in 1973: the Moody Blues, Rod Stewart, David Bowie, Paul McCartney and Wings. I vaguely wonder whether it has been playing on a continuous loop for over 45 years. The music seems none the worse for its longevity, as fresh as before and bristling with atmosphere. I decide to visit my father and grandmother's grave. My sister Marie, who drives up from Cheltenham, joins me at the cemetery. Now I am aware of how important such visits to graves are in Polish culture I feel remiss for not having done this before. My last visit may have been just before I left the town after my sister Marie married in 1973, and I took my bridesmaid bouquet to place on the grave. The black stone marble gravestone with gold lettering is still in pristine condition. My sister Marie and I leave red and white roses in remembrance.

We then visit our first house in Chaddesden, which we left aged six and nine, respectively. The drive there, closer to the cemetery than I remembered, shows familiar landmarks. We pass a carpet shop, still in the hands of a Polish family who are close family friends. My sister and I start remembering who lived in the houses in our street. Mrs Bull, an old lady who lived on the corner and who would give us sweets and I seem to remember played cards with us; the Schwartz family opposite, who were family friends, the parents Polish and German, the three daughters; who would join us for Christmas celebrations, with whom we have recently re-made contact; next door to us, the Tomlinson's large brood, of whom my mother disapproved, but about whom my eldest sister was enthusiastic, and treated as additional siblings; Mrs Bodna, across the road, who had travelled to England from Siberia with General Anders' army, lived with her son, her previous children lost through starvation during the war. Mrs Schwartz complained that Mrs Bodna chased her son Robert with a frying pan – to feed, not punish.

But the vast fields behind our house are now a new housing estate. We found our house. It looked smaller of course than remembered and the modernised windows and new porch were not to my eyes an improvement on the clean 1930s brick and woodwork. The front garden, once supporting lilac and lawn, was paved for a car in the modern fashion. It did not in itself evoke memories. My sister and

I discussed the layout inside. The sitting room with its square, bay window overlooked the street. Our bedroom, at the front, was shared by the three daughters with an additional alcove area where my newborn youngest sister slept when no longer in my parents' room. Their room was on the back overlooking the fields, as was my grandmother's. Curiously, my most vivid memory is of my grandmother's bedroom. This was individualised with small Polish touches: her voluminous feather eiderdown and pillows brought all the way across Europe before duvets became popular, a small Swiss cuckoo clock, a source of early fascination for us; her windowsills full of green and white spider plants; her wickerwork chair and cushion of purple, orange and blue Polish weave; her holy pictures not only of our Lady of Częstochowa, an obligatory icon in Polish households, but also of the less familiar but beautiful Lady of Ostrabrama with radiating star halo. There we would read the Polish comics sent monthly by great-aunt Grazyna. The garden was longer than it was wide and my father planted fruit bushes of red and white currants and raspberries in the further section past the lawn. He was always the keener gardener. There was also an old apple tree blooming in the spring. We remembered a den, an area to the side of the garden covered by bushes in which we could be secret and that opened onto next door's garden – the Tomlinson's – and thereby an escape route.

My mother Christine's 90th birthday celebration is held in spite of her lack of general awareness. Nearly all immediate family come, a couple of English cousins and family friends. The lunch party is held in the hotel with a view of St Mary's Church from the room where we celebrate. This seems appropriate given its long family connection. My mother is on good form and enjoys the socialising, despite little comprehension of who everyone is, but generally enjoying the atmosphere. Her grandchildren who are grown, and her great-grandchildren who are not, crowd around her. My daughter Lucia has made her a memory quilt with photographs printed on to the fabric depicting all her large, immediate family. People crowd round to glimpse themselves and each other as depicted now in fabric. A projection is shown during lunch, of photographs of my mother from different points in her life. Cards bearing a timeline of each of her decades, with corresponding photographs, grace the table. She is honoured with two birthday cakes. Her granddaughter Anastasia who, living in Derby, sees her most often, helps her cut the cake. I make a brief speech and pass on the good wishes sent from my Polish cousins, Małgosia and Piotr, and aunt Marysia in Warsaw; they wish her 100 years (*sto lat*) in traditional style. We all raise our glasses to Christine.

The codicile is that in early January, barely three months after this party, Christine dies in her Derby hospital bed. She has pneumonia and kidney failure. She is not in pain, is calm and recognises family who visit. My eldest sister, Yolanda, who owns the nursing home where my mother stayed, is left to inform me and thereby the rest of the sisters of her death. It is a much sadder occasion than I expected, despite her great age. We hold the funeral in St Mary's and the reception in the same hotel where we celebrated her 90th birthday. Her one surviving sister, Pauline, comes, her other sister Helen having died only two months earlier. A number of my English–Celtic cousins attend, Christine's four daughters and all eight grandchildren. The funeral is sad, but dignified, with a solo *Ave Maria* hauntingly sung by a young family friend, Sam Oram. I give the eulogy. Christine is buried in the same grave with Jurek and Maria, her explicit wish. The reception allows the family to reminisce and there is much laughter. She outlived Jurek by 45 years. She had great resilience and lived those later years with stoicism, acceptance and good humour. A great survivor.

Note

1   www.parliament.uk/about/living-heritage/evolutionofparliament/2015-parliament-in-the-making/get-involved1/2015-banners-exhibition/alinah-azadeh/1965-race-relations-act-gallery/

Photographs section 3

FIGURE 9.3
Christine O'Neill, 1945

FIGURE 9.4
Jurek and Christine marry, Derby 1948

FIGURE 9.5
O'Neill family, with baby Yolanda, Swansea 1949

FIGURE 9.6
Jurek (left) with Gen Bor-Komorowski, Polish Club Derby

FIGURE 9.7
Jurek with Princess Lee Radziwil, Derby 1966

FIGURE 9.8
Christine, Jurek and children, Derby 1962

FIGURE 9.9
Grazyna, Marysia and Maria, Falenica Warsaw, 1958

FIGURE 9.10
Małgosia with family, Warsaw 1961

FIGURE 9.11
Barbara, Karolina and Ania Cygler, Gdansk, 1977

FIGURE 9.12
Jurek and family visit Falenica Warsaw, 1965

FIGURE 9.13
Marie, Joanna, Yolanda, Antonia,
London 2015

FIGURE 9.14
Małgosia and Piotr, Warsaw 2016

10

INTEGRITY

Reminiscence and reflection (1972–2016)

> We cannot leave history entirely to nonclinical observers and to professional historians.
>
> Erik Erikson

Introduction

The final of Erikson's stages, 'integrity', occurs in older age where a capacity for order and meaning is developed. It refers to coming to terms with different facets of oneself and one's life, and facing one's own mortality. The converse is 'despair', as signified by a fear of one's own death, and the death of loved partners and friends, as well as the loss of self-sufficiency. The associated virtue is 'wisdom'. This is encompassed here as reflection and re-evaluation of the family narrative as described in this project. It also has a focus on the present time. In this phase Poland finally gains her independence, first with the fall of communism and resumption of democracy, and second with her accession to the European Union as an equal partner. The rise to independence happens this time without much bloodshed, welcoming a period of potential wisdom on a continental scale. The Polish culture is coming to terms with the past, including both positive and negative experiences, and understanding more about both forgetting and remembering. This is also an individual task in ordering and processing the past.

Warsaw and family, 2016

We were sitting in a wine bar, my sister Marie and I, at the Hotel Bristol, Warsaw, on a hot evening in June 2016, drinking chilled wine with our Anglo-Polish friends from London, Irena and Kazik, and our Polish cousin Piotr. The newly furbished Art Deco hotel provides every luxury, with its interiors recreating those of its 1901 origins. The hotel itself has witnessed the many destructive events to its city, and is also a survivor. I like to think that my father and grandparents came to the bar and restaurant of this elegant hotel in former times. The patio bar overlooks the Krakowski Przedmiescie route to the Royal Castle and the Old Town (Stare Miasto). The medieval and eighteenth-century buildings glow in the evening sun, the pastel and ochre façades providing additional colour. Warsaw is no longer grey. Whilst many of the buildings we can see are mid- to late twentieth-century creations, the careful attention to stonework and architectural embellishment faithfully recreate the old methods. With good Polish craftsmanship and the effects of recent decades of weathering, the effect is indeed that of an old town. A city rebuilt, faithful to its pre-war glory, but new, vibrant and modern.

Warsaw was looking her best in the early summer sunshine. Her wide boulevards, riverside walks, pavement cafés and pedestrianised areas providing a welcome for visitors, and a good quality of life for locals. Its large parks and green areas, including a wildlife area on the east bank of the River Wisła, provide shade and natural greenery. The Saxon and Krasinski gardens now have mature trees grown over the last 70 years, missed on our earlier childhood visits. The Łasienki Palace is restored with its lakes and fountains and luxuriant gardens to offset the cream regency buildings reminiscent of Regent's Park. The Technical University is restored, with a magnificent stucco façade and statues, its dramatic central forum overlooked by multiple arches on its many floors opening to the centre. A statue of Marie Curie guards the entrance.

We visit Zoliborz, where cousin Piotr and his father, Uncle Leszek, still live. It is an affluent and leafy suburb, reached by a wide ring road extending along the River Wisła. It is a popular area to live, with the Old Zoliborz now extended to include new areas of building. White apartment blocks with gardens are under construction, an expensive place to buy housing. The old Powązki cemetery at the end of Krasinski Street still houses tombs from previous eras, commemorating the great and the good of Warsaw, with tree-lined pathways and walled enclosures. The cemetery, frequently visited, is well maintained. Piotr drives us to the cemetery where our cousin, Małgosia, meets us, to visit the Czechowski family graves.

Małgosia is a teacher, now in her late 50s, and my contemporary. I had last seen her when I was aged ten on our first trip to Warsaw. Her mother, my aunt Marysia, a well-known author, is now 85 and no longer in good health. She lives with her younger son, Jan, a talented musician, with her daughter on hand to provide additional care. Piotr, now in his mid-40s, is a medical consultant and pulmonary specialist. He is the grandson of Tadeusz's cousin, Paulina. His father, Leszek, is in his 80s but spritely and still working one day a week as a medical consultant, and has fluent English. The two cousins light candles with us for the Czechowski family, and the related Ancuta and Ostrowski family branches. In the military section, Tadeusz's grave is well maintained and decorated with red and white patriotic colours. The inscriptions are to him, his wife Maria buried in England, and his parents buried alongside him, their names still decipherable. We place our wreath of white flowers and pledge to have Jurek's name added to those who belong with

Tadeusz. We now also need to add Christine's. The cemetery remains a place of calm and tranquillity.

Piotr invites us to his apartment in Zoliborz, not far from where Maria used to live. We feast on tea and Polish cake in an apartment festooned with Polish art form the Tatra Mountains. Piotr shows us his collection of family photographs and documents. He has amassed a great deal of information on the family home in Rudzk, and is now an expert on Czechowski genealogy. He shows us photographs of the long, one-storey manor house and its extensive garden and lands, and various family who have visited it. He shows us pictures of our father Jurek we had never seen before.

Marie and I also meet a handsome young relative, Jas, Ania's son and great, great-nephew to Maria Cygler, who is in his early twenties. Brought up in Gdansk, he studied law at university in Warsaw and works in the Ministry of Justice. He speaks fluent English and is a keen supporter of Manchester United football club. His plan is to enter politics. His mother, Ania, a well-known author (Hannah Cygler) and translator, was in America at the time of our visit seeing her sister Karolina, so Jas was accompanied by his father, Andrzej, a financial expert, previously British Consulate, shortly to be promoted to an ambassadorial role. We eat on the terrace at the Łasienki Palace overlooking the trees, lakes and the new Legere football stadium. The food is excellent, traditional Polish but with a nouvelle cuisine twist.

Later we meet Małgosia at her mother's house, and meet her brother Jan (for the first time) and mother Marysia. Her two sons, new nephews for me, Julek and Maciek, greet us warmly. It is our first meeting. They are engaging, attractive, successful and partnered. Both talented, one published like his grandmother, the other as a photographer like his grandfather. Both work in IT. We have lunch in the house in Falenica where we visited last when I was ten years old, and where my grandmother Maria had met with Marysia and Grazyna nearly 60 years earlier. A fairytale house, full of books and papers, a loft which had been used to reconstruct a famous Wurlitzer pipe organ as a cultural artefact inspired perhaps by Jan, a very accomplished and recorded organ musician (Szypowska, Szypowski and Szypowski, 2009). There are overgrown gardens and a house packed with years of literary and family history. A precious photograph album belonging to my grandmother is casually found among the papers and restored to us. I bring Małgosia an example of the childhood Polish comics we shared, and which she recalled, and copies of letters from her grandmother, which she had never seen. Our hostess, Marysia, now without speech, carries the cultural tradition of her generation, the last in the Czechowski family. Cousin Piotr and Uncle Leszk join us. There is plentiful food, the atmosphere is warm and generous; we have come home and been warmly welcomed, to a lost part of our family.

Memorials

Warsaw is reborn as a vibrant European capital city. It has a commercial and financial centre with the modern skyscrapers common to all capital cities. There is still evidence in the suburbs of the tired communist blocks that provided cheap, but necessary, housing post-war. Warsaw commemorates her history. Restricted under Soviet communism to remember her own recent history, she now expresses it openly with museums, plaques and statues. The city honours the Jewish Ghetto and uprising with its own museum. Around the Moranow area, the outer area of the German-created ghetto, a continuous boundary line marks in the paving stones its whole circumference, for those walking the city to see and remember. The tomb of the Unknown Soldier in the Saxon gardens, the living flame under constant military attendance, notes all the major Polish battles and victories, including those forbidden by the Soviets, such as Grodno where Tadeusz was wounded.

The commemoration of the Warsaw Uprising in both monument and museum form is striking. The monument is on a dramatic larger-than-life scale, formed in metal, showing grim and haggard soldiers emerging from under huge paving stones, with some about to descend into the sewers. It is placed opposite the Garrison Cathedral on Długa Street where Tadeusz's funeral was held. This Cathedral now has a chapel dedicated to the Katyn massacre victims, with all names carved onto the metal plaques lining its walls. Stas Leinweber is amongst them. There is another sad codicil to that awful massacre. Near the hotel where we stayed was a memorial, surrounded by praying people, of the plane crash at Smolensk in April 2010. This was on the occasion of a state visit by Russian invitation, of the late Polish President Lech Kaczinski and key members of the Polish government and clergy, to honour the dead of Katyn. The plane crashed *en route* and all were killed. It was a national catastrophe, depleting the democratic government. Victims included a priest from the West London Polish community who, at the last moment, had been offered a seat. The long shadow of Katyn continues.

Warsaw shows pride in the past but with an acknowledgement of the modern world and its place as a European capital city. Its young population is sophisticated, educated, confident and linguistically talented. They are comfortable with their identity and their rightful place on their continent. They know their history but do not wallow in it. There is a generation grown since the fall of communism who have retrieved their democratic tradition. My father would have been proud of his city and its occupants.

Solidarity and the EU

The central Polish role in the fall of communism in 1989 through the Solidarity movement is now well documented. Emerging in the 1970s, it began not in Warsaw but in the Lenin Shipyard in Gdansk, led by a worker, Lech Wałesa. It received support from the church in Rome from a Polish Pope, John Paul II, inaugurated in 1978. Solidarity was the first independent trades union in the Eastern Bloc, initiated in 1980. It was to change Polish and East European politics. It took time – first a relaxation of communist control, then a period of martial law, then amnesty and finally in 1986 the release of political prisoners. In June 1989 the beginnings of democracy were seen, with a third of the seats in the Polish Sejm subject to election and the establishment of a second elected Senate house. The first non-communist prime minister in the Eastern Bloc was elected. A wave of 'velvet revolutions' rippled across Eastern Europe, culminating in the fall of the Berlin Wall. Wałesa was elected President, ending Poland's communist rule and reinstating democracy. By 1997 Poland was enjoying the highest growth rate in Europe. It joined both NATO and the European Union (EU). In 2004 Poles became able to move freely to live and work between Poland and Britain for the first time.

The EU had begun in 1957 with the Treaty of Rome and six founding members. The UK was to join in 1973, and its largest increase in member states occurred in 2013, bringing the total to 28 members. It was set up with the aim of ending the frequent and bloody wars on the continent, which had culminated in both the First and Second World Wars. It also aimed to end totalitarianism in favour of social democracy and centre ground politics. The last right-wing dictatorships in Europe came to an end in Portugal in 1974, and Spain in 1975. The union was operationalised as an economic union, the Common Market. The resulting drop in custom duties and agreement on food production controls led to economic growth and plentiful food supply. The regional policy transferred huge sums of money to create jobs and improve infrastructure in poor areas within the union. The European Parliament increased its influence, and by 1979 all citizens could elect their members directly. In 1986, the Single European Act increased the free flow of trade across EU borders in a 'Single Market'. With the collapse of communism in 1989, Europeans become closer neighbours. In 1993, the Single Market was completed with the 'four freedoms': of movement, of goods, of services, of money. The 'Schengen' agreement (the UK did not sign) allowed people to travel within member EU countries without passport checks, to benefit communication and easy movement of students. For many in the East it was the first period of true movement across Europe. A new freedom.

The euro became the new currency for many Europeans, although not in the UK. Then after the 9/11 terrorist attacks in New York and Washington, the new 'War on Terror' was instigated. EU countries began to work much more closely together, and with the US, to fight crime and terrorism. No fewer than ten new countries joined the EU in 2004 including Poland, followed by Bulgaria and Romania in 2007. A financial crisis hit the global economy in September 2008 but did not hinder the Treaty of Lisbon, which was ratified by all EU countries, coming into force in 2009. It provided the EU with modern institutions and more efficient working methods. The EU established the 'Banking Union' to ensure safer and more reliable banks.

In 2012, the EU was awarded the Nobel Peace Prize. With Croatia becoming the 28th member of the EU in 2013, enlargement was considered one of the most successful elements of EU foreign policy. A new security policy was established, in the wake of the annexation of Crimea by Russia. Religious extremism increased in the Middle East and various countries and regions around the world, leading to unrest and wars, with many people fleeing their homes and seeking refuge in Europe. The EU was faced with the dilemma of absorbing Syrian and other refugees on compassionate grounds, and having a manageable immigration policy. It has caused dissension in many countries. EU countries also find themselves the target of several terrorist attacks. An unsettled period has set in to challenge the union.

Reflecting on Polish communities in the UK

In the last 25 years there have been waves of Polish newcomers to the UK (Galasinska, 2010). The 1989 immigration wave occurred after the fall of communism, and that in 2004 from the EU enlargement, with the 'accession countries', when Poland became a full member. These, together with the Poles from the Second World War, comprise three overlapping groups, studied by Galasinska, in terms of their interaction in leisure and cultural activities. She investigates their 'grand narratives' that define their immigration. The first post-war migration she identifies as mainly former soldiers and officers and their families who had come to Britain to fight in the war, but prevented from returning due to the communist regime. Their narrative involves escape from persecution and fascism, and their 'long journey' to the UK. Their Polish centres were likened to a Polish home ('Dom Polski') guarded by the members which had some suspicion of newcomers, even later waves of Poles.

The second wave of immigrants, in 1989, were the first to have passports to leave the Eastern bloc post-war, previously marooned from the rest of Europe. These pioneers left Poland, faced challenges of getting to know the West, its economics and traditions, gaining entry and working legally. The narrative of this group was about space being fixed and closed, and freedom of movement something to be fought for. Their difficult journey was seen as a rite of passage, moving between two different political worlds. It involved decision, struggle and determination and was seen as an individual, rather than a group, experience. They did not come through designated 'routes' as the first wave had. Many had additional difficulties in being accepted among the 'old Poles' (being labelled as communists and viewed with suspicion). These newcomers did not have enough power or capital to organise their own new migrant sites.

The latest group, post-EU enlargement, came in 2004 when the UK opened its labour markets for the newly created Europeans. They travelled openly, looked for jobs independently and could move back home easily. They became transnational, keeping a foot in both countries and building identities in both. They had a strong sense of individual achievement, agency and flexibility. These saw themselves as separate to prior waves of Polish settlers. They acted more freely, opened businesses and become useful employers and employees in a range of occupations, as well as academics (students and staff) in universities. The spaces in which they socialised, typically shops and restaurants, served their needs for identity, socialising and the exchange of information just as the Polish clubs did for the older generations.

The 'old Poles' from the post-war period are dying out, and their offspring are assimilated, holding onto some Polish customs and typically bilingual. They identify as British and interact easily with the newer Poles and with return trips to Poland. It has yet to be seen what will happen to the later migrants post-Brexit and whether they begin returning permanently to Poland. It also remains to be seen whether the newly found freedom of movement for Poles in relation to the UK will continue.

Brexit

In June 2016 the UK initiated a referendum on its future in the EU, and whilst the vote was very close, the majority (53.4 vs 46.6 per cent) voted to leave, or 'Brexit'.[1] I participated in an all-day conference on voting day, in London, the conclusion of a three-year, EU-funded research project investigating online abuse among young people and the police response to tackling this. The grant is held by my university at Middlesex (led by a close colleague, Julia Davidson) and with partners in the EU. The conference reporting on our findings goes well and we are proud of the fine collaboration between Italian, Irish, Dutch and British researchers. This has enabled new preventative messages for Europol and Interpol, for educators, psychologists and the academic community in recognising, halting and intervening in online harm to children and teenagers. It is the day of the European Referendum. There is pouring rain, lightning and flooding. Much of London grinds to a halt. The underground trains are delayed and traffic is intense. People still go out to vote.

I awake early the next morning to hear the bombshell that Britain has voted to exit from Europe. We in the UK will no longer be European Union citizens. It saddens and shocks me – a blow to the stomach. The voice of Londoners was overwhelmingly 'remain', but this was at odds with much of the rest of the country, although in line with the Celts and the young. I am content to be in that grouping. But I worry about the 'other' England and the large group suspicious of immigration, acquisitively focused on the greater self-gain and distance and independence from mainland Europe. They waste no tears on the potential destabilising of the great vision of a united Europe and the successful social experiment of bringing together 28 European countries, flourishing under a liberal social system, this having heralded an unprecedented period of peace and prosperity. Nobody raises the issue of whether a British exit might harm the rest of the union; the level of debate is about financial gain and restricted immigration, an argument for the UK autonomy.

The split revealed is right through the UK, since nearly half voted to 'remain' and just over half to exit. Reasons given include anti-immigrant feeling – an objection to EU nationals being able to work freely in the UK, including Poles. It also includes antagonism to Germany's welcoming of Syrian refugee asylum seekers, who can then travel through Europe and can gain entry to other countries.[2] The globalisation agenda is less clear – on the one hand there is a return to localism, and desire for autonomy over British politics and economics, but among some groups a desire for greater global economic activity wider than Europe. It is clear the vote is, on the whole, a protest vote from those feeling disenfranchised – the poorer and less well educated, the older who regret the loss of 'Englishness', and cities in the north and west that suffer deprivation. Wales with England votes to leave. Scotland and Northern Ireland vote to remain. London votes remain. Younger people vote to remain. Academics want to remain, as do many other professionals, and most politicians. It was the party line for both Conservative and Labour, although both had dissenters. At the time of writing, the mechanism for leaving has been activated through Article 50 of the Lisbon Treaty, although the negotiations for the exit are not yet under way. This complicated by a sudden and indecisive election in the UK. The split in the country needs to be understood, and then healed regardless of the political action. A simple yes/no question with a large turnout showed us more about ourselves and our culture than we realised it would. It has certainly raised a passionate response to politics on both sides – I have never seen a political issue so emotionally debated in the UK.

An analysis of Polish immigration to the UK reveals the 'moral panic' expressed by a number of British people that presaged the Brexit vote (Fitzgerald and Smoczynski, 2015). This follows the most recent (2004) wave of immigration and concerns the expressed issue of 'taking British jobs' and 'abusing British social benefits', and underlines the destabilising effects of UK employment insecurities. The later immigrants are typically young, without dependents, and employed in low-skilled jobs with most working for labour agencies. British reactions have varied, but despite trade unions offering help, the British public is now unfriendly or hostile. Those who are anti-immigrant point out that this is a general East European animosity, not Polish specifically. The anti-immigrant feeling occurs across the British Isles, with the highest rates in Northern Ireland. Here, 47 per cent of British people when polled agreed that migrants from East Europe, post-2004, constituted a negative factor for the economy, 76 per cent felt there were too many foreigners in Britain and 76 per cent wanted the British authorities to impose new restrictive measures on immigration (Carby-Hall, 2007). Yet Northern Ireland had a majority vote to remain in the EU, perhaps based on the financial gain for its infrastructure and its long border with the Irish Republic. Clearly the EU referendum decision was a complex one. The moral panic argument of 'disproportionality', with regard to East European migration, claims it to be a risk to social cohesion. No evidence was found, however, for any flood of crime or social housing abuses as outlined (Mawby and Gisby, 2009). After the financial crash of 2008, Poles increasingly have become scapegoats for the financial insecurity faced by workers across the country.

There has been much tolerance and generosity towards Poles in England, and only in more recent debate has an attitude of superiority and hostility began to emerge from the local UK population. There is the usual denigration of the occupations that immigrants take up (building work, care work, restaurant work) and the charge that they take jobs away from British workers, although the case for this during a time of high national employment is hard to sustain. In 2016 the first highly publicised attacks were seen against Polish institutions (POSK in Hammersmith)[3] and individuals, with one loss of Polish life (Arkadiusz Jozwik) in Harlow, Essex.[4] These were linked in the press to the racism emerging from the Brexit campaign. It is hoped these do not increase in the new populist political agenda.

The referendum made me question not whether I feel European, which is very ingrained, but rather whether I feel British. I have no problem, however, identifying myself as a Londoner, having lived here most of my adult life, a more cosmopolitan experience than elsewhere in the country. But I realise many would probably not consider me truly British given my Polish/Irish origins, Catholic upbringing and marriage into an Italian family. I think my childhood in the 1950s and 1960s was a time when these differences were also prominent, and probably disapproved of in some quarters. I was aware as a child that my father was considered a 'foreigner' and I knew early on that my parents were discriminated against when they tried to get housing after the war. I was also aware, from an earlier generation, of discrimination against Catholics. Indeed my Irish grandfather was refused a research position at Oxford University on the basis of his religion in the 1920s. As an adult, however, I have not been aware of any discrimination on this basis. In an academic career there is often evidence of gender bias, which is gradually being addressed, as well as on grounds of Black and minority ethnic communities, but few would expect discrimination against fellow Europeans. Universities have consistently been in favour of including European workers and students to the benefit of academic life, research and teaching.

But perceptions can change, and despite 70 years of assimilation and positive contribution to British society from settled Polish communities, Poles and other East Europeans are increasingly disparaged and considered undesirable. It is an unsettling feeling, and one which erodes a sense of security and belonging. There has been a flurry of Irish and Poles, long settled in England, applying for European passports through their links to these countries. There was a time when a British passport alone was the most prized possession.

I write here of a few other themes relevant to the analysis of this family narrative, its socio-political context and psychological impacts.

Freedom to speak of trauma

The Second World War generation seem to have been stalwart in their survival skills and commonly chose not to describe their trauma experiences to others. For some the barriers have lifted somewhat in older age. For combatants, particularly those in Special Services, the Official Secrets Act inhibited disclosure for many years after the war.[5] There were very real social and legal constraints on speaking out about experiences in addition to the psychological barriers that precluded revisiting emotionally painful episodes. This has led to delays, in some cases across a generation, of wartime trauma stories being revealed. There are differences in the capacity of individuals to speak of trauma, often something psychologically locked away. Trauma research literature suggests that, in the more extreme cases, there is either a level of 'amnesia' with little conscious access to experience or, rather, overwhelming revisiting of the traumatic experience through flashback, nightmares and rumination (American Psychiatric Association, 2013). The experience of symptoms can be delayed by years, and experiences can be accompanied by feelings of shame and guilt (for example, survivor guilt) which creates barriers to disclosure, help-seeking and self-help (Lee, Scragg and Turner, 2001).

There is also the issue of how traumatised populations cope. A recent commentary on Polish national adjustment, post-communism, highlights the twin issues of forgetting and remembering wartime trauma (Misztal, 2009). The argument put forward is that in Europe, deliberate forgetting of traumatic events was common, particularly in East Europe under a communist regime in denial of its culpability. This can also perhaps be applied to some Scandinavian countries, Austria and even France, who had some collaborationist history. However, post-Cold War, there has been a compensatory surplus of memory and when this is institutionalised it can influence the collective identity. The previous politics of 'forgetting' under communism was unsustainable, and in the following era the attempt to recover 'blank spots' and redress wrongs has been extensive, but remembering can also create problems if not well managed. Some degree of forgetting is argued to be conducive to civic health. Health adjustment requires finding an accommodation in processing the information about what happened but being able to move on and develop resilience and even post-traumatic growth (Zoellner and Maercker, 2006).

Applying a mature level of balance to national memory or forgetting may involve challenging the prevailing sense of national identity. This involves not only reporting accurate evidence-based historical information about prior national events, but also the ability to hold a more pluralistic or morally ambiguous representation of the past (Renan, 1990). Collective remembering is argued to be important for creating a democratic community. In order to deal with justice, a community has to know how to deal with its past crimes and with negative information about itself. Misztal argues that forced forgetting under communism was highly organised and strategic in order to justify the communist order (Misztal, 2009). Challenges to the official version of events were eliminated. The mechanism of enforcement was through official ceremonies, re-education and re-socialisation to form a national and class-based interpretation of recent national history. This had the consequence of 'freezing memory', to leave it unscrutinised, and restricting pluralistic debate. Yet when people had access to their own memories of significant events that conflicted with the official view, this also sustained an alternative sense of national identity. People looked toward their private memories for an authentic view of the past, although restricted from publicly challenging the official line.

The official Soviet communist view of the Second World War had two particular gaps relevant to Poland – the narratives of Polish–Russian relations historically and the suffering of Jews. Thus the Katyn massacre was a 'blind spot' because of Russian culpability, unacknowledged, and self-justified by its ideological position on discrimination by social class. But another blind spot was a more in-depth understanding of Jewish experience (Gross, 2006). While communist propaganda assumed that anti-Semitism belonged to the capitalist past and connected it purely to Nazi crimes, there was no acknowledgement of anti-Semitism under Stalin, whether in Russia or Poland. In Poland, Auschwitz was presented as a symbol of Polish martyrdom, a joint experience for both Jew and non-Jew. Anti-Semitism became a taboo topic under the newly democratic Poland. However, finding out about the blind spots or 'refusal of memory' under communism also became an all-consuming investigation in the 'restoration' of memory.

Historical accounts of anti-Semitism in Poland are often contradictory. The two communities (Jewish and non-Jewish Poles) were very close historically and lived in close proximity. There are numerous examples of how the two sets of Poles have helped each other regardless of religion – for example, Jews fighting in the uprisings of the nineteenth century and Catholics helping Jews during the Second World War. This latter scenario was seen to a greater level than in any other European country. However, there are also personal accounts of anti-Semitic experience from Jewish writers which are clearly based on experience. Joanna Olczak-Ronnier, who comes from a family of assimilated Jews from Warsaw, writes of anti-Semitic experiences when growing up during the interwar years (Olczak-Ronnier, 2004). She also relates discrimination and injustice, giving examples in the military such as in Anders' army and with Polish soldiers in Allied forces. She identifies ideological differences – the Jewish-Bolshevik alliance – as one potential source of antagonism between the groups. However, she also describes at length how she and her family survived because of the kindness of Catholic Poles (particularly nuns) who risked their own lives to shelter them. Her immediate family would not have survived without such selfless help, and this was true for many other Jewish families.

A more contentious issue, and one more threatening to national identity, has been the recent uncovering of the wartime Jedwabne massacre of Jews by Poles in June, 1941. An independent Polish investigation has confirmed that around 400 Jews were killed by their non-Jewish Polish neighbours, independently of German action (Gross, 2001; Misztal, 2009). This has been formally acknowledged with an apology made by the Polish government, and a ceremony dedicating a new memorial stone, accepting collective responsibility. Nevertheless, many in the community were upset at this acknowledgement, including the ultra-Catholic and nationalist groups who viewed the admission as a threat to national and religious values. Commentaries have argued that any contemporary anti-Semitism is related to societal unwillingness to admit any former negative attitudes and actions to the Jews. This has caused Poles to look at their past differently and to admit culpability, as any mature democracy needs to do. It represents a point of assimilating both positives and negatives about the cultural beliefs and narratives held, consistent with a more mature democracy.

Discussion of findings

What are the main findings of this single case-study analysis of a family genealogy over three generations? How are the themes of identity, attachment and resilience addressed by the socio-historical and personal information collated over a span of more than 100 years? The following summary and discussion pull together observations from the narrative collected.

Identity

Identity is argued to be varied and multi-layered and, in terms of the cultural aspects, both threatened and strengthened by external assaults and pressures. Thus the cultural identity of Poles is shown to have been under threat during most of the 100 years or more described, apart from a brief period in the 1920s–1930s, and the last 12 years or so with EU accession. Otherwise, Polish national identity was consistently suppressed as a nation from the period covered in this narrative. Yet all these assaults on the cultural identity seem to have become sources of strength. Even 100 years of hostile rule by neighbouring powers did not diminish the use of the Polish language domestically, nor did it stamp out Polish education, culture or values. The Poles are stubborn people, and this is reflected in their hold on their identity and a sometimes hard-headed resistance and resilience. It also taught them as a community a number of skills in both passive resistance and covert organisation, which enabled their continued resistance to the Red Army and the German occupation when needed. It also meant they were far ahead in cryptography, wire-tapping, sabotage and clandestine fighting which benefitted the Allies in the Second World War. Wałesa recognised that Solidarity could not have occurred without the lessons learned from the Warsaw Uprising (Bor-Komorowski, 2010), but the latter could probably not have been as effective without years of a secret state under Partition. This sense of community identity was exported to Polish communities exiled through the politics of the time.

It is clear that my family as described here were consistently clear about their Polish identity and were prepared to sacrifice much in fighting and resisting, for their country. This was patriotic, a term not used much nowadays, and often tainted by nationalism, but also sometimes described as 'attachment to place' whether country, city or social group. Several family members took extreme risk in their vision for national independence and freedom. My grandmother Maria was also solid in her identity as a Polish Catholic and perceived this as a source of resilience and hope, as it was to many in her community. Religious ceremonies were abundant during the war and during the Uprising itself. Of course family members had little choice but to fight or resist – the country was occupied and the population at risk of annihilation more than once. However, several members resisted with passion: Tadeusz, Myszka, Jurek, even Stas, with tales of derring-do, but also with sacrifice.

For my generation, the issue of Polish identity, particularly in a British context, is more complex. My cousins in Poland, who clearly see themselves as Poles, are patriotic about their country (although some critical of its government) and culture, and have no apparent contradictory identities. All of them have parents who are both Polish. I believe they see themselves as European and support the EU vision. My cousin Piotr thanked me for voting 'remain'. All are well travelled, well educated and in middle-class professions. I have only one Polish cousin who has moved abroad (Karolina, née Cygler) and now lives in the USA with her Polish-American husband Steven and two teenage children, Kala and Stefan. They all speak Polish at home, belong to Polish cultural associations in the USA and travel regularly to Poland. I think their Polish identity is strong. I don't know how this will fit with a developing American identity in the children, but I suspect it will be incorporated with some flexibility with Polish communities in the USA.

My sisters and I are in a somewhat different position from many second-generation Poles since we are mixed culture, having Anglo-Irish as well as Polish antecedents. I think we all feel the mix, and at different times of life different elements have emerged more strongly. These have also become intermixed with the families' 'married-in' cultures. This includes Greek, Italian and Jewish. For later generations, partnerships also include Indian, Belizian and American-Jewish-Italian. My eldest sister Yolanda has retained her Polish language, her husband Grigoris is of Greek origin but was born and brought up in communist Poland, and the two visit the country frequently. Since they employ some Polish-speaking carers in their nursing home in Derby, Polish is frequently spoken both at home and at work. My youngest sister Joanna has only retained remnants of her Polish (although it was her first language) but has visited the country and published two novels about Poles in England, one of which is translated (by our cousin Ania) and popular in Poland. I think modern Poles know little of the Second World War diaspora in the UK. My sister Marie is finding her Polish identity with me, on our trips to Warsaw.

I feel a resurgence of Polish identity reflected in the undertaking of this genealogical project; it has been identity-enhancing. My surprise at the warm welcome of our Polish cousins and their families, and their complete acceptance of us as kin, has given me a new 'ready-made' Polish family, not only several cousins and their partners living in Poland, but three young nephews and their partners. More relatives have appeared who are descended from my great-grandparents' cousins, to meet with us. I have been surprised in retrospect how much contact was retained across the Iron Curtain by my grandmother, mother and father. This has only become apparent as I have had the many letters translated, the first time I have known of their contents. My Polish language is reawakening with the help of regular skype lessons by Magda from Polword, who is increasing my 'remembering'. I now have Anglo-Polish friends in West London – Irena, Kazik and Bozena – with whom I dine in Polish restaurants and we co-reinforce identity through discussing family stories. Their parents all came out during the war through different traumatic circumstances, but specifically through the Siberian trek where Irena's family ended up living in Uganda (Malin, 2013). All are very well versed in the cultural narratives and recent history. Bilingual, they have close family in England as well as Poland. All have taken an interest in this narrative, with Bozena undertaking the translation of letters. I now openly tell people I am Polish, which I realise I never did before, since my married name is Italian and I had few Polish contacts. It has also led me to explore academic contacts in Poland. This is to learn further how Psychology is studied and researched in Poland, but also with the sense of 'giving back' some of the experience and privilege of having studied and researched in the UK. Psychology was a banned discipline under communism, so its resurgence post-1989 is under rapid development.

Identity is many-layered, however, and the submergence of my Polish identity in former years may have been partly to do with losing my father early, but also an unintended consequence of taking on Italian identity when I married into a warm and accepting Italian family. This adopted identity is still strong, but has undergone some change since my husband and many of my close in-laws have now died. I still have great empathy with Italian culture and love to visit, and indeed have several collaborations with Italian universities, but I am testing whether a space can be made for a parallel, albeit prior, Polish identity to emerge. Substitution in personal identities is curious: I now think that my very strong attachment to my Italian mother-in-law substituted for the lost attachment to my Polish grandmother. The two were alike. The latter has re-emerged after my mother-in-law's recent death. I have not read theories about such substitute attachments and identity, but it seems to me to be a plausible process.

I have learned more of my Polish family background and have been made to consider what life was like from their point of view, to empathise and sympathise. I am greatly impressed by my relatives and forebears. They present as upright, secure, warm, principled and loyal. While it may not have emerged from the account, they could be fun loving and adventurous. The mania for bridge playing seems to run through the Czechowski family line – my father as well as his aunties played. This family were intelligent but practical folk, tending to be engineers, vets and surveyors as well as military officers. They were highly rooted to their country estates and rural pursuits. I suspect they were not overly devout, but followed all the traditional Catholic rituals and festivities. My grandmother Maria was a Cygler, and very devoutly religious. Since her eldest sister became a nun, it is possible this was a theme running through her family. The Cyglers are certainly a highly intelligent family (they include academics, writers, architects and lawyers), which persists into the recent generation. Writers seem common to both sides of the family, and we have them in each generation going right back to Helena Czechowska in the mid-1800s.

Psychological identity relates to self-image, self-esteem and individuality, and it ties together the past, present and future self and continuity with one's construction of past ancestry (Wienreich and Saunderson, 2003). Identity also includes self-reflection and awareness of self (Leary and Tangney, 2003). One of the things that initially constrained me tackling this narrative concerned the ownership of the account. The narrative seemed to belong to the people who lived it – my grandparents and parents – and was not mine. With increasing age and loss of those involved, I now feel it has come to me to either tell the story or let it go. I myself witnessed none of the events, but parts of it were told to me when I was young, and my sisters and I hold the same, albeit incomplete, story to pass on or not as we choose. It has become a part of me. It has no doubt influenced me in countless unremarked ways. As a friend once said, 'being Polish is half of yourself', so having it hidden for years must have suppressed some facets of my identity of which I was unaware. This exercise of tracing my recent ancestoral experience has expanded my sense of identity. I have found it enriching, and it has led to subtle changes in behaviour and a widening of context.

Identity is now argued to encompasses both exploration and commitment as part of its process of extension (Marcia, Waterman, Matteson, Archer and Orlofsky, 1993). People experience different levels of such exploration and commitment in seeking their identity, and this may be experienced differently at different ages. Some are disinterested while others feel a particular identity without curiosity or any behavioural commitment. 'Identity achievement' – the pinnacle – is described when a person consciously makes identity choices, follows these and then commits to them, thus expanding and clarifying their own identity. Taking this active view of cultural identity means we can, to some extent, choose who we are and, if committed, great benefits can flow from such choices.

DNA analysis

With a recognition of biological explanations for human behaviour, I sent off a saliva sample to a company ('23andme') who provide cultural analysis based on DNA. This was out of curiosity to see whether this could validate the different cultural strands as I understand them from the varied family narratives and secondary sources. There is some debate over its accuracy – it depends on having a large enough pool of individuals analysed all over the world to accurately identify patterns belonging to groups in particular geographic locations. The results seemed surprisingly accurate: my cultural background appears entirely European as expected. The largest proportion (26 per cent) is East European, allied to 2 per cent Ashkenazi Jewish and 2 per cent Iberian/South European. I was surprised the Jewish percentage was not higher, but have little information on the Cygler side of the family. On the other side, 13 per cent was labelled as British and Irish with 9 per cent French and German and 4 per cent Scandinavian. Only the last proportion is not accounted for in family story, but could easily have entered the family from either parent (see Figure 10.1). The health analysis that accompanied the cultural one fortunately held no dire news apart from an unsurprising raised risk for Alzheimer's (this afflicted my mother).

Attachment

The family seems to have had strong attachments and to have the blend of both self-reliance and cooperation that marks out secure attachment style (Bowlby, 1988). My grandparents' and parents' generation had long-lasting stable marriages, when these were not ended by war-related bereavement. I cannot vouch for details of the quality of attachment, but the letters and photographs indicate closeness. In my father's generation, I only know of one aunt who divorced (Danuta) but married again successfully. She had no children. Divorces are more common in my own generation, but no higher than national rates and most conducted amicably. All children in the wider family have been raised by their birth parents, with grand-

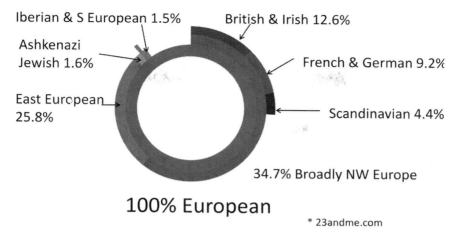

FIGURE 10.1 My DNA cultural analysis

mothers often taking an active role in caregiving. There were rumours of occasional family rifts in the Polish members, but these were healed in time and we don't know the source. There were clearly great kindnesses: Marysia undertaking much of the bureaucracy involved in my grandmother Maria's emigration to England; Maria and Grazyna, sisters-in-law, but more like sisters, helping each other out through war and at times of loss and deprivation; our parcels from England sent not only just after the war but also during the 1970s' periods of deprivation.

There were individuals who cemented the links and served as family 'ambassadors'. Following my younger sister Joanna's lone travel to Poland in 1977 aged 18, my cousin Ania (née Cygler) started corresponding with her and became a frequent visitor to England. A fluent English speaker, she came first alone, and later with her husband Andrzej, spending time in both Derby and London. They were very close to my mother Christine and invited her to Poland on more than one occasion, including to their wedding. They later became involved in many Polish–English activities, including those cultural and ambassadorial, even being invited to Buckingham Palace. Later, cousin Piotr was to come, first with his parents Krystyna and Leszek as a teenager, and later alone after his mother's early death from cancer. He gained work experience as a carer in Yolanda's nursing home as well as visiting London, prior to his study of medicine in Warsaw. He too is fluent in English and is well travelled. These two provided a bridge for the family across the continent.

This has led me to find my cousin Małgosia, who in many ways is my counterpart in Poland but who has been hidden to me over the years. She is nearly the same age as me; she was being looked after by her grandmother Grazyna whilst I was being looked after by my grandmother Maria, so both of us had care from these strong, warm and loving 'sisters' who were born in the late 1800s. I wonder

230 England: the third generation

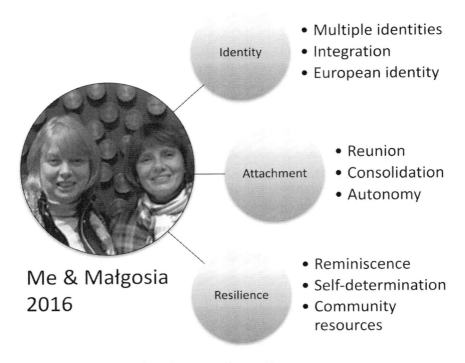

FIGURE 10.2 Summary of the themes in Chapter 10

if it has affected us similarly. There is a film, *The Double Life of Veronique* by Kesłowski, which describes two women living in Warsaw and Paris (played by the same actress), unknown to each other, who have parallel lives and unwittingly share experiences. This is something like finding a close cousin with parallel early experiences rediscovered after 50 years. Whether this develops into a close, long-term relationship is yet to be seen. We are both striving to speak each other's language better and are now in regular email contact. The themes of Chapter 10 are summarised in Figure 10.2.

Resilience

The combination of strong identity and strong attachment more or less equates with resilience in terms of coping with adverse experience. The family has survived a good deal of adversity, both politically and personally. Each generation has had the privilege of good education, good upbringing and a facility for leading or having authority or expertise in their work. However, this does not guarantee resilience under stress and the loss of status can be a further blow to coping. My grandmother perhaps saw the greatest fall in social and economic status and living conditions. She responded with endurance, optimism and faith.

My father Jurek showed resilience, not only during his wartime activities but also in the way he adapted to his new country and put his many talents to use in helping his exiled community organise and look after itself. There was a lot of unused talent in this community, perhaps a general feature of immigrant groups. It seems surprising to me that the English services did not want to make greater use of the extensive training given to my father and men like him – for example, other SOE agents after the war. This lack reflected a general policy. Some of the English women in the SOE lived subsequent quiet lives, never relating their experience, and have only been honoured after their death. This includes Eileen Nearne who lived reclusively in Torquay and her sister Jacqueline (Ottaway, 2013). Talented Poles were rarely utilised by government or security services, due to security constraints because of communism in Poland. As part East European I grew up knowing I could never rise to any significant level in the civil service, police or military. There are no such institutional constraints now.

Another contributor to resilience is outside support. One organisation that has cropped up more than once with wartime aid in this narrative has been the Red Cross. They were active in both world wars. They indexed lists of missing persons and prisoners of war and were able to match family members after the conflict. They created a fund for visiting and monitoring prisoner of war camps. They protested the use of chemical weapons. They organised relief assistance for civilian populations, and administered the exchange of messages regarding prisoners and missing persons. They insisted on the upholding of the Geneva Convention, although the Soviet Union and Japan were not signatories in the second conflict. In the Second World War the Red Cross had been criticised since the German section was Nazi-controlled and refused to cooperate with the Geneva statutes over the deportation of Jews from Germany and the mass murders conducted in the concentration camps. But they were certainly of assistance to Jurek, including acting as courier for letters to Warsaw, getting him released from forced labour and prison in France and Spain, and ultimately providing the certification of Myszka's death in Auschwitz.

One marker of resilience lies in the ability of a family to reproduce and thus survive across generations. This seems to have gone well. Tadeusz and his two siblings only produced one child each, at a time of wartime conflict and early paternal loss. But these have in turn produced six children, who in turn have produced a further thirteen showing sufficient expansion to indicate that the family is growing. All of these are flourishing health-wise despite some temporary setbacks, and show intelligence, talent, good parenting and close family relationships. The family has been resilient and has survived.

There is a danger of idealising previous family members, and the apparent lack of family conflict and breakdown. This may simply be due to missing information, but I suspect not. This is not to say the family was free of tension or disagreement, but this never escalated to levels of separation. My mother and grandmother were both strong personalities who had at times an uneasy relationship in our Derby home. My mother could be domineering, which at times led to conflict with her children. In my generation, as children my sisters often fought, as siblings do. As adults we have had periods of greater or lesser closeness; with age, closeness is increasing. The family in Poland tell of temporary family rifts, gossip and falling out in their letters. But maybe when the external forces are hostile to an extreme, there is no possibility or purpose to sewing discord internally, and no protection if the family falls apart.

Emotional geography

This book opens with a poem by Sara Teasdale, chosen because of the way in which Warsaw has been seen variously as close or distant to England, both politically and emotionally. For Sara Teasdale, an American, the geographical location was literally half a world away. For us in the UK it has never been that far geographically, and politically quite close. But her poem describes how it can seem further or closer depending on the emotional ties. Thus, she writes, when she is close to her lover in Warsaw, she can go 'winged as a bird' but when the relationship turns cold it becomes 'half a world away'.

As a child I knew of the Iron Curtain around East Europe, which I visualised as a rippling metal wall. It was clear that there were major obstacles to travelling to Poland and interacting with family in Poland. My grandmother and mother retained the many carefully handwritten letters they received, indicating their value. There was no effective telephone link, no skype, email or facebook to link relatives as there is now. Poland was distant from 1945 to 1989. Then suddenly, when the Berlin wall came down, the Iron Curtain was pulled aside and, at last, freedom of movement gradually developed, easier interchange was possible. The research narratives tell of the intrepid Poles who came in 1989 to an uneasy settling. Then when Poland joined the EU in the enlargement of 2004 there was ease of movement between the two countries, with many young Poles coming to England for work and to visit family. These latter came as confident Europeans, many with good English skills. In my view, many who came to live in the UK have integrated well and brought traditional family values and a high work ethic with them and have rarely been disruptive, creating few problems with the law. They have taken up jobs for which there is a limited UK workforce (in care homes and hospitals, in services, in agriculture) as well as starting their own businesses in building, gardening and catering. At one time you could hear Polish being spoken wherever you stood in Ealing Broadway – many attracted to West London because of the older community of Poles resident since the 1940s, this in turn because of closeness to Northolt airfield where many had been stationed in the RAF. However, half of the UK now want to stop European immigration. There is thus concern about increasing hostility to Europeans coming from outside the UK. People fear overcrowded services and benefit dependency. Yet it is clear the NHS still actively recruits in Spain and Portugal for nurses to fill posts for which we have no trained UK medical staff. Clearly the country has contradictory needs, or the populace has not accurately identified its needs.

One of the themes of this book has concerned emotional geography which, simply put, is about selecting particular places which are of personal significance (for example, Warsaw or London) – effectively attachment to place. 'Emotional' distance is determined not only by time taken to travel but, more importantly, by the number of close attachments living in those places, and the historical linkages and the emotional charge attached to cities where family have lived. In terms of the former category, Warsaw is now much closer than it has ever been. It takes two hours by jet to get between London and Warsaw, at a relatively low cost and with ease of booking and travel. No visas are necessary, and it is no different from travelling to any other EU capital city. At the beginning of the Second World War when Hitler annexed Czechoslovakia, Chamberlain's comment about 'a quarrel in a faraway country between people of whom we know nothing'[6] served to distance East Europe from British and Western concerns. At that time it took eleven hours to fly from London to Warsaw by propeller plane, which would need to refuel *en route*. Polish people did not speak English and would rarely have visited in those times. Yet even in the First World War in the Russian sector of Poland in 1914, the soldiers fighting with the Allies used British munitions and armoured cars made in the English Midlands. Indeed the Russian Czar, first cousin to the British King George V, visited, so such distances could be spanned by families with relative ease.

As an adult, physical proximity is welcomed and important in attachment, but not essential to the feeling of closeness, which can still exist in some strength at a distance or with more intermittent contact. One can keep a significant other 'in mind' representationally at a distance, secure in the knowledge they will offer emotional support at times of crisis. Feeling attached to someone creates feelings of security and safety. For some this can also apply to family members who have died – a positive representation of them and the feelings of attachment which endure, and can be conducive to psychological well-being. These provide more positive 'go-to' memories for sustenance in adversity.

Conclusions

This approach to investigating psychological themes, through intensive study of secondary family data, has served as exploration of context as it affects family behaviour. It is an exploratory method of drawing political and social context into the actions of the family, and the resulting family narratives. It could be similarly undertaken with any family for which there was sufficient systematic information, against the social era in which they lived. Different themes would emerge. These may be illuminating, identity-enhancing or identity-destructive for the participant researcher, but all would hold great interest regardless of time, place, social class or cultural identity.

The method has limitations. One cannot be truly independent in viewing people who are close and who are a product of a shared cultural narrative. The closeness gives the motivation and the access to materials, including personal memory, but this can also obscure any negative information or interpretation. There are selection processes in what to include, and gaps where not much is known. In this narrative there is no personal account as collected by interview, although there are biographic writings. Letters may distort the truth – censorship may restrict what is said, and the form of a letter is not very open to disclosure, and responses are too slow. There are also bound to be factual errors in this account – the historical context is vast and much has been written. Here there is only room for a brief summary as a backdrop, and this is not of a critical academic level. The sources are, I hope, of good enough quality but are limited in number. The account also misses many important historical events and the harsh treatment of other groups who did not happen to follow the same path or location of my family. I hope this is not seen as dismissive: there was no such intention.

A potential limitation lies in the choice of themes and sub-themes and the exclusion of others. For example, I have not discussed response to trauma, traumatic disorder or secondary trauma from witnessing or having trauma impacts transmitted in families. This is because I did not observe it in my family or have any documentary evidence of it. It did affect others who went through related experiences, and there is some indication that this at times does move through the generations – a Polish friend queries whether her younger sister's suicide attempt in young adulthood and her other sister's early death from cancer may have been an expression of the trauma experienced by their parents during the war. This is an important topic, but not one which arose in my family as far as I am aware.

Another potential limitation is the extent to which this psychological study has excluded personal analysis. It was not my intention to analyse my personal experiences and memory in order to see how these have affected me as an individual. Some would argue that I should have. Similarly I have not written much about my feelings about my family, nor their individual perceptions of their identity or upbringing. My generation has been described only in very general terms to preserve privacy and to prevent overextending the project. Again I could have taken a different approach and considered their experiences in depth. I can admit, however, that finding out about traumatic events and bereavements that occurred in my earlier family, and the horrors of war they experienced, felt painful. One of my sisters cried when reading it. Whilst this is not uncommon when one sees television programmes about genocide or the Holocaust, there is an additional dimension when you are aware that people biologically related to you are among those masses. An uncle shot at Katyn, a stepmother dying in Auschwitz, a bomb landing on my grandmother's house, these things you take personally. I do not know whether reliving such history is generally helpful, but it may motivate people to stop it happening again and to understand the catastrophe of war. Maybe one will see the ongoing bombing of Aleppo, Syria in these terms and feel sorrow and empathy for the refugees being forced out of that country and losing their homes.

Paula Nicolson approached this same method slightly differently in her innovative genealogical study of her family (P. Nicolson, 2017). She used a wider range of individuals than I, covering a breadth of different relationships and extending it to her husband's family. She has then picked out different stories, themes and conflicts to illustrate different psychological issues. For example, she covers anti-Semitism, domestic violence, single parenthood, social class and cultural differences. Some of her ancestors were publicly known figures, a number of whom lived in parts of London she knows well and for whom she had felt an affinity. Her personal proximity to many of the issues described by her kin has the benefit of removing stigma and increasing empathy. It is easier to put one's self 'in the shoes' of a family member who gets into difficulty, than a stranger. 'There by the grace of God, go I.'

Nicolson asks herself how her narrative investigation has affected her self-view. She describes the discoveries as affecting her differently at different times. Overall she describes that her feelings of warmth and closeness to her extended family increased. She also sought to re-evaluate her relationship with her father and her mother and noticed in writing she had said less of her mother. She emphasises that the self is dynamic, and changing. This is psychological, physical, geographical and social and underpins our narrative and the meaning it holds. She writes:

> Knowledge of our ancestors provides valid information because these individuals are the means and the reason we are alive and in the place (in every sense) we find our self. . . . Most of what I discovered represented thwarted ambitions, frustrated lives and more than anything that so many of us live with, loss and grief. It may be that we can learn from the mistakes our forbear's made. I hope so because there are things to tell my grandchildren.
>
> P. Nicolson, 2017, p. 159

So has the exercise changed my sense of identity, expanded my cultural awareness and led to any increased commitment to such exploration? Has it increased my well-being? The answer is 'yes' on all counts. This is despite some elements of the research and narrative being painful as I imagine myself in situations of duress. But it feels like finding a missing part of a familiar puzzle – the picture emerges as the pieces are slotted together. Suddenly I feel more connected to my childhood, which had been disconnected by bereavement and then geographical distance. There is behavioural commitment in travelling to Poland, learning Polish and retaining contacts with my cousins. Suddenly the distance is inconsequential – two hours from nearby Heathrow and ready email contact. I feel my family to be expanded. With my mother's Anglo-Irish family, this has also occurred as cousins now start to congregate regularly in London around joint activities. I like the cousin relationship – close enough to allow informality and shared contexts, but more novel and less complex than sibling relationships. I also feel connection now with those close to me who have died. This honouring of their story has brought them much closer to mind. It is a benevolent acquisition. I now feel I have a whole group of my forebears positioned with me to take my part. Even being alone now feels quite lively, as these various voices accompany me in my daily life. A small army of ready-made support, attachment, identity and resilience all rolled into one.

Notes

1. www.bbc.co.uk/news/uk-politics-32810887
2. www.independent.co.uk/news/world/europe/refugee-crisis-germany-asylum-seekers-numbers-drop-600000-in-2016-angela-merkel-syria-middle-east-a7521191.html
3. www.theguardian.com/uk-news/2016/jun/27/brexit-polish-centre-london-reeling-after-graffiti-attack
4. www.theguardian.com/commentisfree/2016/sep/05/death-arkadiusz-jozwik-post-referendum-racism-xenophobes-brexit-vote
5. http://researchbriefings.parliament.uk/ResearchBriefing/Summary/CBP-7422
6. Broadcast (27 September 1938), quoted in 'Prime Minister on the Issues', *The Times* (28 September 1938), p. 10.

REFERENCES

Ainsworth, M.D.S., Blehar, M., Waters, E. and Wall, S. (1978). *Patterns of Attachment: A Psychological Study of the Strange Situation*. Hillsdale, NJ: Lawrence, Erlbaum.
Aksamit, B. (2015). *Batory: Stars, Scandal and Love on the Transatlantic Liner*. Warsaw: Adam Mickiewicz Institute.
Allison, S.T. and Goethals, G.R. (2011). *Heroes: What They Do and Why We Need Them*. Oxford: Oxford University Press.
American Psychiatric Association (2013). *The Diagnostic and Statistical Manual of Mental Disorders* (5th edn; DSM–5). Washington, DC: American Psychiatric Association.
Andrzejewski, A. (1965). Housing situation, Warsaw. *Polish Perspectives*, VII, 11–20.
Beard, G. (1869). Neurasthenia, or nervous exhaustion. *The Boston Medical and Surgical Journal*, 80, 217–221. doi: 10.1056/NEJM186904290801301.
Becker, S.W. and Eagly, A.H. (2004). The heroism of women and men. *American Psychologist*, 163–78.
Bifulco, A. (2009). Risk and resilience in young Londoners. In D. Brom, R. Pat-Horenczyk and J. Ford (eds), *Treating Traumatised Children: Risk, Resilience and Recovery*. London: Routledge, pp. 117–31.
Bifulco, A. (2015). Attachment and adversity across the lifespan. *New Directions in Psychotherapy and Relational Psychoanalysis*, 9, 201–18.
Bifulco, A., Bernazzani, O., Moran, P.M. and Ball, C. (2000). Lifetime stressors and recurrent depression: preliminary findings of the Adult Life Phase Interview (ALPHI). *Social Psychiatry and Psychiatric Epidemiology*, 35, 264–75.
Bifulco, A., Harris, T. and Brown, G.W. (1992). Mourning or early inadequate care? Reexamining the relationship of maternal loss in childhood with adult depression and anxiety. *Development and Psychopathology*, 4, 433–49.
Bifulco, A., Moran, P.M., Jacobs, C. and Bunn, A. (2009). Problem partners and parenting: exploring linkages with maternal insecure attachment style and adolescent offspring internalizing disorder. *Attachment and Human Development*, 11(1), 69–85.
Bifulco, A. and Thomas, G. (2012). *Understanding Adult Attachment in Family Relationships: Research, Assessment and Intervention*. London: Routledge.
Blom, P. (2008). *The Vertigo Years: Europe 1900-1914*. New York: Basic Books.
Bor-Komorowski, T. (2010). *The Secret Army. The Memoires of General Bor-Komorowski*. Barnsley, UK: Frontline.

Borowiec, A. (2015). *Warsaw Boy: A Memoire of a Wartime Childhood*. Random House, UK: Penguin.

Bowlby, J. (1958). The nature of the child's tie to his mother. *International Journal of Psycho-Analysis*, *39*, 350–73.

Bowlby, J. (1988). *A Secure Base: Clinical Application of Attachment Theory*. London: Routledge.

Brown, G.W. and Harris, T. (1978). *Social Origins of Depression: A Study of Psychiatric Disorder in Women*. London: Tavistock.

Budiansky, S. (2000). *Battle of Wits: The Complete Story of Codebreaking in World War II*. New York: Free Press.

Budnik, A. and Liczbin, G. (2006). Urban and rural differences in mortality and causes of death in historical Poland. *American Journal of Physical Anthropology*, 129(2), 294–304.

Calvocoressi, P. (2011). *Top Secret Ultra*. Kidderminster, UK: M&M Baldwin.

Carby-Hall, J. (2007). The treatment of Polish and other A8 Immgrants in European member states. Hull: Report for the Commisioner for Civil Rights Protection of the Republic of Poland.

Ciano, G. (1945). *The Ciano Diaries 1939-43*. San Antonio, TX: Simon Publications.

Crowdy, T. (2016). *SOE: Churchill's Secret Agents*. Oxford: Shire Publications.

Czechowska, H. (1895). *Wedding at Rudzk*. Krakow, Poland: Academy of Sciences.

Czechowska, J. (2006). *Black Madonna of Derby*. Chippenham, UK: Silkmill.

Czechowska, J. (2012). *The Sweetest Enemy*. Chippenham, UK: Silkmill.

D'Abernon, E.V. (1931, 1977). *The Eighteenth Decisive Battle of the World, Warsaw 1920*. London: Hyperion.

Davidson, J., Smith, M. and Bondi, L. (2007). *Emotional Geographies*. Aldershot, UK: Ashgate.

Davies, N. (1972, 2003). *White Eagle, Red Star. The Polish-Soviet War 1919-1920 and the 'Miracle on the Vistula'*. London: Pimlico edn., Random House.

Davies, N. (2004). *Rising '44' The Battle for Warsaw'*. Basingstoke and Oxford: Pan Books, Macmillan.

Davies, N. (2005). *God's Playground* (revised 2nd edn). New York: Columbia University Press.

Davies, N. (2015). *Trail of Hope: The Anders Army, An Odyssey Across Three Continents*. Oxford: Osprey.

de Waal, E. (2010). *The Hare with Amber Eyes: A Hidden Inheritance*. London: Chatto and Windus.

Eberhardt, J., Williams, M. and Jackson, M. (2008). Not yet human: implicit knowledge, historical dehumanization, and contemporary consequences. *Journal of Personality and Social Psychology*, *94*(2). doi: 10.1037/0022-3514.94.2.292.

Eichsteller, G. (2009). Janusz Korczak – his legacy and its relevance for children's rights today. *International Journal of Children's Rights*, *17*, 377–91.

Erikson, E. (1950). *Childhood and Society*. New York: Norton.

Farmer, S.B. (2004). *Foreign Labor in Vichy, France: The Groupements de Travailleurs Etrangers, Symposium 2004*. Paper presented at the United States Holocaust Memorial Museum, Centre for Advanced Holocaust Studies.

Figes, O. (2007). *The Whisperers. Private Life in Stalin's Russia*. London: Allen Lane (Penguin Books).

Finlay, L. (2002). Negotiating the swamp: the opportunity and challenge of reflexivity in research practice. *Qualitative Research*, *2*(2), 209–30.

Fitzgerald, I. and Smoczynski, R. (2015). Anti-Polish migrant moral panic in the UK: Rethinking employment insecurities and moral regulation. *Sociologický časopis/Czech Sociological Review*, *51*(3), 339–61. doi: 10.13060/00380288.2015.51.3.180.

Fivush, R., Bohanek, J.G. and Duke, M. (2008). The intergenerational self: Subjective perspective and family history. In F. Sani (ed.), *Individual and Collective Self-Continuity*. Mahwah, NJ: Erlbaum, pp. 131–43.

Fivush, R. and Zaman, W. (2011). Intergenerational narratives: How collective family stories relate to adolescents' emotional well-being. *Aurora. Revista de Arte, Mídia e Política*, 10, 51–63.

Fonagy, P., Steele, M., Steele, H., Higgitt, A. et al. (1994). The Emanuel Miller Memorial Lecture 1992: The theory and practice of resilience. *Journal of Child Psychology and Psychiatry and Allied Disciplines*, 35(2), 231–57.

Freedman, J. and Combs, G. (1996). *Narrative Therapy: The Social Construction of Preferred Realities*. New York: W.W. Norton.

Frost, N. (2016). *Practising Research. Why You're Always Part of the Research Process Even When You Think You're Not*. New York: Palgrave.

Frost, N.A. (2011). *Qualitative Research Methods in Psychology: Combining core approaches*. Milton Keynes, UK: Open University Press.

Fugate, M., Landis, L., Riordan, K., Naureckas, S. and Engel, B. (2005). Barriers to domestic violence help seeking. Implications for intervention. *Violence Against Women*, 11(3), 290–310. doi: 10.1177/1077801204271959.

Furst, A. (1995, 2005). *The Polish Officer*. London: Phoenix.

Galasinska, A. (2010). Gossiping in the Polish Club: An emotional coexistence of 'Old' and 'New' migrants. *Journal of Ethnic and Migration Studies*, 36(6), 939–51.

Giddens, A. (1995). *Politics, Sociology and Social Theory: Encounters with Classical and Contemporary Social Thought*. Redwood, CA: Stanford University Press.

Gregory, D. (2011). *The Dictionary of Human Geography*. Hoboken, NJ: John Wiley and Sons.

Gross, J.T. (2001). *Neighbours. A Destruction of the Jewish Community in Jewabne, Poland*. Princeton, NJ: Princeton University Press.

Gross, J.T. (2006). *Fear: Anti-semitism in Poland after Auschwitz. An Essay in Historical Interpretation*. Princeton, NJ: Princeton University Press.

Gumkowski, J. and Leszcynski, K. (1961). *Poland under Nazi Occupation*. Warsaw: Polonia.

Harff, B. and Gurr, T.R. (1988). Toward empirical theory of Genocides and Politicides: Identification and measurement of cases since 1945. *International Studies Quarterly*, 32, 359–71.

Haslam, N., Kashima, Y., Loughnan, S., Shi, J. and Suitner, C. (2008). Subhuman, inhuman, and superhuman: Contrasting humans with nonhumans in three cultures. *Social Cognition*, 26(2), 248–58. doi: 10.1521/soco.2008.26.2.248.

Heineman, J.L. (1994). *Readings in European History, 1789 to the Present: A Collection of Primary Sources*. Duboque, IA: Kendall Hunt.

Herbert, J.M. (1944). *G for Genevieve*. New York: Roy.

Holmes, J. (1993). *John Bowlby and Attachment Theory*. London and New York: Routledge.

Hoover, H. (1951). *The Memoirs Of Herbert Hoover 1874–1920: Years of Adventure*. London: Macmillan.

Household, G. (1939, 2014). *Rogue Male*. London: Orion.

Karski, J. (1944, 2012). *The Story of a Secret State. My Report to the World*. London: Penguin Classics.

Koa Wing, S. (ed.) (2007). *Mass Observation: Britain in the Second World War*. London: The Folio Society.

Kulski, J. (2014). *The Color of Courage: A Boy at War: The World War II Diary of Julian Kulski*. Los Angeles, CA: Aquila Polonica.

Kynaston, D. (2008). *Austerity Britain, 1954-51*. New York: Walker.
Leary, M.R. and Tangney, J.P. (eds) (2003). *Handbook of Self and Identity*, 2nd edn. New York: Guilford.
Lee, D.A., Scragg, P. and Turner, S. (2001). The role of shame and guilt in traumatic events: A clinical model of shame-based and guilt-based PTSD. *British Journal of Medical Psychology*, 74(4), 451–66.
Lightbody, B. (2004). *The Second World War: Ambitions to Nemesis*. London: Routledge.
Lukas, R.C. (2001). *Forgotten Holocaust: The Poles Under German Occupation, 1939-1944*. New York: Hippocrene.
Main, M. and Hesse, E. (1990). Parents' unresolved traumatic experiences are related to infant disorganized attachment status: Is frightened and/or frightening parental behavior the linking mechanism? In M. Greenberg, D. Cicchetti and M. Cummings (eds), *Attachment in the Preschool Years: Theory, Research, and Intervention*. Chicago, IL: University of Chicago Press, pp. 161–82.
Malin, J. (2013). *Faith, Hunger and Song*. London: Tewksbury.
Marcia, J.E., Waterman, A.S., Matteson, D.R., Archer, S.L. and Orlofsky, J.L. (1993). *Ego Identity: A Handbook for Psycho-Social Research*. New York: Springer-Verlag.
Maresch, E. (2010). *Katyn 1940 – the Documentary Evidence of the West's Betrayal*. Stroud, UK: The History Press.
Masten, A.S. and Curtis, W.J. (2000). Integrating competence and psychopathology: pathways toward a comprehensive science of adaptation in development. *Development and Psychopathology*, 12, 529–50.
Mawby, R. and Gisby, W. (2009). Crime, media and moral panic in an expanding European Union. *The Howard Journal*, 48(1), 37–51.
Mayhew, H. (1851). *Mayhew's London*. London: Spring Books.
McAdams, D.P. (1988). *Power, Intimacy and the Life Story: Personological Enquiries into Identity*. New York: Guilford.
Mcgoldrick, M. (2011). *The Genogram Journey: Reconnecting With Your Family*. London: W.W. Norton.
Misztal, B. (2009). The banalisation and the contestation of memory in postcommunist Poland, in M. Anico and E. Peralto (eds), *Heritage and Identity: Engagement and Demission in the Contemporary World*. London, New York: Routledge.
Moller, A.C. and Deci, E.L. (2010). Interpersonal control, dehumanization, and violence: A self-determination theory perspective. *Group Processes and Intergroup Relations*, 13, 41–3.
National Archives. (2014). *SOE Manual. How to be an Agent in Occupied Europe. Special Operations Executive*. St Ives, UK: William Collins.
Neuner, F., Schauer, M., Klaschik, C., Karunakara, U. and Elbert, T. (2004). A comparison of narrative exposure therapy, supportive counseling, and psychoeducation for treating posttraumatic stress disorder in an African refugee settlement. *Journal of Consulting and Clinical Psychology*, 72, 579–87.
Nicolson, J. (2016). *A House Full of Daughters*. London: Chatto and Windus.
Nicolson, P. (2017). *Genealogy, Psychology and Identity: Tales From a Family Tree*. London: Routledge.
Nord, P. (2015). *France 1940. Defending the Republic*. New Haven, CT: Yale University Press.
Ohler, N. (2016). *Blitzed: Drugs in Nazi Germany*. London: Penguin.
Olczak-Ronnier, J. (2004). *In the Garden of Memory: A Family Memoire*. London: Weidenfeld and Nicolson.
O'Neill, H. (1995). *The Autobiography of Hugh O'Neill*. Printed by Christopher O'Neill.
O'Neill, H. (1967). Mixed metal memories. A biographical note. *Metals and Materials*.

Ottaway, S. (2013). *Sisters, Secrets and Sacrifice: The True Story of WWII Special Agents Eileen and Jacqueline Nearne*. New York: Harper Element.
Quin, S. (1995). *Marie Curie: A Life*. Portsmouth, NH: Heineman.
Renan, E. (1990). What is a nation? In H.K. Bhabha (ed.), *Nation and Narration*. London: Routledge.
Rosenberg, S.E. (1988). Self and others: Studies in social personality and autobiography, in L. Berkowitz (ed.), *Advances in Experimental Social Psychology, Vol. 21*. New York: Academic Press, pp. 57–95.
Rutter, M. (2007). Resilience, competence, coping. *Child Abuse and Neglect*, 31, 205–09.
Scotland Liddell, R. (1915). *The Track of the War*. California: University of California Libraries.
Seathoff, G. (2009). *'A Mutual Responsibility and a Moral Obligation': The Final Report on Germany's Compensation Programs for Forced Labour and Other Personal Injuries*. London: Palgrave Macmillan.
Shaw, R.L. (2010). Embedding reflexivity within experiential qualitative psychology. *Qualitative Research in Psychology*, 7, 233–43.
Spiegleman, A. (1996, 2003). *Maus: A Survivor's Tale*. London: Penguin.
Struk, J. (2013). *Photographing the Holocaust: Interpretations of the Evidence*. London: I.B. Tauris.
Szhlachetko, G. (2015). *Wira of Warsaw: Memoir of a Girl Soldier*. London: Emedal.
Szypowska, M. and Szypowski, A. (2005). *As You Enter the Old Warsaw Track*. Warsaw: Artibus Foundation.
Szypowska, M., Szypowski, A. and Szypowski, J. (2009). *The Dramatic History of the Warsaw Wurlitzer Organ*. Warsaw: Artibus Foundation.
Travers, M. (2001). *Qualitative Research through Case Studies*. London: Sage.
Tucholski, J. (1984). *Cichociemni*. Warsaw: Warsaw Institute Wydawniczy Pax.
Valentine, I. (2006). *Station 43. Audley End House and SOE's Polish Section*. Stroud, UK: The History Press.
White, A. (2011a). *Polish Families and Migration since EU Accession*. Bristol, UK: The Policy Press.
White, A. (2011b). *Polish Immigration in the UK – Local Experiences and Effects*. Paper presented at the AHRC Connected Communities symposium: Understanding local experiences and effects of new immigration, 2011, 9, 26.
Wienreich, P. and Saunderson, W. (2003). *Analysing Identity: Cross-cultural, Societal and Clinical Contexts*. London: Routledge.
Wittenberg, J. (2016). *My Dear Ones: One family and the Final Solution*. London: William Collins.
Young, M. and Willmott, P. (1957, 2007). *Family and Kinship in East London*. London: Penguin Classics.
Zamoyski, A. (2008, 2014). *Warsaw 1920: Lenin's Failed Conquest of Europe*. London: William Collins.
Zerubavel, E. (2011). *Ancestors and Relatives: Genealogy, Identity and Community*. Oxford, UK: Oxford University Press.
Zoellner, T. and Maercker, A. (2006). Posttraumatic growth in clinical psychology: A critical review and introduction of a two-component model. *Clinical Psychology Review*, 26(5), 626–53.

INDEX

Ainsworth, Mary 13
AK (Armia Krajowa) resistance movement 110–11, 112–15, 142–3, 147, 148–50, 149–50, 154
Anders, Władyław, General 167–8, 185
attachment: attachment theory 13–14; family relations 46, 92–3, 151–2, 205, 206, 228–30; mourning process 184; parental loss 70; separation through war 104–9, 155; trust and life experience 16, 25; trust and military relations 69; war, hazardous haven 51, 57–8, 65–7, 114–15
Augustow 19, 65
autonomy: developmental implications 25–6; heroism 69, 114–15; parental encouragement 36–7; technology and social change 27–8

Battle of Narwik, 1940 122
Beck, Josef 89
Bifulco, Antonia (née Czechowska): birth 189; cultural identity 226–8, 235; Derby revisited, 2016 206–8; DNA analysis 228, 229; education 204; family photographs 211, 213; Małgosia, connection to 229–30, 230; personal identity 222; Warsaw and family, 2016 214–16
Blom, Philip 42
Bowlby, John 13
Brexit, analysis behind 220–2
Britain: French Resistance support 128; Poles mixed transition 166–9; Polish ally (1939–45) 89–90, 98, 101, 120, 125–6, 132–3; Polish communities established 17, 18, 167, 184–5, 202–4; Polish Government in Exile 167–8; post-1945 economic struggles 165, 166, 187; post-war immigration 187, 204, 219–20, 232; reaction to Warsaw uprising 156–7; Second World War involvement 122–3; Sheffield Irish community 83–4; Special Operations Executive (SOE) 137–41; Warsaw uprising, role in 141–2, 145, 146, 147–8
Bryan, Julien 99–100

Chamberlain, Neville 89, 91
Chełmno 79
Churchill, Winston 138, 146, 148, 152–3
Ciano, Galeazzo 90
Ciechanów 19, 32
confusion (social identity): Erikson's concept 97; separation through war 104–9; Warsaw siege 99–100
cultural identity: British born and multicultural 219–20, 222, 226; displacement, adapting to 119–20, 134; family narrative xiii, 226–8; group membership 14–15; Nazi dehumanisation, Jews and Slavs 100–1, 104, 111–12, 116, 117; patriotism 40–1, 69; Polish resistance movement 110–11, 112–15; private education 34–5; traditional festivals 37–8; transmission through narratives 17
Cygler family: family traits 227; origins 33; secure family attachments 34, 37, 42

Cygler, Felicija 33, 48
Cygler, Jadwiga 38, 77, 191, 192, 196–7, 199
Cygler, Jan 33, 77, 104, 191, 193
Cygler, Karolina 193, 212
Cygler, Teofil 33
Cygler, Wacek 33, 77, 104, 189, 200–1
Czechowska, Christine (née O'Neill): birth 83; family photographs 210, 211; family visit to Poland, 1965 199–202; final celebration and death 208–9; formal documents 11; Jurek, first meeting and courtship 175–80; marriage and early family life 180–3, 189, 210; 178
Czechowska, Danuta 82, 145
Czechowska, Joanna 189, 204, 211, 213, 216, 226
Czechowska, Maria (née Cygler): biographic details 33, 34; education 38; emigration to England 1, 2–3, 189–91, 191–3; English life and death 197–8; family escape from Bolsheviks 57–8; family photographs 48–50, 81, 154, 212; Grazyna 42, 52, 92, 190–1, 192, 198, 229; letters to Jurek and post-war life 170–4; life under communism 188–9; life under German occupation 103–4; marriage and family life 44, 45, 48, 59; personal character 42; Płock, family connections 19, 26, 33; religious identity 33, 34, 45, 225; Tadeusz's wounding and death 65–7; Warsaw uprising and life after 142, 144–5, 148, 150–2, 153; widowhood in Warsaw 76–7, 77, 92–3
Czechowska, Maria-Victoria (née Rodziewiczes) 16, 19, 29, 31–2, 48
Czechowska, Marie-Christine 183, 204, 207–8, 211, 213, 214–16, 226
Czechowska, Myszka (née Janiszewska): death confirmed 173; life under occupation (letters to Jurek) 105–9; marriage to Jurek 50, 82–3, 102; photograph 116, 161; sacrificial resistance 114–15
Czechowska, Paulina 31
Czechowska, Yolanda 181, 204, 211, 213, 226
Czechowski family: country estate at Rudzk 30–1, 57, 78, 80; family traits 227; family trees 32, 193; identity and patriotism 40–1, 69, 79, 225; life under German occupation 104; move to Warsaw (1912-13) 44–5, 52; Poland 1900 16; relocation within Warsaw (post-1925) 76–7; secure family attachments 32, 37, 46–7, 92–3; upper class identity 29–31, 38, 46–7
Czechowski, Henryk 31, 80
Czechowski, Jurek: birth 19, 45; career moves 189, 192, 204; Christine, first meeting and letters 175–80; death 205; Derby's Polish community 18, 175; escape to England 1943 128–30, 137; family escape from Bolsheviks 57–8; family photographs 23, 49–50, 81, 206, 210–11, 213; family visit to Poland, 1965 199–202, 213; formal documents 11–12; job and life in London 179, 180–1; French Resistance 126–8, 133, 162, 185; letters from Myszka 105–9; marriage and early family life 180–3, 189, 210; marriage to Myszka 50, 82–3; military service 82–3; Myszka's death 176, 184; personal character 92, 133–4, 183; Polish Airforce Association 202–3, 211; post-war reconnection with mother 170–4, 184; Race Relations Board 204; relations with Stas 78, 80, 92, 93; resettlement and acceptance 184–5; retreat to France 102, 118–19, 120–1, 122, 162; Special Operations Executive (SOE), role in 137–8, 140–1, 148, 153–4, 163, 185; Warsaw childhood 76–7, 77
Czechowski, Justin 31, 57
Czechowski, Olgierd 16, 32, 59, 65–7, 104
Czechowski, Tadeusz: biographic accounts 10, 36–7; birth 19, 28, 32; education as boarder 38, 39; family escape from Bolsheviks 57–8; family photographs 48–9; First World War involvement 52–4, 55, 56–7; heroism 69–70; marriage and family life 44–5, 48, 52, 71; military career 44–5, 52; neurasthenia diagnosis 41; personal autonomy 36–7, 41–2, 45–6; personal character 68, 69, 70–1; photographs 23; Płock, family connections 19, 26; Polish army role 59; Polish patriotism 40–1, 45–6; war against Red Army 62, 64–7; wounding and death 65–7
Czechowski, Władysław 32; biographic details 31; biography of Tadeusz 10, 36; family portrait 1900 16; photograph 48; Tadeusz's wounding and death 65–7; Warsaw, career and family life 45, 59, 64
Częstochowa 19, 44, 59, 62

Davis, Norman 20
Dawes Plan 1924 76, 90

Derby: Irish community 88; Polish community 18, 167, 174–5, 202–3
Dunant, Henry 43

Eden, Anthony 131
emotional geography 8–9, 232–3
emotional history xiii–xiv, 6, 9
Erikson, Erik: autonomy 25, 26; confusion (social identity) 97; generativity 186; identity, development theory xiv, 14–16, 15; industry 72; initiative 51; integrity 214; intimacy 136, 164; isolation 136; trust 16
Europe: European Union membership 218–19; fall of communism, 1989 217–18; First World War origins 52; post-1945 economy and boundaries 165–6; scientific revolutions 42–3; technology and social change 27–8, 42; Treaty of Versailles, 1919 59, 90–1

family narratives: psychology and genealogical study 5–7
First World War: Germany army 52–6, 58–9; origins of 52; Poland's direct involvement 52–7; Russian army in Poland 52–6
France: Allied support for Poland 89–90, 98, 101; Battle of Narwik, 1940 122–3; French Resistance 126–8; German invasion, 1939 124–5; Paris liberated 146; Vichy regime 124–5, 127
Freud, Sigmund 43
Frost, Nollaig 7

Gaulle, Charles de 61, 71, 124–5, 128, 146
Gdansk 19
Gdynia 2, 19
generativity: Erikson's concept 186; family life in Derby 189; family visit to Poland, 1965 199–202; grandmothers as carers 192–3, 195–6; Maria's emigration to England 191–3
Germany: Berlin Wall's fall 218; First World War 52–6, 58–9; Hitler and rise of Nazi Party 90–1; invasion of France, 1940 124–5; invasion of Poland, 1939 97–100; Jews, Nazi oppression and killings 91; Katyn massacre discovered 131–2; mass murder and expulsion of Poles 100–1, 116–17; Nazi aggression towards Poland 89–90; Polish atrocities, belated apology 9; post-1918 economic crisis 76, 90; post-1945 economy and boundaries 165; Warsaw siege 99–100; Warsaw uprising, 1944 142–50, 152, 155–6
Great Depression (1930's) 76
Grodno 19, 29, 64–5

Hartley, Jozef 122, 137, 138
Hartman, Jozef 139
Herbert, J. M. 120
heroism 69–70, 114–15
Hitler, Adolf: Master Plan and ideology 100–1; Nazi aggression towards Poland 89–90; Nazi Party leadership 90–1; Warsaw, annihilation plan 145, 149, 152; Warsaw visit 101
Holocaust 9
Hoover, Herbert 60
Horowitz, Maks 74
Hungary 120–1

identity: concealment and subterfuge 118, 126–30, 133; cultural links 14–15; development through life-stages (Erikson) 15; personal sense 14–15, 97, 205, 222; social class differences 40, 45–6, 73; *see also* cultural identity; national identity
industry (creativity): Erikson's concept 72; Hugh O'Neill's industrial links 87, 89; O'Neill family firm 84, 85; Second Republic reconstruction 73, 75–6, 81, 91; Warsaw's regeneration 78–9, 81
initiative: Erikson's concept 51; Polish fight for independence 58–9, 62–4, 67–8, 70; Tadeusz's military experience 54, 55, 57–8, 59, 62, 70–1
integrity: Erikson's concept 214; family connections maintained 215–16; Poland's return to democracy 217–18; traumatic events, challenging accounts 222–4; Warsaw memorials 216–17
intimacy: Erikson's concept 136, 164; Jurek and Christine, courtship 175–80; Jurek and Christine, marriage and family 180–3; Maria and Jurek's post-war reconnection 170–4
isolation: Erikson's concept 136; Maria's life 142, 144–5, 148, 150–2, 153; SOE and Jurek's role 137–41; Warsaw uprising, 1944 141–50

Jews: Germany's oppression and killings 91; Holocaust 9; Nazi dehumanisation 100–1, 104, 111–14, 116, 117; Polish anti-Semitism 224; Polish status and attitudes towards 33–4, 73–5; Warsaw Ghetto 111–12

Kanthak, Ania (née Cygler) 11, 191, 193, 212, 229
Karski, Jan 102, 110, 112, 128–9
Katyn massacre 103, 115, 117, 131-2, 135, 217
Komorowski, Tadeusz 'Bor': Polish Government in Exile 167, 185, 203; war against Red Army 64; Warsaw occupation 114; Warsaw uprising, 1944 142, 145, 146, 147, 148, 153, 155–6
Korczak, Janusz 79, 113–14
Koscuiszko, Tadeusz, General 40–1

Leinweber, Julia (née Czechowska) 31, 49, 57, 78, 104
Leinweber, Stas: army call-up, Russian capture and death 102–3, 115–16; birth 78; family photographs 23, 49, 161; relations with Jurek 78, 80, 92, 93; sporting achievements 80
Liddell, Robert Scotland 55–6
lifespan psychology 4
Łódz 19, 44
Lubienska, Barbara (Basia) 150, 191

Malin, Jola 17, 203–4
Marshall Plan 165
Miliskiewicz, Małgosia (née Szypowska) 193, 195–6, 212, 215–16, 229–30, 230
Mohylew 19, 31–2

narrative therapy 6
national identity: hidden due to oppression 26–7, 34–5, 225; patriotism 69, 114–15, 225; Polish fight for independence 58–9, 62–3; Polish resistance movement 110–11, 112–14; Warsaw's reconstruction post-1945 169–70
neurasthenia 41
Nicolas II, Tsar 44, 54
Nicolson, Paula 5, 234–5

Olczak-Ronnier, Joanna 74–5, 112, 224
O'Neill, Aloysuis 84–5
O'Neill, Barbara (née Friend) 83, 86–7, 192
O'Neill, Christine *see* Czechowska, Christine (née O'Neill)
O'Neill, Daniel 84, 85, 174
O'Neill, Hugh: Anglo-Polish Society 174; biographic accounts 10–11, 83–4, 85; birth 85; career in metallurgy 87, 88, 175; education 86, 87; family ancestry 84–6, 87; German visits, 1936 89; marriage and family life 87, 88–9; Polish visit, 1927 87–8; war work 174
O'Neill, Pauline 175–6
Ostrowska, Grazyna (née Czechowska): birth 32; family photographs 49, 212; family portrait 1900 16; life under communism 189; Maria 42, 52, 92, 190–1, 192, 198, 229; Marysia's family 194–6; Warsaw, family life 59; Warsaw occupation 104; Warsaw uprising, 1944 148

Paderewski, Ignacy Jan 63
peace initiatives 43
Pétain, Phillipe, Marshal 124–5
Piłsudski, Józef: Jews, attitudes towards 73, 74; Polish independence leadership 58–9; Second Republic leadership 75–6; war against Red Army 61, 62–5, 68–9, 71
Płock 19, 26, 32
Poland: communist rule during 1950's 187–8; country at war, people's resilience 3–4; democracy reinstated, 1989 218; Enigma Code breakers 130–1; epidemics, late 1800s 33; European Union membership 218; First World War, direct involvement 52–5; gentry 29–30; German and Soviet invasions, 1939 97–8; immigration to Britain 219–20, 232; independence 1918 58–9; Jews, status and attitudes towards 33–4, 73–5; map 20; modern history 18–21; Allies support 89–90; partition and Russification 26–7, 27, 34–5; Poles in British forces 137–8, 139–42, 147–8, 153; political conflict, early 1900s 43–4; post-1918 hardships 60; post-war Stalinist regime 166, 167; Red Army invasion and Polish retaliation 60–5, 67–8; Second Republic, reconstruction challenges 73, 75–6, 91; Second World War narratives 17–18; Solidarity movement 217–18; traditions and cultural identity 37–8; troop retreat and Romanian internment (1939) 102, 118–20; Uprising Museum, Warsaw 157; war compensation lost 165–6; wartime anti-Semitism 224; women and feminism 35
psychology and genealogy 5–7
psychotherapy 6

246 Index

Radwan-Rohrschef, Piotr 11, 193, 215–16, 229
Radziwil, Lee, Princess 203, 211
Red Cross: founding of 43; services in wartime France 126, 127, 131, 133; services in wartime Poland 105, 231
Rejewski, Marian 130–1
research study: ethical considerations 10; limitations identified 233–4; qualitative analysis and reflexivity xiv–xv, 7–8; social context 5; source materials xiv, xvi–xvii, 10–12; thematic analysis 12–16, 15, 16; themes and methodology xiv–xvi; time period 5
resilience: conceptual elements 14; family support 205–6, 231–2; fighting skills and tactics 70, 132–3, 231; national identity under oppression 26–7, 133, 185; outside support 231; Polish resistance movement 110–11, 112–14; resettlement and acceptance 184–5; Second Republic reconstruction 73, 75, 81, 91; Warsaw under occupation 104–5, 110; Warsaw uprising, 1944 143–5
Rodziewicz, Maria 31, 32
Romania 57–8, 101, 102, 119–20
Roosevelt, Franklin D. 131, 146, 152–3
Roosevelt, Theodore 113
Russia: Bolshevik revolution 57; partition and Russification of Poland 26, 27, 35, 43–4; Red Army invasion of Poland 60–5, 67; Russian army in Poland, First World War 52–6; *see also* Soviet Union

Second World War: Battle of Narwik, 1940 122–3; Enigma Code breakers 130–1; Fall of France, 1940 123–5; French Resistance 126–8; German and Soviet invasions of Poland, 1939 97–9; Nazi genocide and politicide 100–1; Polish army evacuations 118–22, 125–6, 128–30; Polish personal accounts 17–18; Special Operations Executive (SOE) 137–41; traumatic events, challenging accounts 222–4; Yalta Conference, 1945 152–3
Sheffield 84–5
Sikorski, Władysław, General 63, 64, 113, 129–30, 131
Skłodowski, Władysław 35
Sosnkowski, Kazimierz 62, 63
Soviet Union: expansion post-1945 152–3; famine in Ukraine 76; forced forgetting, wartime 'blind spots' 223–4; invasion of Poland, 1939 98–9; Polish resistance to communism 90; Stalinist regime in Poland 166, 167; Stalin, the Great Purge 76, 90; *see also* Russia
Special Operations Executive (SOE) 137–41
Stalin, Joseph 76, 90, 145, 146, 147, 152–3
Stefan Batory, MS (liner) 1–2, 101, 123
Struk, Janina 125–6
Suttner, Bertha von 43
Suwałki 19
Szlachetko, Danuta (Wira) 17, 99, 104, 110, 111, 149–50, 168, 169
Szypowska, Marysia (née Ostrowska): family gathering, Warsaw 2016 216; family photographs 212; Jurek's wedding 82; life under communism 189; literary career 193, 199, 201; marriage and family life 194; post-uprising 151–2; Warsaw occupation 104; Warsaw resistance 111, 145, 148

technology and social change 27–8, 42
Trotsky, Leon 60–1
trust: development and life experience 16, 25; military relationships 69; wartime alliances 89, 133
Tukhachevsky, Mikhail 60, 64, 90
Turner, Alan 179

United Kingdom (UK) *see* Britain
United States: economic aid to Europe 165

Versturlund, Ivar 150

Warsaw: battle against Red Army 62–4, 67–8; First World War accounts 55–6, 58; German invasion, 1939 97–8; Jewish Ghetto 111–12; life under German occupation 104–5, 110; memorials 216–17; Polish independence 58; political conflict, early 1900s 44; reconstruction and economy, post-1920s 78–9, 81; reconstruction, post-1945 169–70, 215; siege and surrender, 1939 99–100; threatened city 4; Uprising and aftermath, 1944 17, 141–50, 152; Zoliborz 77, 103, 110, 142, 148
willpower 26, 67–8

Yugoslavia (Croatia) 121

Zerubavel, Eviatar 5
Zygalski, Henryk 130–1